Leckie

e education publisher

or Scotland

National 4 & 5
MODERN STUDIES

T0340416

Course Notes

Elizabeth Elliott, Jenny Gilruth,
Jenny Reynolds

001/06012019

10 9 8 7

ISBN 9780008282189

Published by
Leckie
An imprint of HarperCollinsPublishers
Westerhill Road, Bishopbriggs, Glasgow, G64 2QT
T: 0844 576 8126 F: 0844 576 8131

leckiescotland@harpercollins.co.uk   www.leckiescotland.co.uk

HarperCollins Publishers
Macken House, 39/40 Mayor Street Upper, Dublin 1, D01 C9W8, Ireland

A CIP Catalogue record for this book is available from the British Library.

Acknowledgements
We would like to thank the following for permission to reproduce their material:
Images: Fig 1.5: This fi le is licensed under the Creative Commons Attribution-Share Alike 3.0 Unported license; Fig 1.7 Brendan Howard/Shutterstock.com; Fig 1.12: © LINGTREN IMAGES / Shutterstock.com; Fig 1.13: AFP/Getty Images; Fig 1.14: Ken Jack - Corbis / Contributor; Fig 1.17 LESLEY MARTIN / Stringer / Setty images; P27 © DrimaFilm / Shutterstock.com; Fig 1.21 (top) © Gina Power / Shutterstock.com; Fig 1.21 (bottom) © John Selway / Shutterstock.com; Fig 2.4: This fi le is licensed under the Creative Commons Attribution-Share Alike 3.0 Unported license; Fig 2.6 © WENN Ltd / Alamy Stock Photo; Fig 2.7 © Steven Scott Taylor / Alamy Stock Photo; Fig 2.8: AFP/Getty Images; Fig 2.12 © Jeff J Mitchell / Staff / Getty Images; Fig 3.4: AFP/Getty Images; Fig 4.3 AFP/Getty Images; Fig 4.5 © Jeff J Mitchell / Staff / Getty Images; Fig 4.6: AFP/Getty Images; Fig 4.7 © Jeff J Mitchell / Staff / Getty Images; Fig 4.10: AFP/Getty Images; Fig 5.8: AFP/Getty Images; Fig 5.13: AFP/Getty Images; Page 96–97 (Police and EDL): veroxdale/Shutterstock.com; Fig 5.20: Open Government Licence v3.0 ; Fig 5.21: Open Government Licence v3.0 ; Fig 6.2: Scottish Government; Fig 9.2 © ROBERT PERRY / Stringer / Getty Images; Fig 9.3 © Creative Commons Attribu-tion-ShareAlike 2.0 license ; Fig 9.8 Scottish Government; Fig 9.9: Scottish Government; Fig 10.5 © UIG via Getty Images; Fig 10.13: Scottish Government; Page 148–149: Getty Images; Fig 11.1: fpolat69/Shut-ter-stock.com; Fig 11.2: CC BY-SA 4.0; Fig 11.4: © Dave Thompson / Stringer / Getty Images; Fig 11.5: Getty Images; Fig 11.7: Getty Images; Fig 11.8: Getty Images; Fig 11.10: Getty Images; Fig 11.11: Getty Images; Fig 12.1: Getty Images News; Fig 12.2: Bloomberg via Getty Images; Fig 13.2: This fi le is licensed under the Open Government Licence v1.0; Fig 13.3 DANIEL SORABJI / Staff / Getty Images; Fig 13.5: Boston Globe via Getty Images; Fig 13.7: Getty Images; Fig 14.1: Getty Images; Fig 14.2: Spirit of America/Shutterstock.com; Fig 14.3: AFP/Getty Images; Fig 14.5: Northfoto/Shutterstock.com; Fig 14.6: Spirit of America/Shutterstock.com; Fig 15.2: Getty Images; Fig 15.3: s_bukley/Shutterstock.com; Fig 15.6 Anadolu Agency / Contributor; Fig 15.8: MidoSemsem/Shutterstock.com; Fig 17.2: 360b / Alamy Stock Photo; Fig 17.4: Sadik Gulec/ Shutterstock.com; Fig 17.5: Mark III Photonics/Shutterstock.com; Fig 17.10: AFP/Getty Images

All other images from Shutterstock.com

Text: Impact spreads © Scottish Qualifi cations Authority; P89 Reproduced with permission of Herald and Times group; P102-103 Reproduced with permission of Herald and Times group; P131 Reproduced with permission of Herald & Times Group; P139 Reproduced courtesy of STV; P140 Reproduced courtesy of the Daily Record; P200 © Telegraph Media Group Limited 2012

This book contains FSC™ certified paper and other controlled sources to ensure responsible forest management.

For more information visit: www.harpercollins.co.uk/green

Introduction

About this book

This book is designed to lead you through the National 4/National 5 Modern Studies course. The book has been organised to map the course specifications and is packed with examples, explanations, activities and features to deepen your understanding of the topics and help you prepare for the assessment.

At the beginning of each section you will find the National 4 assessment outcomes. Underneath this you will find the Course Assessment Specification for each section. These tell you the different areas you may be assessed on in the National 5 exam. There is also a list of things you may have studied as part of your broad general education in S1–S3 that you will build upon as you progress through the Modern Studies course.

In Modern Studies there is a choice in the topics you study for each section. This book covers the following topics:

Section 1: Democracy in the UK and Scotland

Section 2: Crime and the law in the UK

Section 3: International Issues: Terrorism

The final two chapters focus on the Added Value Unit (National 4), Assignment (National 5) and exam skills, and include lots of useful advice about the skills and techniques you will need.

Features

LEARNING INTENTIONS

This is a list of what you will learn as you work your way through the chapter.

What you will learn in this chapter

- How the political system operates in Scotland and the UK.
- The main rights and responsibilities of citizens in Scotland.

HINT

Hints give you advice and tips to support your learning.

 Hint

Constituency MSPs are elected by the FPTP system in exactly the same way as MPs are elected to the House of Commons.

THINK POINT

Think points ask you to consider the implications of what you are learning and help you to develop critical thinking skills.

 Think point

What do you think are the advantages and disadvantages of having a direct democracy?

MAKE THE LINK

Make the Link helps you to connect what you are learning to other sections within the course and to other subjects you might be studying. Modern Studies is about what is happening around the world today and you will find that what you learn has links to lots of other subjects like History, Geography, English, Maths, RMPS and many more.

> ### ✦ Make the Link
>
> In History you may learn about the factors that led to the Act of Union.

WORD BANK

Words which you might not be sure of are highlighted in the text in red and a definition is given in the Word Bank box; this should help you to become familiar with them and how they are used.

> ### 📖 Word bank
>
> • **Consensus**
>
> A general agreement, reached by a group as a whole.

ACTIVITY

Activities will get you thinking about what you have learned and help you to practise and develop the skills you will need for your assessment. There are different kinds of activities, including individual research work, paired discussion and class debates.

> ### GO! Activity
>
> **Discuss**
> Discuss with your shoulder partner which government (UK or Scottish) you think sets the age limits associated with certain rights.

QUESTIONS

Questions are included throughout each chapter to test your knowledge and understanding of what you have learned. Many of these questions will also help you to develop and practise the skills you will need for your assessment.

? Questions

1. What is a constitution?
2. Why is the British constitution different?

CASE STUDY

There are lots of interesting case studies in every chapter of this book. Each case study shows you how what you have been learning has an impact on the wider world by telling you about a real organisation, person or event. We have also included lots of newspaper articles so you can see how the topics you are studying are reported by the press in real life. These case studies will give you lots of great examples which you can use as evidence to back up the points you make as part of your assessment.

> **Vulnerable Witnesses Bill**
>
> Michael Matheson, Cabinet Secretary for Justice, introduced a bill on 12th June 2018.
>
> 'An Act of the Scottish Parliament to make provision about the use of special measures for the purpose of taking the evidence of child witnesses ...'

LEARNING CHECKLIST

Each chapter closes with a summary of learning statements showing what you should be able to do when you complete the chapter. You can use the checklist to check that you have a good understanding of the topics covered in the chapter; you can make a note of how confident you feel using the traffic lights so that you know which topics you might need to revisit.

> Now that you have finished the **Power and decision-making in the political system in the UK** chapter, complete a self-evaluation of your knowledge and skills to assess what you have understood. Use the checklist below and its traffic lights to draw up a revision plan to help you improve in the areas you identified as red or amber.
>
> • I can explain what a democracy is.
>
> • I can state the main political rights and responsibilities of citizens in Scotland.

NATIONAL 5

There are some parts of this book that might be more appropriate for National 5 learners; these sections are shaded as below.

> **N5 Legislative Consent Memorandums**
>
> Legislative Consent Memorandums can be lodged in the Scottish Parliament by the Scottish government, or by any MSP, giving the Westminster Parliament the power to legislate on a devolved matter. Westminster will not pass bills on devolved matters.

Course Assessment Specification

National 4 *(Democracy in Scotland and the UK)*

Outcome 1

1 Use a limited range of sources of information to detect and explain bias and exaggeration relating to democracy in the Scottish and United Kingdom political systems by:

1.1 Detecting bias or exaggeration using up to two sources of information.

1.2 Briefly explaining bias or exaggeration using evidence from up to two sources of information.

Outcome 2

2 Draw on a straightforward knowledge and understanding of democracy in the Scottish and United Kingdom political systems by:

2.1 Giving straightforward descriptions of the main features of a political issue which draw on a factual knowledge of democracy in Scotland or the United Kingdom.

2.2 Giving straightforward explanations relating to a political issue in Scotland or the United Kingdom.

National 5 *(Democracy in Scotland and the UK)*

Option 1: Democracy in Scotland

Power and decision-making
- features of a democratic political society
- devolved and reserved matters
- role and powers of Scottish First Minister

Participation
- rights and responsibilities of individuals
- opportunities for individuals
- elections and campaigning (role of individuals, political parties and the media)

Influence
- the media *and* **either**
  ◦ pressure groups *or*
  ◦ trade unions

(Study of the group/organisation chosen should focus on role, purpose, aims, methods and critical evaluation of the extent to which influence is exercised in democracy.)

Representation
- role of MSPs
- representation of women and minority groups
- purpose, function and composition of Committees in the Scottish Parliament

Voting systems
- key features and outcomes of the system used to elect MSPs to the Scottish Parliament, including the strengths and weaknesses of this system

Option 2: Democracy in the UK

Power and decision-making
- features of a democratic political society
- devolved and reserved matters
- role and powers of Prime Minister

Participation
- rights and responsibilities of individuals
- opportunities for individuals
- elections and campaigning (role of individuals, political parties and the media)

Influence
- the media *and* **either**
  ◦ pressure groups *or*
  ◦ trade unions

(Study of the group/organisation chosen should focus on role, purpose, aims, methods and critical evaluation of the extent to which influence is exercised in democracy.)

Representation
- role of MPs
- representation of women and minority groups
- purpose, function and composition of the House of Lords

Voting systems
- key features and outcomes of the system used to elect MPs to the UK Parliament, including the strengths and weaknesses of this system

Democracy in Scotland and the United Kingdom

Level 3 and 4 experiences and outcomes relevant to this topic

The Democracy in Scotland and the United Kingdom section naturally builds upon the knowledge already secured in the third and fourth level experiences and outcomes, and in particular:

❖ I can use my knowledge of current social, political or economic issues to interpret evidence and present an informed view. **SOC 3-15a**

❖ I can understand the arrangements for political decision-making at different levels and the factors that shape these arrangements. **SOC 3-18a**

❖ I can debate the reasons why some people participate less than others in the electoral process and can express informed views about the importance of participating in a democracy. **SOC 4-18b**

❖ I can evaluate the role of the media in a democracy, assess its importance in informing and influencing citizens, and explain decisions made by those in power. **SOC 4-17b**

1 Power and decision-making in the political system in the UK

What you will learn in this chapter

- How the political system operates in Scotland and the UK.
- The main rights and responsibilities of citizens in Scotland.
- How the Scottish and UK political systems are structured.
- The relationship between the Scottish and British political systems.
- The ongoing debates regarding the future of Scotland within the United Kingdom constitutional structure.
- The position of the UK within the EU.

Figure 1.1: *The road to democracy*

Think point

What do you think are the advantages and disadvantages of having a direct democracy?

Think point

Think about why the government sets age limits before people can legally have certain rights.

Democracy

The word 'democracy' has its origins in two Greek terms – demos (people) and kratia (rule by) – and translates as 'rule by the people'.

A democracy is where the people have a say in how the country is run. In a direct democracy, the citizens assemble to make decisions for themselves, rather than electing representatives to make decisions on their behalf.

A representative democracy is where citizens within a country elect representatives to make decisions on their behalf. The UK is a representative democracy.

In a democracy, citizens have opportunities to participate in the political process and to influence the decisions that are made in parliament. The success of a democracy depends on the participation of its citizens.

Rights and responsibilities in the UK

We all have rights, things we are entitled to by law, and responsibilities, things we are obliged to carry out.

Within our rights and responsibilities the government decides that we cannot be given certain rights until we reach a particular age, e.g. students have the right to leave school at 16 years old, and at 18 years old citizens have the right to vote in all elections.

Activity

Discuss
Discuss with your shoulder partner which government (UK or Scottish) you think sets the age limits associated with certain rights.

Citizens living in a democracy have many political rights and responsibilities that give them the power to participate directly or indirectly in how the country is run.

Political rights	Responsibilities
Right to freedom of speech and expression: to say and do what you want within the law.	Respect the right of others to express themselves and their points of view. Do not break the law, e.g. do not tell lies or be slanderous.
Right to vote, over the age of 18 in all elections; over the age of 16 in some elections.	Ensure you use your vote in order to gain appropriate representation.
Right to stand as a candidate in an election, over the age of 18.	To allow others to exercise their rights and accept the result of the election.
Right to campaign, for example, to send a petition, demonstrate etc.	Not pressurise people to support your cause.

Figure 1.2: *Declaration of Human Rights*

Think point

What do you think happens if a citizen does not uphold their responsibilities?

Questions

1. **Explain** what is meant by a democracy.
2. Create a table to show some of the political rights and responsibilities people in the UK have.

Rights	Responsibilities

3. **Explain, in detail**, which right you think is the most important to have in a democracy.
4. **What do you think** the UK would be like if we didn't live in a democracy? **Explain** your answer.

The constitution

A constitution is the rules and fundamental political principles on which a country is governed (run). Some of the principles are about procedures such as how often elections must be held. Others are concerned with the amount of power the government has and therefore specify what those governments can or cannot do.

Unlike most other democratic countries, such as the United States of America and India, the British constitution is not written down in a single formal document. Instead the rights and responsibilities we have as individuals and as a society have come through people

Figure 1.3: *An old poster calling for votes for women*

⚛ Make the Link

The EU will be looked at in greater detail in the International Issues section on page 198.

Figure 1.4: *The Union flag*

⚛ Make the Link

In History you may learn about the factors that led to the Act of Union.

📖 Word bank

• **Parliamentary sovereignty**

The main legislative body has absolute sovereignty (power) and is supreme over all other government institutions. It may change or repeal any previous legislation.

• **Consensus**

A general agreement, reached by a group as a whole.

• **Referendum**

A vote in which the electorate is asked whether to accept or reject a particular proposal.

• **Motion of 'no confidence'**

A vote in which members of a group are asked to indicate that they do not support the person or group in power, usually the government.

standing up for their rights in the past, such as the suffragettes who fought for the right of women to vote, through acts of parliament and from European law.

Parliamentary sovereignty

Parliamentary sovereignty is the most important principle of the UK constitution.

It makes the UK Parliament at Westminster the supreme legal authority, which means that it can create, change or end any law. However, over the years they have passed laws that limit the application of parliamentary sovereignty. One such law is the devolution of power to the Scottish Parliament.

Scottish Parliament

Until 1707 Scotland had its own parliament and governed itself accordingly. However, the **Act of Union** that year brought about the joining of the Kingdom of England with the Kingdom of Scotland to create Great Britain. Westminster Parliament, where the English Parliament had sat, became the heart of political power in the new 'United Kingdom'.

Ever since then, debate has continued about Scotland's position in the United Kingdom. By the 1970s there was political consensus that political power should be returned to Scotland in some form.

The 1979 referendum

In 1979 a referendum was held in Scotland to establish whether people wanted their own devolved assembly. However, a last minute addition by Labour backbench MP George Cunningham meant that 40% of those eligible to vote (not all of whom would turn out to vote) had to vote in favour in order for a 'Yes' vote to count. In spite of 51.6% of voters voting in favour of the Scottish Assembly, the number was not enough for the proposal to go forward, as this total represented only 32.9% of the registered electorate as a whole.

Figure 1.5: *Calton Hill, Edinburgh, the proposed site for the parliament*

Following the result, the Scottish National Party (SNP) members of parliament submitted a motion of 'no confidence' in the UK government (a Labour–Liberal coalition at that time). The 1979 election led to a Conservative government with Margaret Thatcher as Prime Minister. Throughout the 1980s and 1990s the demand in Scotland for more say in how Scotland was governed grew. After the 1979 referendum defeat a pressure group known as the Campaign for a Scottish Assembly was formed; this led to the creation of the Scottish Constitutional Convention, which was to lay the foundations for the re-establishment of the Scottish Parliament.

? Questions

1. What is a constitution?
2. Why is the British constitution different?
3. 'Scotland has a history of popular sovereignty'. **Explain** what this means.
4. What is devolution?
5. What was the outcome of the 1979 referendum?

The 1997 referendum

In the 1997 UK general election campaign, the Labour Party included a referendum on the re-establishment of a Scottish Parliament in their manifesto. Following a landslide Labour victory, in September of that year a referendum was held to re-establish a Scottish Parliament with devolved powers, and to ask whether or not that parliament should have tax-varying powers.

This time the turnout was 60% and 74.3% voted in favour of the establishment of a devolved Scottish Parliament in Edinburgh. In addition to this, 63.5% of voters agreed that a Scottish Parliament should have tax-varying powers.

Establishment of the Scottish Parliament

In 1998 the UK government passed the **Scotland Act 1998**, thereby re-establishing the Scottish Parliament. The first Scottish Parliament election was held on 6th May 1999, leading to the election of 129 Members of the Scottish Parliament (MSPs). At the time of publication, there have been five subsequent Scottish Parliament elections since 1999; the next scheduled election is to take place in 2021.

On Saturday 9th October 2004, in the presence of Her Majesty the Queen, the new Scottish Parliament building was officially opened. The building is located on the Royal Mile in the Holyrood area of Edinburgh; this is why the parliament building is sometimes referred to as Holyrood. In her speech, The Queen described Holyrood as a 'landmark for 21st century democracy'.

Hint

Devolution essentially means the transfer of powers from the UK parliament in London to assemblies in Cardiff and Belfast, and the Scottish Parliament in Edinburgh.

Make the Link

The work of pressure groups will be looked at in more detail later in this section on page 75.

Figure 1.6: *Casting votes for a devolved Scottish Parliament*

Word bank

- **Manifesto**
A public declaration of intent, policy, aims, etc., as issued by a political party.

Think point   N5

The Scottish government has the power to vary (up or down) the Scottish rate of income tax. They have introduced different bands in the 2018/19 year for the first time. This increased the amount of tax paid by 30% of the paying population.

Hint

On the Scottish Parliament website you can access introductory information on the parliament by visiting http://www.parliament.scot/visitandlearn/education.aspx

Figure 1.7: *The entrance to the Scottish Parliament building in Holyrood*

Devolved and reserved powers

The Scotland Act (1998, amended 2012) gave the Scottish Parliament the power to legislate (make laws) on a range of issues. These issues are known as devolved matters. However, the UK Parliament has retained the power to make laws on certain issues. These issues, which generally have a UK-wide or international impact, are known as reserved matters.

Word bank

• **Legislate**
To create or pass law.

Make the Link

Education being a devolved power is the reason why you are learning a new curriculum and are studying different qualifications from the rest of the UK.

Devolved matters	Reserved matters
Health	The constitution
Education	Benefits and social security
Justice	Immigration
Police and fire services	Defence
Housing	Foreign policy
Local government	Employment
The environment	Broadcasting
Sports and the arts	Trade and industry
Social work	Nuclear energy, oil, gas and electricity
Agriculture	Consumer rights
Many aspects of transport, including roads and buses	Data protection

Figure 1.8: *Education: a power devolved to Scotland*

Make the Link

You will learn more about Justice in Section 2 and more about Defence and Foreign Policy in Section 3.

The fact that the Scottish Parliament has the power to make decisions over many devolved matters means that the Scottish people can have a say in these issues. The Scottish Parliament has passed a number of laws that Scottish people are in support of, such as free university tuition and free prescriptions. On the other hand, although the Scottish

Parliament can hold debates on reserved matters it cannot change the law or make decisions on these matters. For example, MSPs debated Brexit in 2018. However, they had no say on the vote which was held in the House of Commons in London. Many people think it is unfair that the Scottish Parliament cannot pass legislation on reserved matters as they feel that these important aspects of Scottish people's lives shouldn't be controlled by Westminster.

N5 Legislative Consent Memorandums

Legislative Consent Memorandums can be lodged in the Scottish Parliament by the Scottish government, or by any MSP, giving the Westminster Parliament the power to legislate on a devolved matter. Westminster will not pass bills on devolved matters without first obtaining the consent of the Scottish Parliament. The consent itself is given through a motion (a Legislative Consent Motion), which is taken in the Chamber. This is done because in certain circumstances it can be sensible and advantageous, for example it might be more effective to legislate on a UK basis in order to put in place a single UK-wide regime, e.g. powers for the courts to confiscate the assets of serious offenders. It might also be used when the UK Parliament is considering legislation for England and Wales which the Scottish government believes should also be brought into effect in Scotland, but no parliamentary time is available at Holyrood, e.g. legislation to strengthen protection against sex offenders.

As of July 2018, 131 Legislative Consent Memorandums had been passed by the Scottish Parliament: 39 in the first session (1999–2003), 38 in the second (2003–07), 30 in the third (2007–11), 34 in the fourth (2011–2016), and, when this book was published in 2019, 9 so far in the fifth (2016–21).

📖 Word bank

- **Bill**
  A draft of a proposed law presented to parliament for discussion.

GO! Activity N5

Research
Using the Scottish Parliament website, research Legislative Consent Memorandums that have been lodged recently.

N5 Holocaust (Return of Cultural Objects) (Amendment) Bill CASE STUDY

Fiona Hyslop, Cabinet Secretary for Culture, Tourism and External Affairs, lodged a memorandum in relation to the **Holocaust (Return of Cultural Objects) (Amendment) Bill** that was introduced in the House of Commons on 13th March 2018.

'That the Parliament agrees that the relevant provisions of the Holocaust (Return of Cultural Objects) (Amendment) Bill, introduced in the House of Commons on 13 March 2018, relating to the repeal of [the bill at the end of 10 years], so far as these matters fall within the legislative competence of the Scottish Parliament, should be considered by the UK Parliament.'

The Scotland Act 2016

The Smith Commission was established following the Scottish Independence referendum in 2014 and gave recommendations for further devolution and amendments to the Scotland Act 2008. The resulting legislation was the **Scotland Act 2016**. The 2016 act implemented new powers but also strengthened some of the powers devolved in the 2012 act.

The Scottish Parliament is now able to pass legislation on the following issues:

- abortion
- consumer advocacy and advice
- equal opportunities
- gaming machines
- parking
- policing of railways in Scotland
- speed limits
- traffic signs

The act made changes to the way Scotland generates income, including control over certain taxes, such as Air Passenger Duty and income tax.

The act also recognised the Scottish Parliament and a Scottish government as permanent among the UK's constitutional arrangements, with a referendum required before either can be abolished.

Figure 1.9: *The interior of the Scottish Parliament*

❓ Questions

1. What was the outcome of the 1997 referendum?
2. What are devolved matters? Include some **examples**.
3. What are reserved matters? Include some **examples**.
4. Briefly outline some of the new powers given to the Scottish Parliament by the Scotland Act 2012 and 2016.

N5 5. **Explain** what a Legislative Consent Memorandum involves.

Activity

Class debate: 'The Scottish Parliament has been given enough devolved powers'

Your teacher will now divide your class into two groups. Your challenge is to research either the Proposition's (supporting the motion) or the Opposition's opinion (opposing the motion). Even if you do not agree with the viewpoint that you have been given, a good debater should be able to argue from any perspective.

1. You should try to find evidence from the internet on the powers of the Scottish Parliament. You may wish to focus on:

   - Scotland Act 2016

   - Scotland Act 2012

   - Scotland Act 2008

   - the independence debate (see page 27 for further information)

2. Once you have gathered your evidence, use it to make a valid point.

3. Produce a structured paragraph which uses the 'Point, Explain, Example' structure (see page 236).

You will now all be able to make a contribution to the debate. After everyone has made a point your teacher will invite you to participate in debating the issues that have been raised. Your teacher will explain how the debate is to be structured to allow everyone the opportunity to contribute to the discussion.

Following the debate your teacher may take a vote and may ask the class which side of the debate they now agree with.

Reflect on your learning

Underneath the paragraph you produced above, reflect upon your class debate.

- Has the debate changed your opinion on the topic?

- Did you feel that you were able to contribute in a confident manner?

- What might you change if you were to debate in the future?

The structure of the UK political system

The UK Parliament is based in the Palace of Westminster in the capital city of London. There are three elements that make up the UK Parliament: the House of Commons, the House of Lords and the monarch.

The House of Commons is the part of parliament where 650 elected Members of Parliament (MPs) represent the interests and concerns of their constituents. Parliament has responsibility for checking the work of the government and examining, debating and approving new laws.

The House of Lords is the second chamber of the UK Parliament. It is independent from, and complements the work of, the elected House of Commons. The Lords shares the task of making and shaping laws and checking and challenging the work of the government. Currently, there are about 760 unelected members who are eligible to take part in the

Figure 1.10: *The Houses of Parliament in Westminster, London*

work of the House of Lords. Many members, known as peers, have a political background, some don't. They represent a wide range of professions – in medicine, law, business, the arts, science, sports, education etc.

In the UK, power lies with parliament, not the monarch. However, the monarch does play a role in the processes of parliament, including:

- appointing a government: the day after a general election the Queen invites the leader of the party that won the most seats in the House of Commons to become Prime Minister and to form a government
- in the annual State Opening of Parliament ceremony, the Queen opens parliament in person and addresses both Houses in The Queen's Speech. Neither House can proceed to public business until The Queen's Speech has been read
- during The Queen's Speech, the Queen informs parliament of the government's policy ideas and plans for new legislation. Although the Queen delivers the speech, it is the government who writes it
- meeting with the Prime Minister once a week to discuss current business
- when a bill has been approved by a majority in the House of Commons and the House of Lords it is formally agreed to by the Queen. This is known as the Royal Assent. This turns a bill into an act of parliament, allowing it to become law in the UK
- the Queen dissolves (dismisses) parliament before a general election is held

📖 Word bank

- **Majority**

A number that is more than half of the total.

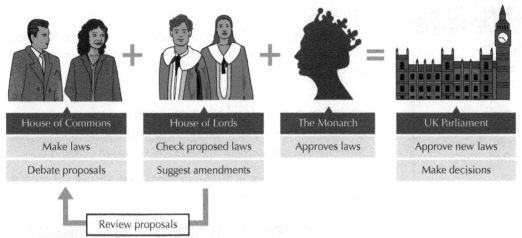

Figure 1.11: *The UK's political structure*

Forming a government

The government runs the country and has responsibility for developing and implementing policy and for drafting laws on reserved matters. After an election, if a party has won more than half the seats in parliament they can form a 'majority government'. This means they find it easier to get bills passed through parliament. Alternatively there may be a 'hung parliament', where no single party has won more than half the seats. In this situation either the party with the most seats forms a 'minority government' or two or more parties can work together to create a coalition government.

UK General Election Results 2017			
Party	Seats	% of vote	% of seats
Conservative	317	42.4	48.8
Labour	262	40.0	40.3
SNP	35	3.0	5.4
Liberal Democrats	12	7.4	1.8
Others	22	3.7	3.4
			Turnout = 69.1%

As the 2017 general election resulted in a hung parliament, the Conservatives chose to govern as a minority government and signed a 'confidence and supply' agreement with the Democratic Unionist Party (DUP). This means that the DUP agreed to support the Conservatives in votes on key areas of legislation without the DUP being part of the government.

 Hint

Government policy is a plan of action that the government proposes to take.

📖 **Word bank**

- **Implement**
  To put something (a decision, plan, agreement, etc.) into effect.

- **Coalition**
  When two or more political parties work together.

The Prime Minister

The leader of the party with the most seats becomes Prime Minister, the head of the UK government, and the person ultimately responsible for all policy and decisions. The Prime Minister:

- oversees the operation of the Civil Service and government agencies, such as the Food Standards Agency
- appoints members of the government to be in the Cabinet
- is the principal government figure in the House of Commons

The current Prime Minister, in 2018, is Theresa May MP. She is based at 10 Downing Street in London.

Figure 1.12: *Theresa May outside 10 Downing Street*

The UK Cabinet

The Cabinet is made up of the senior members of government. Every Tuesday during parliament, members of the Cabinet meet to discuss the most important issues for the government.

Ministers are chosen by the Prime Minister from the members of the government in the House of Commons and House of Lords. They are mainly responsible for specific government departments, such a health, transport, education etc.

The structure of the Scottish political system

In the Scottish Parliament there are 129 elected Members of the Scottish Parliament (MSPs) who represent the interests and concerns of their constituents. MSPs consider and propose new laws on devolved matters, and can scrutinise government policies by asking ministers questions about current issues either in the Chamber or in committees.

The Scottish Parliament was shaped by four founding principles.

1. That parliament should be **accessible and participative** by being easily accessible to the public and involving the people of Scotland in its decisions as much as possible.

2. That the Scottish government should be **accountable** to the parliament and that both should be accountable to the Scottish people.

3. That parliament should promote **equal opportunities**; everyone should treat all people fairly.

4. That parliament should promote the **sharing of power**, among the Scottish government, Scottish Parliament and the people of Scotland.

The Scottish government

The relationship between the Scottish government and the Scottish Parliament at Holyrood is similar to the relationship between the UK government and the UK Parliament at Westminster.

The Scottish government is the devolved government in Scotland. It is a separate organisation from the Scottish Parliament. The Scottish government is responsible for formulating and implementing policy on devolved matters whereas the Scottish Parliament passes laws on devolved issues and scrutinises the work of the Scottish government.

> ### 📖 Word bank
>
> - **Scrutinise**
> To examine or inspect closely and thoroughly.

Figure 1.13: *The Scottish government building in Leith, Edinburgh*

The Scottish government is formed from the party or parties holding the most seats in the Scottish Parliament. The SNP won the election in 2016 and secured a third term in government. However, the party was two seats short of securing a majority. At the time of publication, the SNP governs as a minority government and seeks individual MSP support for bills.

The First Minister of Scotland

The First Minister of Scotland is the political leader of Scotland and the head of the Scottish government. The First Minister is responsible for the creation and development of Scottish government policy. Additionally,

> ### Activity
>
> **Research**
> Research the names and political parties of Scotland's previous first ministers.

Figure 1.14: *Nicola Sturgeon and her Cabinet outside Bute House, Edinburgh*

the First Minister promotes and represents Scotland at home and abroad. The First Minister appears at First Minister's Questions (FMQs) every Thursday to answer questions from MSPs.

MSPs take part in an exhaustive ballot to vote for the First Minister. Under the exhaustive ballot the elector simply casts a single vote for his or her favourite candidate. However, if no candidate is supported by an overall majority of votes then the candidate with the fewest votes is eliminated. Further voting takes place until one candidate has a majority. The winning candidate is then appointed by the monarch. Nicola Sturgeon is the current (as of 2018) First Minister of Scotland. She lives at Bute House, Charlotte Square, in Edinburgh.

The Scottish Cabinet

The Scottish Cabinet is chaired by the First Minister who selects members of the government to join. The Scottish Cabinet normally meets weekly at Bute House in Edinburgh.

The Scottish Cabinet operates on the basis of collective responsibility. This means that all decisions reached by ministers, individually or collectively, are binding on all members of the government.

Each government department is run by a Cabinet Secretary who works on behalf of all ministers and all departments in the government to manage Cabinet business and facilitate collective decision-making.

The Presiding Officer of the Scottish Parliament

The Presiding Officer is the MSP who has been elected by other MSPs to chair meetings of the Parliament. The Presiding Officer is supported in their duties by two Deputy Presiding Officers.

The Presiding Officer remains politically impartial in everything that he/she does, which means he or she does not favour any party, even when a member of one. They therefore take the interest of all members equally into account and act on their behalves. The Deputies are also required to act impartially when they are undertaking their official duties.

⁙ **Make the Link**

You will learn more about Brexit later in this section.

Gender equality in the Scottish Cabinet   CASE STUDY

When she was elected as First Minister, Nicola Sturgeon pledged to put gender equality at the heart of government. She announced her first cabinet with a 50/50 gender balance in November 2014 and maintains this balance. Nicola Sturgeon said in 2014 that her cabinet was 'a clear demonstration that this government will work hard in all areas to promote women, to create gender equality and it sends out a strong message that the business of redressing the gender balance in public life starts right here in government'.

In 2018, Nicola Sturgeon increased the size of the cabinet from 10 to 12, but kept the 50/50 gender balance. She stated that more cabinet ministers were needed in order to address the issues presented by Brexit.

GO! Activity

Research
Use the Scottish Parliament website (http://www.parliament.scot/abouttheparliament/presiding-officer.aspx) to create a fact file on the Presiding Officer.
Make sure your fact file includes the answers to the following questions:

1. Who is the current Presiding Officer?
2. What are the main roles for the Presiding Officer in the Scottish Parliament?
3. Why does the Presiding Officer give up his or her party political role?
4. Three responsibilities of the Presiding Officer?

? Questions

1. **Explain** the role of the House of Commons, the House of Lords and the monarch in making up the UK political structure. You may wish to create a diagram to **exemplify** your points.

2. Briefly **describe** the work of the UK government, the Prime Minister and the Cabinet.

3. Briefly outline the four founding principles of the Scottish Parliament.

4. Outline the differences between the Scottish Parliament and the Scottish government.

5. **Describe** the roles of the First Minister and the Scottish Cabinet.

Figure 1.15: *The Scottish and UK Parliaments do not always agree on what is best for Scotland*

The relationship between the Scottish and UK Parliaments

The main elements of the relationship between Westminster and Holyrood are set out in a Memorandum of Understanding (MOU). The MOU emphasises the principles of good communication, consultation and co-operation.

During the first two sessions of the Scottish Parliament, the parliament worked in co-operation with Westminster and there was not much conflict. This may have been due to the fact that the Labour party was in power in both parliaments. However, since 2007 there have been different parties in power in Holyrood and Westminster and this has created some conflict between the two parliaments as the two governments have different ideological views about what is best for Scotland.

Legislation issues

The Scottish Parliament has chosen to adopt a different approach to many issues from that applied in England. For example, Scotland does not have tuition fees for those attending Higher Education establishments.

The Scottish Parliament has also clashed with Westminster over reserved policy areas. For example, the UK Trident programme involves Faslane naval base in Scotland storing Britain's fleet of nuclear-powered and nuclear-armed submarines. The continued use of Trident nuclear weapons is opposed by the majority of MSPs. However, because Westminster controls defence legislation (it is a reserved power) MSPs have no say in this matter.

Finance issues

Tax

The Scottish Parliament has the power to set a Scottish rate of income tax. From April 2018, Scottish taxpayers and employers are deducted tax at the rates set by the Scottish Parliament, making it the first time in recent history that Scotland has paid a different rate of tax to the UK. The Finance Secretary, Derek Mackay, raised the higher and top rate of tax by 1p each, Scotland's lowest earners have a new starter rate of 19p, and the basic rate is frozen at 20p. There is a new 21p intermediate rate of tax for those earning more than £24,000, increasing the taxes paid by middle and higher-rate employees. This means that the Scottish government has more money to use for devolved areas and that the lowest earners now pay less tax than their counterparts in the rest of the UK.

Annual budget

The Scottish Parliament has the financial power to decide how to spend its annual budget. Most of this money comes from a 'block grant', which comes directly from the UK government. The Scottish people pay taxes on their earnings, which are used to fund the 'grant'. If the UK government decided to reduce the block grant then the Scottish government would have to make cuts in spending in Scotland.

Figure 1.16: *Spending cuts might result if the block grant is reduced*

> **N5** The Barnett formula is a mechanism used by the UK Treasury to determine the amount of public expenditure allocated to Scotland. For the financial year 2016–17 the budget was approximately £30 billion. Many English people think Scotland gets too much money from the formula as spending per person is higher in Scotland. Some English MPs resent the greater finance Scotland receives under the Barnett formula, which has allowed the funding of various policies such as free prescriptions.
>
> The SNP would like to see the Barnett formula replaced by 'fiscal autonomy'. This would involve the Scottish Parliament using its full tax-raising powers to allow Scotland to earn and spend its own money.

The relationship between the First Minister and Prime Minster

The relationship between the First Minister and Prime Minister should be one of mutual respect. However, with two very different political ideologies in power across the two parliaments, relationships may be strained.

In 2018, the relationship is strained due to the fact that both leaders – Nicola Sturgeon and Theresa May – have opposing views about the future of both Scotland and the UK: the First Minister would like Scotland

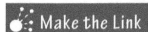

Make the Link

Conflict among the different political parties will be examined in more detail later in this section.

Make the Link

You will study formulas in Maths.

to be an independent country and to remain part of the EU and the Prime Minister would like Scotland to remain part of the UK and for the UK to leave the EU. The leaders also disagree on the terms of leaving the EU and are currently (as of 2018) disputing the Brexit agreement.

After the Brexit referendum Nicola Sturgeon said: 'The UK wide vote to leave the EU is one that I deeply regret. It remains my passionate belief that it is better for all parts of the UK to be members of the European Union…

I want to make it absolutely clear that I intend to take all possible steps and explore all options to give effect to how people in Scotland voted – in other words, to secure our continuing place in the EU and in the single market in particular.'

Speaking about Scotland's position after the UK leaves the EU, Theresa May said: 'we want to ensure … that people, businesses here in Scotland are able to continue to trade freely across the whole of the United Kingdom … there are real opportunities for the United Kingdom when we leave the European Union.'

Figure 1.17: *Theresa May and Nicola Sturgeon*

Ultimately, the UK Parliament has sovereignty and can therefore extend or reduce the areas for which the Scottish Parliament can make laws. However, it is unlikely that powers would ever be taken away from the Scottish Parliament as this would lead to the UK government being unpopular in Scotland.

? Questions

1. **Explain** the relationship between the Scottish and UK Parliaments. Mention legislation and finance issues in your answer.
2. 'The First Minister and Prime Minister don't agree on anything.' Give one reason why this statement is **exaggerated**.

Figure 1.18: *An independent Scotland separate from the rest of the UK*

The future of the UK constitutional arrangement

Scottish Independence Referendum

The idea of Scottish independence has caused major tension between the two parliaments in recent years. The concept of Scottish independence is a constitutional affair that is reserved to Westminster. **The Edinburgh Agreement** is the agreement between the Scottish government and the UK government, signed on 15th October 2012 at St Andrew's House, Edinburgh, of the terms for the Scottish independence referendum that was held in September 2014. Both governments agreed that they would respect the result of the referendum.

The Scottish Independence Referendum (Franchise) Bill was introduced on 21st March 2013. It set out arrangements for the conduct of the referendum, including the date of the vote and campaign spending limits. The bill stated that a referendum would be held on Thursday 18th September 2014. **The Scottish Independence Referendum (Franchise) Bill** was passed on 27th June 2013 giving a person aged 16 or over the right to vote in the referendum.

BALLOT PAPER
Vote (X) ONLY ONCE
Should Scotland be an independent country?
YES ☐
NO ☐

Figure 1.19: *The ballot paper for the September 2014 referendum*

🔵GO! Activity

Group work

In small groups, create a presentation discussing the arguments for and against giving citizens over the age of 16 the right to vote.

- Create a list of the arguments for and against allowing 16-year-olds to vote.
- Research the main political parties' stances on the issue of voting at 16.
- Look at voter turnout in countries where 16-year-olds have the vote.
- Investigate public opinion on the matter.

The independence debate

Two cross-party campaigns were established to persuade the people of Scotland which way they should vote in the referendum. The 'Better Together' group campaigned for a 'no' vote while the 'Yes Scotland' group pushed for a 'yes' vote.

The 'Better Together' campaign promoted the view that Scotland is a better and stronger country as part of the United Kingdom. The campaign was established with the support of the three main pro-union political parties in Scotland: Labour, the Conservative Party and the Liberal Democrats. Alistair Darling, Labour MP, was the head of the campaign.

The 'Yes Scotland' campaign believed that independence would allow Scotland to create a fairer and more prosperous country. The campaign was established with the support of the SNP, the Scottish Green Party and the Scottish Socialist Party, as well as the Independent members of parliament. Blair Jenkins OBE (former head of News at BBC Scotland) was the head of the campaign. The 'Yes Scotland' campaign continues to organise marches and protests in support of a second referendum.

A pro-independence billboard in Stornoway

'Better Together' said …	'Yes Scotland' said …
A strong Scottish Parliament within the UK gives Scotland real decision-making power and a key role in the UK.	Decisions about Scotland's future should be taken by a government that the people want.
As part of the UK we share resources and ideas. The NHS was founded by a Welshman. Partners in these islands are better working together.	Being independent means the revenue from our vast offshore renewable energy will come to Scotland.
The size, strength and stability of the UK economy is a huge advantage for Scotland's businesses. Scotland's largest market is the rest of the UK.	We can work more effectively to attract companies to Scotland, and help businesses already here to grow, allowing us to create more jobs.
Scotland's security will be strengthened as part of the UK. The British Armed Forces are the best in the world. The UK is an important part of the UN, NATO and the EU, and has Embassies around the world.	While the UK government plans to spend £100 billion on new nuclear weapons in the years ahead, we can choose to use our £8 billion share of this money more wisely.

Result of the Scottish independence referendum

	Number of votes	% of vote
No	2,001,926	55
Yes	1,617,989	45

Analysis

The turnout at the referendum was a record-breaking 85%, with the majority of people (55%) voting for Scotland to remain part of the United Kingdom. The vote was counted by each local authority area and then the total number of votes combined to give a Scotland-wide result.

N5 There was a majority vote in favour of independence in four of Scotland's 32 local authorities: Glasgow, Dundee, North Lanarkshire and West Dunbartonshire. These results support the view that the 'Yes' campaign was more successful in local authority areas with higher levels of poverty and unemployment. The opposite was true for the 'No' campaign. The 'No' vote was greater in local authority areas where levels of poverty and unemployment were lower.

Younger voters and local authorities with greater numbers of people born in Scotland were more likely to vote 'Yes'. In areas with greater numbers of voters born outside Scotland (such as England or other European countries), the 'No' campaign was more successful. Older voters were also more likely to vote 'No'.

Immediate impact of the referendum

In the lead-up to the referendum, most public opinion polls showed the 'No' campaign to be well ahead but in the last few weeks of the campaign the gap between the 'Yes' and 'No' campaigns narrowed. One opinion poll even placed 'Yes' ahead.

In the days before the referendum, the leaders of the three main UK parties – Labour, the Conservatives and the Liberal Democrats – offered a 'vow' to the people of Scotland. The vow stated that, in the event of a 'No' vote, the Scottish Parliament could expect to be given further powers over and above those detailed in the Scotland Act 2012. When the result of the referendum was announced, the parties quickly came together to discuss which powers should be given. This led to the establishment of the Smith Commission. The results of the commission were published in November 2014 and were used by the UK Parliament as the basis of the Scotland Act 2016.

Some people were happy with the Scotland Act 2016 but others were not. Those continuing to seek Scottish independence feel the extra powers in the act still fall short of what was promised in the 'vow'. SNP and Labour MPs submitted many amendments to the bill which would have given more power to the Scottish Parliament, but they were rejected by MPs in the House of Commons.

The SNP claims too little time was spent considering the detail of the bill. However, David Mundell, the Conservative Secretary of State for Scotland, claimed the bill would make the Scottish Parliament the most powerful devolved assembly in the world and that the UK government had delivered on the promises (the vow) made before the referendum.

Further consequences of the referendum

With so many areas of policy devolved to the Scottish Parliament, many MPs representing constituencies in England called for legislation to allow only English MPs to vote on laws affecting England. This is known as 'English votes for English laws'.

A form of 'English votes for English laws' was introduced in October 2015. Under the new system, any law discussed by the UK Parliament which affects only England needs to be approved separately by a majority of English MPs, in addition to being passed by the House of Commons as a whole.

The decision-making powers held by the Welsh and Northern Ireland assemblies may also be reviewed in light of the new powers granted to Scotland. Many may see it as inconsistent to grant further powers to one devolved part of the UK and not to the others.

Long-term impact of the referendum

The level of public political engagement in the referendum process was very high by modern standards. Of the 4.29 million registered voters (the largest electorate in Scottish voting history), there was a record turnout of 85%. Some suggest that the referendum led to a greater turnout at the 2015 general election in Scotland and Scottish Parliament election in 2016. At the 2016 Scottish Parliament election the turnout was 5% higher than in 2011.

Following the extension of the franchise to allow 16- and 17-year-olds to vote in the independence referendum in 2014, there is growing support for the voting age across the UK to be lowered to 16. In June 2015, the Scottish Parliament passed the **Scottish Elections (Reduction of Voting Age) Act**, allowing 16- and 17-year-olds to vote in Scottish Parliament and local council elections.

📖 Word bank

• **Electorate**
The number of people entitled to and registered to vote in an election.

❓ Questions

1. What was the result of the referendum in 2014?
2. What were the characteristics of the typical people who voted 'no'?

3.   What were the characteristics of the typical people who voted 'yes'?

4.   What impact did the referendum have on the rest of the UK? Mention at least two things in your answer.

Figure 1.20: *The UK voted to leave the EU in 2016*

Referendum on UK membership of the European Union

The European Union (EU) is a group of 28 countries in Europe whose governments work together. It was set up to help make trading, as well as travel and immigration, easier between European countries. EU laws affect many areas of our lives, such as health and safety rules and even how many fish we are allowed to catch in European waters.

There has always been a lot of debate about the UK's membership of the European Union. In their manifesto for the 2015 general election, the Conservatives promised to hold a referendum on membership of the EU if they were elected.

On Thursday 23rd June 2016, the Prime Minister at the time, David Cameron, asked people to vote on whether the UK should remain a member of the European Union.

BALLOT PAPER	
Vote (X) ONLY ONCE	
Should the United Kingdom remain a member of the European Union or leave the European Union?	
Remain a member of the European Union	☐
Leave the European Union	☐

Figure 1.21: *The ballot paper for the June 2016 European Union referendum*

The 'Remain' campaign argued that being part of a bigger 'club' makes the UK richer and more important. The 'Vote leave' campaign argued that the EU takes away power from Britain, that it costs Britain too much money to be a member and that people who aren't British shouldn't be making laws for this country.

The debate

'Remain' said …	'Vote leave' said …
The amount of funding that was given to local projects by the EU, including the ability to take part in trade, meant the cost was not important.	Leaving the EU would result in an immediate cost saving, as the country would no longer contribute to the EU budget.
The UK would lose trade with its neighbours and reduce its negotiating power with the rest of the world if it left the EU.	Leaving the EU could more than compensate for the disadvantages of losing trade with neighbours because the UK would be free to establish its own trade agreements.
Free passage within Europe has allowed UK citizens to save money and has allowed UK citizens to emigrate to European countries, while also allowing European citizens to enrich the communities in the UK.	There are too many immigrants who are hindering UK society and that Britain should 'tighten' its borders.
Leaving the EU would mean Britain would miss out on vital security information, especially relating to terrorists etc.	Leaving the doors open to immigration means that the UK is vulnerable to a terrorist attack.

GO! Activity

Research
Use the internet to research the other arguments surrounding the EU referendum. You can use the advice on page 222 to help you conduct a detailed search.

Result of the referendum

	Number of votes	% of vote
Leave	17,410,742	52
Remain	16,141,241	48

More than 33 million people voted in the referendum. Turnout was high once more, at 72%.

N5 *Analysis*

England and Wales voted to leave the EU while Scotland and Northern Ireland voted to remain. The areas that voted to leave most heavily were more likely to be affluent and have a high level of formal education, while the areas that voted to remain were more likely to be less affluent and have a lower level of formal education.

Older voters were more likely to vote to leave, whereas younger voters were more likely to vote remain. In fact, over-65s were more than twice as likely to have voted 'Leave' as under-25s.

Figure 1.21: *Vote Leave and Britain Stronger in Europe were designated as the official Leave and Remain campaigns in the EU referendum*

Immediate impact of the referendum

Prime Minister David Cameron was in favour of staying in the EU and resigned from the post following the referendum. Theresa May succeeded him in July 2016. The political instability meant that the pound was worth a lot less in the world immediately after the referendum.

The Labour party also suffered in the aftermath as Jeremy Corbyn was accused of campaigning badly for 'Remain' and he faced a vote of no confidence as leader. He won the vote and continued as leader.

There was a lot of debate in parliament about the 'deal' that should be struck between the EU and the UK and this led to Theresa May calling a snap general election. She said:

'Division in Westminster will risk our ability to make a success of Brexit and it will cause damaging uncertainty and instability to the country ... we need a general election and we need one now, because we have at this moment a one-off chance to get this done while the European Union agrees its negotiating position and before the detailed talks begin. I have only recently and reluctantly come to this conclusion.'

The snap election resulted in a hung parliament with the Conservative Party continuing as the largest party but losing its overall majority. This has led to further political turmoil as the Conservatives now need an agreement with the Democratic Unionist Party in order to pass legislation. It has also weakened the UK's position in the negotiations with the EU.

Theresa May invoked Article 50 on 29th March 2017. This started a two-year negotiation to decide on the UK's future relationship with the EU. Now that Article 50 has been triggered, there is no way back into the EU unless all of the other EU members agree. There is currently, in 2018, a lot of debate calling for a second referendum.

Long-term impact of the referendum

The UK will leave the EU on 29th March 2019. Theresa May has visited Brussels several times to negotiate the terms of Brexit. Decisions reached so far include:

- People who are already in the UK have been given a guarantee that they can stay. The same applies to anyone from the UK who has moved to another EU country.

- The Republic of Ireland is a member of the EU so the border with Northern Ireland would be the only land border where the UK and the EU meet. Theresa May says an agreement has been reached which will guarantee that there will be no 'hard border' with lots of checks on people and goods going backwards and forwards over the border between the two countries.

However, both the UK and the EU have not yet agreed how trade will work between them once the UK has left the EU. The delay in dealing with this issue has been partly blamed on disagreements within the Conservative Party about how Brexit should work.

In July 2018, Theresa May announced that she wanted the UK to have a closer relationship with the EU than did many other Conservatives. Some of her cabinet members – including Boris Johnson (Foreign Secretary) and David Davis (Secretary of State for Exiting the European Union) – said they didn't agree with her decision and that they no longer wanted to be part of her government. At the time of publication of this book, the Brexit bill has not been finalised.

? Questions

1. What was the result of the 2016 referendum?
2. Why did some people want to remain in the EU?
3. Why did some people want to leave the EU?
4. What happened in the immediate aftermath of the referendum? Mention at least two things in your answer.
5. What terms of Brexit have been agreed so far?

GO! Activity

Research
Use the internet to research the latest news on Brexit. You can use the advice on page 222 to help you conduct a detailed search.

Summary

In this chapter you have learned:

- how the political system operates in Scotland and the UK
- the main rights and responsibilities of citizens in Scotland
- how the Scottish and UK political systems are structured
- the relationship between the Scottish and British political systems
- the ongoing debates regarding the future of Scotland within the United Kingdom constitutional structure
- the ongoing changes regarding the future of the UK within Europe

Learning Summary

Now that you have finished the **Power and decision-making in the political system in the UK** chapter, complete a self-evaluation of your knowledge and skills to assess what you have understood. Use the checklist below and its traffic lights to draw up a revision plan to help you improve in the areas you identified as red or amber.

- I can explain what a democracy is.

- I can state the main political rights and responsibilities of citizens in Scotland.

- I can describe how the UK and Scottish governments are set up.

- I can state the role of the Prime Minister and the UK Cabinet.

- I can explain the difference between the Scottish Parliament and the UK Parliament.

- I can state the role of the First Minister and the Scottish Cabinet.

- I can explain the relationship between the Scottish government and the UK government.

- I can explain the relationship between the First Minister and Prime Minster.

- I can discuss the debates about change to the current UK constitutional arrangement, including the position of Scotland within the UK and the position of the UK within the EU.

Examples

In Modern Studies it is essential that you are able to back up any point you make with relevant evidence. When you are considering the statements above try to think of relevant examples for each response. You may wish to note these examples under each statement in your revision notes.

2 Representation

What you will learn in this chapter

- The names of the different types of political representatives.
- The work of an MSP in the parliament and constituency.
- How a constituent can contact their MSP.
- How local councils are organised in Scotland.
- The work of a local councillor representing their constituents.
- The representation of women and ethnic minorities.

Representation

Scotland is a representative democracy. A representative is an individual who has been elected to act, speak or make decisions on behalf of other people.

There are different representatives to represent us at different levels of government.

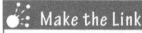

Make the Link

You may have learned about the skills and qualities that are needed for specific jobs in subjects like PSE and Business Management.

Member of European Parliament (ending in 2019)

Member of Parliament (MP)

Member of Scottish Parliament (MSP)

Local Councillors

Figure 2.1: *Representatives at EU, national and local levels*

In the Scottish Parliament elected representatives are called Members of the Scottish Parliament (MSPs). They were elected to represent the people of their constituency.

Word bank

- **Constituency**
An electoral area where a group of voters live.

Activity

Discussion

Think, pair, share with your shoulder partner the skills and qualities that you think representatives need to have to make them good at their job. Think about what would make you vote for a candidate and the characteristics they might have.

 Hint

You need to know which constituency and region you live in so you can understand who represents you. You will learn more about how MSPs are elected later in this section.

 Activity

Research

Use the Scottish Parliament website to find who your MSPs are. Follow the step-by-step instructions below to do this:

* visit the Scottish Parliament website at http://www. parliament.scot

* click on: MSPs
* enter your postcode

Once there, answer the following questions:

1. What is the name of the Scottish parliamentary constituency you live in?
2. What is the name of your constituency MSP?
3. What political party is your MSP a member of?
4. What is the name of the Scottish parliamentary region you live in?
5. Write down the names of your seven regional MSPs and which political parties they belong to.

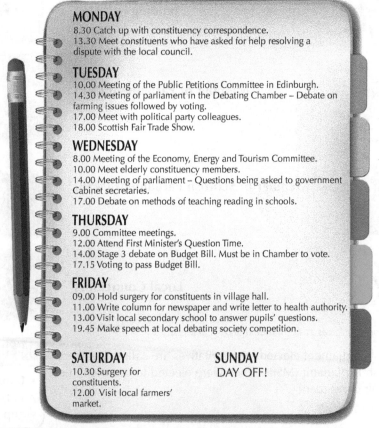

MONDAY
8.30 Catch up with constituency correspondence.
13.30 Meet constituents who have asked for help resolving a dispute with the local council.

TUESDAY
10.00 Meeting of the Public Petitions Committee in Edinburgh.
14.30 Meeting of parliament in the Debating Chamber – Debate on farming issues followed by voting.
17.00 Meet with political party colleagues.
18.00 Scottish Fair Trade Show.

WEDNESDAY
8.00 Meeting of the Economy, Energy and Tourism Committee.
10.00 Meet elderly constituency members.
14.00 Meeting of parliament – Questions being asked to government Cabinet secretaries.
17.00 Debate on methods of teaching reading in schools.

THURSDAY
9.00 Committee meetings.
12.00 Attend First Minister's Question Time.
14.00 Stage 3 debate on Budget Bill. Must be in Chamber to vote.
17.15 Voting to pass Budget Bill.

FRIDAY
09.00 Hold surgery for constituents in village hall.
11.00 Write column for newspaper and write letter to health authority.
13.00 Visit local secondary school to answer pupils' questions.
19.45 Make speech at local debating society competition.

SATURDAY
10.30 Surgery for constituents.
12.00 Visit local farmers' market.

SUNDAY
DAY OFF!

Figure 2.2: *On Tuesdays, Wednesdays and Thursdays MSPs work in the Scottish Parliament*

Interview with Kezia Dugdale, MSP

Q. Why did you want to become an MSP?

A. I spent a few years as a welfare adviser after I graduated. My job was about trying to help people with difficult housing or financial situations. I was constantly trying to make the system work for them but soon realised it was the system that needed to change and that only politics could deliver that sort of change. So I stood for election for the first time in 2007 and came fourth in my party's regional list. Four years later, I did the same again and came second. That was enough to get me elected for the first time as a Labour MSP for the Lothians aged 29.

Q. Can you describe a typical day in parliament?

A. Most MSPs spend their weekday mornings in committees. They all have a theme. Some are about subjects like health and justice. Others are about procedures – like Standards or what we call subordinate legislation – that's where you can alter little bits of existing laws to keep up with the times without having to crack open the whole thing again.

In the afternoons we go into the Chamber to debate contemporary issues and then vote at 5 o'clock. After 5pm most MSPs will attend cross-party groups or evening receptions related to their interests.

Q. Can you describe a typical day in the constituency?

A. Mondays and Fridays are constituency days. These are the days when you hold advice surgeries, inviting members of the public to come and talk to you face-to-face about any problems they are having or any political issues they have strong opinions about. I also like to do a lot of visits on these days, going into schools or businesses, meeting with charities or campaigning groups. This informs my speeches in parliament and makes sure I'm on top of all the local issues which are brewing away.

Q. How do you ensure that you represent the members of the electorate that voted for you?

A. You don't always know who voted for you and many people don't like to be asked. It doesn't matter to me one bit. My job is to represent everyone who lives in the Lothians to the best of my ability. If I do that – there's a chance they might vote for me next time.

Obviously my party stands for the interests of working people. That's the vast majority of the British public who aren't wealthy landowners and just want to work hard, be treated fairly and ensure their children have more opportunities than they did. I do a better job of representing them because their values are my values.

Figure 2.3: *Kezia Dugdale*

CASE STUDY

Q. What committee(s) are you a member of?

A. I was until very recently a member of the Economy Jobs and Fair Work committee. During that time I secured an inquiry into bank branch closures in Scotland. We looked at the impact that was having on town centres and what could be done about it.

Q. What do you think is the most enjoyable part of your job?

A. It sounds clichéd but I love meeting people. I'm interested in ideas, technology and progress. I want to make sure that as exciting as the future is, it's fair for everyone.

Because of those three letters after my name I get access to real leading thinkers, experts and activists. I love asking them questions and I'm constantly learning and refining my own views and opinions.

Q. Do you think the Scottish Parliament effectively represents women and ethnic minorities?

A. I think we're ok at representing women and terrible at representing ethnic communities. There have only ever been four non-white MSPs. They were all men of Pakistani origin. While I'm glad they were there, Scotland is much more diverse than our Parliament looks.

We are also very poor at representing disabled people.

I support affirmative action mechanisms to change this because I think our politics and our political systems would be more representative of the country if it looked more like them. There are still too many white, middle-aged, middle-class men in politics.

The work of MSPs

MSPs work on behalf of their constituents in two main ways:

1. The work they do in the Scottish Parliament.
2. The work they do in their constituency.

Committee work

Committees are small, cross-party groups of MSPs who meet on a regular basis to scrutinise the work of the Scottish government, conduct inquiries into subjects within their remit and examine legislation. There are many committees in the parliament, e.g. the Economy, Energy and Tourism Committee. Committees can be created during parliamentary sessions to deal with specific issues.

MSPs represent constituents in parliamentary committees by various means.

- Committees have the power to introduce bills (draft laws) which are specific to the committee. These are known as Committee Bills. If there is enough support in parliament Committee Bills are passed and become acts of law.

- When an amendment (change) to a law is being considered or a new law is being created, the bill is sent to the appropriate committee. This gives the committee the chance to scrutinise and propose any changes to the bill before it goes to the parliament.

- Committees conduct inquiries – this is where they investigate issues to find out if there are problems and if changes are needed to bills. Committees can call on outside groups, such as trade unions, and witnesses to present evidence to help them to develop informed opinions and to represent the views of a wide range of people. During this time the questions answered and the evidence given helps the committee understand the issues more clearly. **For example, in 2016 the Health and Sport Committee was seeking evidence as part of the Scottish Government Palliative and End of Life Care Strategy. The committee took written evidence from the BMA Scotland and the Care Inspectorate.**

- Committees discuss and write reports for the parliament to consider. Reports will recommend whether the parliament should agree to a bill. Committee reports can have an influence on how MSPs vote in parliament. **For example, in 2017 the Education and Skills Committee published its report on teacher workforce planning for Scotland's schools. The report looked at what could be done to make teaching an attractive profession.**

- When a petition is being examined by the Public Petitions Committee the group must carry out an investigation into what should be done. If the committee finds that the law should be changed it then reports to the parliament and asks for the law to be changed.

- Committees can check the work of the Scottish government by asking Cabinet Secretaries to answer questions and give evidence at committee meetings or inquires. A Cabinet Secretary could be asked to justify money they have spent or received. Minutes (notes) from all committee meetings are available on the Scottish Parliament website and members of the public can sit in on meetings.

 Make the Link

In Section 2 you will learn about new and possible changes to the law. For example, the **Criminal Justice (Scotland) Bill**, which sets out the powers of the police.

 Word bank

- **Petition**
A written request, signed by many people, submitted to authority in support of a cause.

? Questions

1. **Describe** what a committee is.
2. **Explain, in detail**, the work of committees in the Scottish Parliament.
3. 'Committees cannot check the work of the Scottish government.' Give one reason to show why this statement is **exaggerated**.

[N5]

The work of MSPs inside the Chamber of the Scottish Parliament

The Chamber is the part of the Scottish Parliament where MSPs are able to debate, discuss and vote on bills. The Chamber is the only part of the parliament where a bill can be passed and become a law. The seats in the Chamber are arranged in a half circle which reflects the desire to promote debate and encourage consensus among MSPs.

Activity

Research
Using the Scottish Parliament committees webpage: http://www.parliament.scot/ parliamentarybusiness/ Committees.aspx (QR code below), create a list of the current committees in the Scottish Parliament. Choose two committees you are interested in and find an **example** of the work that is going on within each committee.

Figure 2.4: *The Scottish Parliament Chamber*

Figure 2.5: *The House of Commons*

MSPs can represent constituents in the Chamber by:

- putting forward a motion (idea) to be debated
- speaking and voting in the Chamber
- questioning Ministers and the First Minister
- suggesting an amendment (change) to be made to a bill
- introducing a Members' Bill (according to the parliament's rules every MSP has the right to introduce two bills in the term of the parliament)

Stages of a bill

A major function of the Scottish Parliament is to make laws. All legislation must pass through three basic stages before it can become an act of law:

First stage	The most appropriate committee will scrutinise the bill and take evidence. It will then produce a report that will say whether the committee agrees with the general principles or not. The whole of the parliament will then consider the report and decide whether the bill should proceed to the next stage.
Second stage	If the bill makes it to the second stage it is scrutinised further by committee members or sometimes by all MSPs. Usually a number of amendments will be made at this stage, which can result in changes being made to the final legislation.
Third stage	Finally, the bill goes back to the main Chamber and all the MSPs to consider the amended bill. Again, amendments can be made at this point. After a debate MSPs will vote for or against the bill. It will then be scrutinised by law officers to ensure that it falls within the devolved remit of the Scottish Parliament.

 Think point

The Chamber in Westminster is set up so that the government faces the opposition. Why do you think this is? Which parliament do you think is arranged in the best way?

When MSPs are satisfied, the Presiding Officer will seek Royal Assent from the Queen. It is only after the Queen has given her assent that a bill becomes an act of the Scottish Parliament. The power to withhold Royal Assent is permitted but it is not expected that this would happen.

For example, each year the Cabinet Secretary for Finance introduces the **Budget Bill**. The purpose of the bill is to seek parliamentary approval for the Scottish government's spending plans for the financial year. The bill goes through the same three legislative stages as other bills. However, there is an accelerated timescale: no stage 1 report is required and only the Scottish government may lodge amendments to the bill.

Debates

Issues concerning the whole country will be discussed during a debate. MSPs can contribute to debates, particularly if they are of direct concern to their constituents. Debates are useful because solutions to problems can be identified and new bills can be created. During a bill's passage through parliament on its way to becoming an act, MSPs can use the Second Reading to debate the principles or ideas of the bill. During the debating process the issue may be raised by the mass media and attract the public's attention. For example, MSPs debated the **Alcohol (Minimum Pricing) (Scotland) Bill** to make provisions about the price at which alcohol may be sold from licensed premises. The bill received Royal Assent on 29th June 2012 but was not fully introduced until 1st May 2018 due to legal challenges outside of parliament.

Voting

At the end of each business day in the Chamber, MSPs need to vote. This is called 'decision time' and the results of the vote can decide whether an issue or bill passes on to the next stage of the legislative process (this depends on the stage of the bill). MSPs must consider the views of their constituents when voting, as well as the view of their political party. In the Scottish Parliament, MSPs vote by electronic keypad and the results can be seen by the Presiding Officer.

 Make the Link

You may learn more about the minimum pricing of alcohol in subjects which look at health and wellbeing, such as PE and PSE.

 Hint

You can watch debates in the Scottish Parliament by accessing the webpage: www.scottishparliament.tv

 Activity

Research
Voting records for all current MSPs are published on the Scottish Parliament website. To find out when and how a MSP has voted in the Chamber:

- go to the Scottish Parliament website: http://www.parliament.scot

- click on 'MSPs' then 'current MSPs'
- choose an MSP
- the information is found under 'parliamentary activities'

 N5 Whips

Parties in the Scottish Parliament have 'whips'. A whip is an MSP whose job is to make sure that MSPs vote how their party tells them to. Whips instruct MSPs to vote as a group, regardless of what the MSP's constituents want.

If an MSP ignores these instructions they may find that they are not promoted in the future, or that they might not be reselected as a candidate at the next election. This means if a party has a majority in parliament, and the party whips instruct their MSPs to vote together in a particular way, then it is very likely that the bill would be passed.

 Think point

This raises the question as to whether or not MSPs really represent the interests of their constituents. What do you think?

Activity

Homework
Watch First Minister's Question Time online or on the Parliament Channel to see how this process takes place and how the Scottish Parliament is arranged.

Question Time

Question Time is the main chance for MSPs to question and hold to account the actions of the Scottish government. This is where MSPs can ask questions and raise issues on behalf of their constituents. Question Time is one of the key ways in which parliament can hold the First Minister and individual ministers to account. This means the parliament can 'check' the Scottish Government and make sure they have to answer for decisions they are making and are doing their job correctly.

First Minister's Question Time (FMQs) takes place every Thursday between 12 and 12.45pm. It is broadcast on the TV, internet and radio by BBC Scotland. The main leaders of the other political parties and some MSPs are able to question the First Minister. The First Minister is therefore directly accountable to the other party leaders. Because FMQs can become quite lively, when the Presiding Officer deems the subject to be exhausted he/she will move on to the next question.

Figure 2.6: *Question Time in the Scottish Parliament*

Question Time to Scottish Ministers takes place on a Thursday afternoon. It is a 60-minute session which allows MSPs to ask questions of relevant Scottish ministers on a pre-determined theme for 40 minutes, followed by a general question time lasting 20 minutes. Questions to Scottish ministers can be tabled 8–14 days before Thursday's question time. Questions are randomly selected by the Presiding Officer. For example, the Cabinet Secretary for Health and Sport could be asked about a local hospital closure during this time.

Members' Bills

According to the Scottish Parliament's rules, every MSP has the right to introduce two Members' Bills during one parliamentary session (which is usually four years). These bills may be the result of a constituent contacting their MSP about an issue in an attempt to get them to change the law. Many Members' Bills are unsuccessful, especially if they come from an opposition MSP, but they may impact upon future government legislation. For example Stewart Maxwell, SNP MSP, introduced a bill to ban tobacco smoking in enclosed public places in February 2004. The Labour–Liberal Democrat coalition at first opposed this proposal but were eventually forced to accept the idea after it received widespread support. The coalition eventually published a bill that was passed on 30th June 2005 and the ban came into effect on 26th March 2006.

Members' Bill

In August 2017, Monica Lennon MSP first submitted legislation to end 'period poverty'. The proposal is for a bill to ensure free access to sanitary products, including in schools, colleges and universities. Ninety-six per cent of responses to the initial consultation on her draft proposal were supportive and the bill has now been submitted as a final proposal with the support of the five parties in the Scottish Parliament.

Her proposed **Sanitary Products (Free Provision) (Scotland) Bill** would create a statutory duty for free provision of sanitary products. Ms Lennon said: 'Scotland can lead the world on period poverty – and it is a positive step that all the parties at the Scottish

Figure 2.7: *Monica Lennon*

Parliament have united behind these proposals. Access to sanitary products should be a basic right but sadly in Scotland we know not everyone can afford or obtain what they need.'

The main provisions of the bill are:

- A duty on Scottish Ministers to introduce a universal system of free provision of sanitary products.
- A duty on all schools to provide free sanitary products in school toilets.
- A duty on all colleges and universities to provide free sanitary products in campus toilets.
- Measures to allow Scottish Ministers to extend these duties to other bodies in future, following a period of review, if deemed appropriate or necessary.

GO! Activity

Research

Research a current Members' Bill using the internet. Discuss in small groups the following questions:

- do you **support** the main aim of the proposed bill? **Explain the reasons** for your response
- what do you think are the advantages and disadvantages of the proposed legislation?
- if you were an MSP would you vote for or against this bill? **Explain the reasons** for your choice

---

? Questions

1. Draw a flow chart to show the different stages a bill must pass through before becoming a law.
2. **Why do you think** there are so many stages involved in passing a bill?
3. Create a table showing the work of an MSP in the Scottish Parliament. Use the structure below:

Work of MSP in the Parliament	Explanation	Example

Activity

Group work
In groups, create a role-play exercise demonstrating the work of an MSP in parliament. Choose one example of the work of an MSP from the list below:

- committees
- debating
- voting
- asking a question at Question Time
- creating a Members' Bill

Groups should write and perform a role-play based on their chosen example. All members of the group should be given a part to play to demonstrate their understanding.

Figure 2.8: *A Labour constituency office*

 **Activity**

Research
Using the Scottish Parliament website, find out the contact details of your MSPs.

The work of MSPs in the constituency

All citizens of Scotland have one constituency MSP and seven regional list MSPs.

For example, Fulton MacGregor (SNP) is the current (2018) constituency MSP for the constituency of Coatbridge and Chryston. This constituency is in the region of Central Scotland that is currently represented by the following regional list MSPs:

- Richard Leonard (Labour)
- Mark Griffin (Labour)
- Monica Lennon (Labour)
- Graham Simpson (Conservative)
- Elaine Smith (Labour)
- Margaret Mitchell (Conservative)
- Alison Harris (Conservative)

All MSPs work in their constituency on Mondays and Fridays.

MSPs can be contacted about issues that are related to devolved matters, such as housing, transport etc.

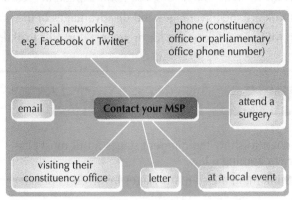

Figure 2.9: *Ways in which a constituent can contact their MSP*

During their time in the constituency MSPs will do a variety of things.

- **Work from their local constituency office** replying to correspondence, such as letters, emails and phone calls they have received. Constituents have the right to contact their MSPs and MSPs have a duty to respond to constituents and proceed as appropriate. More and more MSPs are using social networking sites such as Facebook and Twitter to reach out to their constituents.

- **Hold surgeries.** A surgery is when people go along to talk to their MSP face-to-face about problems or issues they might have in the constituency. Issues can be about any devolved matter. Surgeries take place on a regular basis in the constituency and the MSP is duty bound to take up the issue and report back to the constituent with the outcome.

- **Attend local meetings.** MSPs attend local meetings of local people to find out about things that are of concern to them in the constituency. MSPs might use their influence to talk to business people, the police or council departments.

- **Attend local events.** MSPs are often asked to local schools, hospitals, factories etc. At these events MSPs can learn about the concerns of their constituents and find out about projects that could affect their constituents.

- **Meet with other representatives.** MSPs may meet with the MP, local councillors and MEP to discuss issues of common concern in the area or to resolve constituents' issues.

- **Organise fact-finding visits.** When a constituent raises an issue, the MSP may have to visit somewhere to see first-hand what the problem is. Afterwards, the MSP might arrange more meetings to resolve the problem or raise it as an issue in parliament.

- **Contact the mass media.** An MSP may also work with the media, such as local TV and newspapers, to highlight an issue within their constituency. The publicity may result in the issue being resolved. Additionally, MSPs will use the media to try to maintain a positive public profile.

> **Jenny Gilruth MSP**
> Mid Fife and Glenrothes
> is holding a public surgery on
>
> **Saturday 26th**
> **April**
> **1130–1230**
>
> **GLENROTHES**
> **Rothes Halls**
>
> **No appointment necessary**

Figure 2.10: *Poster of an MSP's surgery details*

? Questions

1. What days of the week do MSPs work in their constituency?
2. List the various ways that a constituent can contact their MSP.
3. Create a table showing the work of an MSP in their constituency. Use the structure below:

Work of MSPs in the constituency	Explanation	Example

🔵 Activity

Research
Research some specific examples of the MSP working in the constituency where you live.

4. Copy and complete the below weekly timetable for the work of an MSP. Include the work they do in the parliament and the work they do in the constituency. Use Figure 2.2 on page 36 to help you.

Day		Work
Monday	AM	
	PM	
Tuesday	AM	
	PM	
Wednesday	AM	
	PM	
Thursday	AM	
	PM	
Friday	AM	
	PM	

5. Design a webpage, leaflet or poster detailing your MSP's constituency work. You will need to include the following:

- your MSP's name and their political party
- how constituents can contact the MSP, e.g. phone number, email address, constituency office details and opening hours
- examples of the MSP's recent work in the constituency
- information telling constituents what issues they can contact their MSP about

Local councils in Scotland

Local councils are often referred to as local government or authorities. Local councils provide a range of services and play an important part in the everyday lives of people in Scotland. There are 32 local council areas in Scotland. Glasgow City Council is the largest council with almost 600,000 people and Orkney is the smallest with under 20,000 people.

Each council area is made up of councillors who are directly elected by the residents in the area they represent. These areas are called council 'wards'.

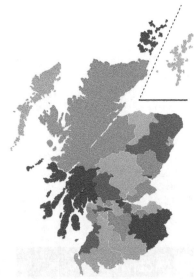

Figure 2.11: *Map of local authorities in Scotland*

Each ward will have three or four councillors and in total there are 1,222 elected councillors in Scotland. For example, in Glasgow City Council there are 21 wards with 79 councillors.

Following the introduction of the **Local Governance (Scotland) Act 2004**, local elections are held using the Single Transferable Vote (STV) system, with this first taking place in 2007. STV asks voters to rank the candidates in order of their preference.

 Hint

Electoral systems will be covered in more detail later in this section on page 52.

Activity

Research
Using the webpage https://www.gov.uk/find-your-local-council find out the following information:

1. Which local authority area do you live in?
2. What is the name of the council ward in which you live?
3. What are the names and political parties of the councillors who represent you?

Local council services

Local government is a devolved matter (see page 14); the Scottish government decides policies and laws in this area and local councils deliver them.

Local councils are responsible for planning, resourcing and delivering key public services. Mandatory services are those that councils must provide by law, such as education, fire services and social work services. Discretionary services are those that councils do not have to provide but may do if they have enough money. These include recreation services, such as parks and museums.

The work of local councillors

The main role of local councillors is to represent the interests of the people in their ward. As most councillors are part-time they do most of their work in the evenings and at weekends.

Councillors find out the views of local people by holding surgeries in their wards. Local people can speak to their councillor who will decide the best course of action to take in order to solve their problem. A local councillor can approach the relevant council department on behalf of the local people. Additionally, councillors can contact other representatives for the area, such as the local MP and MSP, and pass on the concerns of people living in that community.

Councillors have to attend meetings to deal with the major decisions taken by the council. This is a chance for councillors to try to ensure that the decisions made are in the best interests of their constituents.

Councillors may also work on committees wherein small groups of councillors make decisions on behalf of local people. There is usually a committee for each of the various council departments. Committees work to develop new policies for the council or scrutinise existing ones.

Councillors may also be asked to attend local events. During this time they are able to interact with local residents and gain publicity in the media.

 Activity

Research
Create a fact file on the services your local council offers by visiting their webpage. Your fact file should include the council's name and logo, an explanation of the difference between mandatory and discretionary services, a list of the services provided by the council and appropriate images.

Think point

Should the role of a councillor be a part-time or full-time role?

❓ Questions

1. How many local councils are there in Scotland?
2. What is a local councillor?
3. What is the name given to the area which councillors represent?
4. How many councillors will represent each ward?
5. Name the voting system used to elect local councillors.
6. Describe the work of a local councillor. Mention at least 4 things they do.

Representing Scottish women and minorities

Most of the major parties in Scotland have made commitments to improve the representation of women and members from black, Asian and minority ethnic (BAME) communities. As of 2018, the leaders of Scotland's two largest parties (the SNP and the Scottish Conservatives) are both women. The Labour Party had a female leader until Kezia Dugdale stepped down in 2017.

Figure 2.12: *Nicola Sturgeon, leader of the SNP with Ruth Davidson, leader of the Scottish Conservatives*

	No. of MSPs	% of Parliament	% of Scottish population
Female	45	35.0	51.0
Openly identify as LGBT	10	7.0	2.2
BAME	2	1.5	4.0
Privately educated	26	20.0	4.4

Think point

Why might some people think all-women shortlists for elections are unfair?

In terms of men and women, the Scottish Parliament is slightly more representative than the UK Parliament (32% female) but it still falls short of the ideal 50/50 split. All of the major parties are committed to improving the representation of women and many have introduced all-women shortlists for selecting candidates for election.

Female MSPs by party (2016 Scottish Parliament election)	
Party	% of female MSPs
Labour	46
SNP	43
Conservative	19
Green	17
Liberal Democrat	0

In 2017, 2.2% of Scotland's population identified their sexual orientation as lesbian, gay, bisexual or other. This means that the Scottish Parliament reflects LGBT interests well. Scotland has also been applauded by LGBT charities and organisations for introducing progressive policies such as recognising gay marriage and pledges to legislate for non-binary gender recognition for the transgender community.

In 2017, minority ethnic groups represented 4% of the Scottish population. With only two MSPs from ethnic minority backgrounds (1.5% of Parliament), there is still work to be done to ensure these interests are fairly represented.

One-fifth (20%) of MSPs were privately educated compared with just 4% of the Scottish population. This is a large difference and raises questions about how well the Scottish Parliament represents the population.

? Questions

1. How have Scottish political parties tried to improve representation of women?

2. Copy and complete the table to compare the Scottish Parliament with the Scottish population.

	% of Scottish Parliament	% of Scottish population
Female		
BAME		
LGBT		
Privately educated		

3. 'The Scottish Parliament accurately represents the Scottish population.' Give one reason to **support** and one reason to **oppose** this statement.

Summary

In this chapter you have learned:

- the names of the different types of political representatives
- the work of an MSP in the parliament and constituency
- how a constituent can contact their MSP
- how local councils are organised in Scotland
- the work of a local councillor, representing their constituents
- the representation of women and ethnic minorities

Learning Summary

Now that you have finished the **Representation** chapter, complete a self-evaluation of your knowledge and skills to assess what you have understood. Use the checklist below and its traffic lights to draw up a revision plan to help you improve in the areas you identified as red or amber.

- I can list the main types of political representatives I have learned about.

- I can name my local constituency MSP, the party they belong to and at least one of my local councillors and their respective political party.

- I can explain the ways in which MSPs can represent their constituents in committees in the Scottish Parliament.

- I can explain the different ways in which MSPs represent their constituents in the Chamber of the Scottish Parliament.

- I can outline the stages of a bill.

- I can list the ways in which constituents can contact their MSP.

- I can explain the ways in which MSPs represent their constituents in the constituency or region.

- I can explain how local councils in Scotland are organised.

- I can explain the ways in which local councillors can represent their constituents in their ward.

- I can list the ways a constituent can contact their local councillor.

- I can describe the under-representation of women and ethnic minorities

Examples

In Modern Studies it is essential that you are able to back up any point you make with relevant evidence. When you are considering the statements above try to think of relevant examples for each response. You may wish to note these examples under each statement in your revision notes.

3 Electoral systems

What you will learn in this chapter

- What an electoral system is.
- The main features and outcomes of the electoral system used for Scottish Parliament elections.
- The advantages and disadvantages of the Scottish electoral system.
- The main features and outcomes of the electoral system used for local council elections in Scotland.
- The advantages and disadvantages of the electoral system used for local council elections in Scotland.

Figure 3.1: *Voting: casting a sealed vote*

What is an electoral system?

An electoral system, also known as voting system, is a method used during an election to allow voters to make a choice based on who they wish to represent them. Different electoral systems are used for different elections and can result in very different outcomes.

Scottish Parliament elections

Scottish Parliament elections have fixed four-year terms except if this clashes with the UK election which is why the current parliamentary term is 5 years. The **Fixed-term Parliaments Act 2011** introduced fixed-term elections for the first time to the Westminster Parliament. Under the act a UK Parliament general election will normally be held on the first Thursday in May every five years. However, with the support of two-thirds of the House of Commons it is possible to hold an early election, as happened in May 2017. This means the next general election will be in 2022, rather than 2020.

The Additional Member System (AMS)

The electoral system used to elect the 129 Members of the Scottish Parliament (MSPs) is called the Additional Member System (AMS). AMS is a hybrid system that combines elements of the First Past the Post (FPTP) system and Proportional Representation (PR). Under the AMS system voters are given two ballot papers.

The constituency ballot paper

The ballot paper to elect constituency MSPs uses the FPTP system. Scotland is divided into 73 constituencies and each constituency elects one MSP.

The constituency ballot paper contains a list of the names of candidates and their political parties who are standing for election. Voters have to put one cross next to the name of the candidate they wish to vote for

Word bank

- **Ballot paper**
A paper used to register a vote.

Hint

Constituency MSPs are elected by the FPTP system in exactly the same way as MPs are elected to the House of Commons.

on the ballot paper. When the results of the election are counted, the candidate with the most votes is elected as the MSP for the constituency. This is why FPTP is known as a single winner voting system.

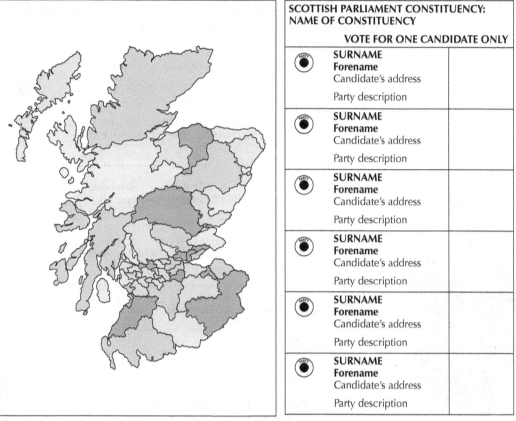

Figure 3.2: *Scottish Parliament 73 constituencies map and constituency ballot paper*

Advantages and disadvantages of the FPTP system

Advantages of FPTP	Disadvantages of FPTP
It is an easy system for voters to understand. FPTP is a fair system as the candidate with the most votes wins. For example, in 2016 Tavish Scott (Liberal Democrats) won the Shetland Islands seat with 67.4% of the vote.	The winning candidate doesn't need to get a minimum number of votes; they only need more votes than any other candidate. This can result in more people actually voting against the winning candidate. For example, in 2016 Alexander Burnett (Conservatives) won the Aberdeenshire West constituency with just 38% of the vote.
There is a strong link between the MSP and the people of the constituency. The MSP is accountable to the voters and has a duty to help them with any problems.	Many votes do not make a difference, especially in constituencies where a candidate wins with a large majority. This can lead to voter apathy. For example, in the 2016 election turnout was only 55%.
It can discourage candidates from extremist parties as it is very hard for them to be elected, even if they do achieve a sizeable number of votes. For example, the British National Party has never won a seat in the Scottish Parliament.	It is unfair on candidates from smaller parties as they usually do not receive enough votes to secure a seat in parliament. Only the SNP, the Scottish Labour Party and the Scottish Conservative Party had candidates in all constituencies.

The regional ballot paper

The second ballot paper uses a form of PR to elect 56 additional members to the Scottish Parliament. Scotland is divided into eight parliamentary regions, each comprising a number of whole constituencies. The initial regions for the parliament were the same as the European Parliament constituencies. Each region elects seven regional MSPs.

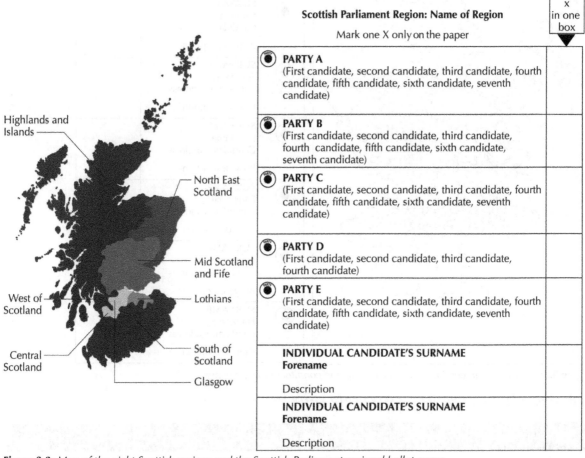

Figure 3.3: *Map of the eight Scottish regions and the Scottish Parliament regional ballot paper*

On the regional ballot paper, voters indicate their choice by placing an 'X' next to their preferred party or individual candidate to represent the region. The votes are counted for each political party. As a system of PR is in place, the percentage of votes a party receives is then converted into seats. The formula takes into account the number of regional votes that a party has received and the number of constituency seats it has already won – this helps to make the overall result more proportional.

For example, if the SNP received 40% of the vote then they get around 40% of the seven seats. 7 × 40% = 3 MSPs

Regional MSPs are selected from lists compiled by the parties. Each party produces a list of candidates numbered one to seven before the election. If a party receives three MSPs through the regional vote then the candidates numbered one to three on the list become MSPs. This is why regional MSPs are sometimes referred to as Party List MSPs.

If a regional seat becomes vacant, the next candidate on the party list becomes an MSP. For example, in December 2016 Alex Johnstone,

Conservative list MSP for the North East region, died. He was replaced by Bill Bowman who was the next name on the Conservative Party list for the region.

This is different from a constituency MSP resigning or dying, as this would trigger a by-election. In the Ettrick, Roxburgh and Berwickshire by-election, after the resignation of John Lamont MSP in 2017, the Conservative candidate Rachael Hamilton won after beating the SNP candidate by more than 9,000 votes.

Summary of the make-up of the Scottish Parliament

1 constituency MSP for each constituency	73 constituencies = 73 constituency MSPs
7 regional list MSPs for each region	7 MSPs × 8 regions = 56 regional list MSPs
	Total MSPs = 129 Therefore a political party needs to secure **65 seats** to win an overall majority in Holyrood.

GO! Activity

Discuss
Think, pair, share with your shoulder partner what type of individuals you think political parties might put at the top of their Party List. **Why do you think** this might be the case? (Hint – it might be useful to think about female candidates, or candidates from an ethnic minority.)

❓ Questions

1. Name the electoral system used to elect MSPs.
2. How many ballot papers are Scottish voters given?
3. **Explain, in detail,** how constituency MSPs are elected to the Scottish Parliament.
4. List some advantages and disadvantages of electing constituency MSPs using FPTP.
5. **Explain, in detail,** how regional MSPs are elected to the Scottish Parliament.
6. Can you **explain** why by-elections are not held to replace regional MSPs?
7. Copy out the summary of the make-up of the Scottish Parliament.

The outcome of AMS

After the 1999 and 2003 Scottish Parliamentary elections, the Labour Party and the Liberal Democrats formed a coalition in the Scottish Parliament. By joining forces they had a majority of MSPs and formed the Scottish Executive (now called the Scottish Government). After the 2007 elections, however, the SNP won more seats than any other party, but only by one seat – they did not have an overall majority. The SNP decided to form a minority government, which meant that every time it wanted to pass legislation it had to agree with the other parties in the parliament on an issue-by-issue basis. The same situation arose following the 2016 election. The SNP argue that this approach has led to more consensus politics in the third and fifth Scottish Parliament electoral terms (2007–11 and 2016–21).

The 2011 Scottish Parliament election results					
Party	Constituency MSPs	Regional MSPs	Total MSPs	% of votes	% of seats
SNP	53	16	69	44.7	53.5
Labour	15	22	37	29	28.7
Conservative	3	12	15	13.15	11.6
Liberal Democrats	2	3	5	6.55	3.9
Green	0	2	2	2.2	1.6
Margo MacDonald	0	1	1	0.45	0.8
					Turnout = 50.6%

Figure 3.4: *SNP leader Alex Salmond, jubilant after the historic 2011 election result*

The results of the 2011 election were historic because for the first time in the history of the Scottish Parliament one party, the SNP, were able to achieve an overall majority. AMS was designed to prevent this from ever happening – indeed, one of the many advantages often cited of AMS is the fact that it produced governments that need to work in coalition, be that formally, as with the Labour – Liberal alliance from 1999, or more informally, as in the SNP's 2007–11 term.

The 2016 Scottish Parliament election results						
Party	Constituency seats	Regional seats	Total seats	% of votes (constituency)	% of votes (regional)	% of seats
SNP	59	4	63	46.5	41.7	48.8
Conservative	7	24	31	22.0	22.9	24.0
Labour	3	21	24	22.6	19.1	18.6
Green	0	6	6	0.6	6.6	4.7
Liberal Democrats	4	1	5	7.6	5.2	3.9
Independent	0	0	0	0.5	4.5	0
						Turnout = 55.6%

In 2016 the SNP won the election and a third term in government but fell two seats short of a second overall majority. The Conservatives saw an increase in support and replaced the Labour Party as the second-largest party and main opposition in the Scottish Parliament. This was the first time that Labour had finished in third place at a Scottish election in 98 years. The Scottish Greens won six seats on the regional list and overtook the Liberal Democrats, who remained on five seats.

Although the SNP lost its majority, it was still by far the largest single party in the Scottish Parliament, with more than double the seats of the Conservatives. Nicola Sturgeon announced that she would form a minority SNP government as the party had done in 2007.

It is clear to see that under AMS the percentage of votes a party gains is closely related to the percentage of seats they gain in parliament. In both the 2011 and 2016 elections the Greens had a better chance of being elected and doing well out of AMS as they only fielded candidates in the regional election. This is because their votes were spread out geographically rather than being concentrated in specific constituencies.

 Think point

Try to think of some disadvantages and advantages of AMS.

 Activity

Use your skills
Using only the results from the Scottish Parliament elections, what **conclusions** can be drawn about AMS?

You must make and justify a **conclusion** about each of the following headings:

- fairness in representation – do all political parties receive a proportionate (equal) number of seats in relation to the number of votes secured?
- overrepresentation of parties – which parties do well under AMS?
- underrepresentation of parties – which parties do not do well under AMS?
- trends/patterns over time – has support increased or decreased for some parties?

The advantages and disadvantages of AMS

Advantages of AMS	Disadvantages of AMS
AMS is a fair system because there is a link between the number of votes a party receives and the number of seats it gets. This results in fewer wasted votes and should improve turnout.	AMS is more difficult for voters to understand. In the 2007 election there was a lot of confusion – around 140,000 ballot papers were not filled out properly and were therefore disqualified.
AMS usually results in a coalition government. Some people think that coalition governments are more representative of the way people have voted.	Coalition governments may be less stable than a majority government. If the coalition parties disagree over too much, the coalition can be torn apart and the government can fall.
AMS prevents large parties from getting more seats than the share of the vote they received. This has prevented Labour from potentially governing Scotland permanently. PR helps smaller political parties gain seats and representation in the parliament.	AMS is unfair to larger parties. Parties that win a lot of constituencies lose out on seats from the regional lists. For example, in 2007 Labour won only nine regional members because they performed well on the constituency vote.
AMS gives voters greater representation. It is a way of keeping the link between voters and their constituency representative as well as giving voters additional representatives who are accountable to them in their region.	Scottish voters have eight representatives, very often from different political parties. This can lead to confusion about who is responsible for what and who they can go and see if they have a problem.

? Question

Explain the advantages and disadvantages of AMS. Use the election results above and your knowledge of AMS to give examples to support as many of your points as possible.

Local council elections in Scotland

Scottish local government elections are a matter devolved to the Scottish Parliament under the **Scotland Act 1998**. The Scottish government is responsible for setting the rules for the conduct of local government elections. Local authorities themselves are responsible for organising and conducting these elections in their own areas.

Local government elections elect local councillors who represent the voters who live in the council area. In May 2007 the Single Transferable Vote (STV), a form of PR, was first used in Scotland. Before 2007, councillors had been elected using the FPTP electoral system.

Figure 3.5: *The sign points to a polling station, where voters can cast their vote*

N5 How does STV work?

Within the 32 local councils in Scotland, each council is divided into areas called 'wards', often referred to as 'multi-member constituencies'. Under STV, constituencies are normally larger than they were under FPTP, however each elects several representatives; depending upon its size up to four councillors are elected for each ward.

Under STV, voters rank candidates in order of preference by marking '1', '2', '3' and so on next to the names of candidates on a ballot paper. A voter can rank as many or as few candidates as they like or just vote for one candidate. It is simple for the voters to cast their votes, but it is complicated to count the votes in the STV system.

Figure 3.6: *A STV ballot paper as used in the 2012 local council elections*

(continued)

N5 Each candidate needs a minimum number of votes to be elected. This number is calculated according to the number of seats and votes cast, and is called a quota. The quota is calculated by dividing the number of votes cast by one more than the number of seats available, and then adding one.

$$\left(\frac{Votes\ cast}{Number\ of\ seats\ available + 1} \right) + 1 = Quota$$

E.g. in a four-member constituency where 150,000 votes were cast, a candidate would require 30,001 votes in order to be elected:

$$\left(\frac{150,000}{5(4\,seats + 1)} \right) + 1 = 30,001$$

> ### 📖 Word bank
>
> **• Quota**
> A limited or fixed number or amount of people or things.
>
> **• Surplus votes**
> The amount of votes that exceed the quota needed for a candidate to be elected.

The first preference votes for each candidate are added up and any candidate who has achieved this quota is elected. If a candidate has more votes than are needed to fill the quota, that candidate's surplus votes are transferred to the remaining candidates. Votes that would have gone to the winner instead go to the second preference listed on those ballot papers.

If candidates do not meet the quota, the candidate with the fewest first preference votes is eliminated and the second preference votes are transferred to other candidates. These processes are repeated until all the seats are filled.

The advantages and disadvantages of the STV system

Advantages	Disadvantages
Fewer votes will be wasted as a number of candidates will be elected in each constituency. This means that a variety of parties may win some representation. This may encourage more people to vote if they know that their vote will count.	STV is a complicated system for voters to understand. This may stop people from voting because they do not understand how candidates are to be elected.
There is greater choice for voters as they can choose between different candidates from the same party. This means that less effective candidates will not be guaranteed election and keeps elected politicians on their toes as there are no longer 'safe seats', where established politicians can, in some case, rely on being re-elected.	Each constituency being able to elect a number of representatives may cause confusion. If a voter has a problem, it may be difficult to work out which representative to consult. Furthermore, larger constituencies may result in less representation of local issues.
STV gives smaller parties a greater chance of getting elected, resulting in a more diverse range of views being represented. For example, many Green Party and Independent candidates were elected to Scotland's councils in 2007 when STV replaced FPTP as the electoral system.	

Figure 3.7: *A Labour–Conservative coalition was the way forward for Stirling Council in 2012*

? Questions

1. How often do local council elections usually take place?
2. Name the electoral system used to elect local councillors.

N5 3. **Describe, in detail,** how the STV works.

4. **Explain, in detail,** some advantages and disadvantages of STV.

Summary

In this chapter you have learned:

- what an electoral system is

- the main features and outcomes of the electoral system used for Scottish Parliament elections

- the advantages and disadvantages of the Scottish electoral system

- the main features and outcomes of the electoral system used for local council elections in Scotland

- the advantages and disadvantages of the electoral system used for local council elections in Scotland

Learning Summary

Now that you have finished the **Electoral systems** chapter, complete a self-evaluation of your knowledge and skills to assess what you have understood. Use the checklist below and its traffic lights to draw up a revision plan to help you improve in the areas you identified as red or amber.

- I can explain what is meant by an electoral system.

- I can state how often Scottish Parliament elections are held.

- I can name the electoral system used to elects MSPs to the Scottish Parliament.

- I can describe the features of the electoral system used to elect MSPs.

- I can explain what is meant by proportional representation.

- I can outline when by-elections are held.

- I can explain the outcome of recent Scottish Parliament elections.

- I can explain the advantages and disadvantages of the AMS.

- I can state how often local council elections are held in Scotland.

- I can name the electoral system used to elect local councillors in Scotland.

- I can describe the features of the electoral system used to elect local councillors. (N5 only)

- I can explain the advantages and disadvantages of the STV system. (N5 only)

Examples

In Modern Studies it is essential that you are able to back up any point you make with relevant evidence. When you are considering the statements above try to think of relevant examples for each response. You may wish to note these examples under each statement in your revision notes.

4 Participation

Participation

The word 'participate' means 'to take part'. As Scotland is a democracy, people can participate in making decisions for the country and try to influence representatives.

There are various ways to participate, such as:

- voting in elections
- joining a political party
- standing as a candidate
- contacting a representative, e.g. at a surgery
- signing a petition
- contacting the media, e.g. writing to a newspaper
- taking part in a protest or demonstration
- joining a pressure group
- joining a trade union

Figure 4.1: *Joining a protest or demonstration is one way to participate in a democratic country*

Voting in the UK

One of the most important ways people can participate in a democracy is by voting. Voting usually takes place at election time when the whole country is given the opportunity to choose who they want to represent them. In Scotland we have the right to vote in elections for local councils, the Scottish Parliament, the Westminster Parliament, and the European Parliament.

Citizens have the right to vote when they are:

- 18 years of age or over on polling day (16 years of age or over for Scottish government and Scottish local council elections)
- a British citizen, a Commonwealth citizen or a citizen of the Irish Republic (and resident in the United Kingdom)
- on the electoral register (see below)

> **✦ Make the Link**
>
> You may have learned about pressure groups and trade unions in Business Management.

The following citizens do not have the right to vote:

- anyone under 18 years old (under 16 years old for Scottish government and Scottish local council elections)
- people who are visiting the UK
- those who are in prison (for sentences longer than 5 years)
- anyone found guilty within the previous five years of electoral malpractice
- under common law, people with learning disabilities or a mental illness if, on polling day, they are incapable of making a reasoned judgement

Figure 4.2: *Citizens who are in prison cannot vote*

The responsibilities associated with voting

Each year the local council sends every house in the UK a list of people registered to vote at that address. The form should contain the names of those who live in the house and are eligible to vote. You can register to vote from the age of 16. These names are then submitted to become part of what is known as the 'electoral register'.

If an individual is unable to vote in person they may choose to have someone vote on their behalf. This is called a proxy vote. Alternatively, a voter may choose to apply to make their vote by post. Postal voting takes place before election day, so that the results can be counted with the others.

The responsibility of voting lies with the individual voter. Voters should use their vote wisely when selecting a candidate/party to best represent their interests.

🧠 Hint

Many people think that members of the Royal Family are not able to vote. This is not the case – however, in practice, most choose not to do so because it would be considered unconstitutional.

Turnout

Voter turnout is the percentage of eligible voters who cast a ballot in an election. It is often used as an indicator of how engaged or disengaged with democracy the people are; for many, turnout is viewed as the most important measure of the health of a democracy.

Scottish Parliament elections	Turnout
1999	59%
2003	49.4%
2007	50.6%
2011	51.7%
2016	55.6%

Figure 4.3: *Voters turning out to vote at their polling station*

Voter turnout at Scottish Parliament elections is usually over 50%. This is lower than turnout at UK general elections but higher than other elections. For example, turnout in the 2017 UK general election was 68.7%, up from 65.1% in 2010, but down compared to 1950 when it was 83.9%.

Think point

The fine for failing to attend a polling place in Australia is the equivalent of just over £10. Do you think this is a reasonable punishment for not voting?

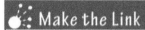

Make the Link

You will learn about different types of punishments in Section 2.

Make the Link

In History you may have learned how the suffragettes fought for a woman's right to vote. You may also have studied dictatorships such as Nazi Germany; you will learn more about dictatorships in Section 3.

Compulsory voting

The right to vote is a freedom fiercely sought by people all over the world, yet in some countries, for example Australia, voting is not a choice, it is compulsory. Under such a system voters are obliged to vote in elections or attend a polling place on voting day, although once there they can choose not to use their vote. Additionally, many voters spoil their ballots – they either mistakenly or intentionally submit a ballot that is blank or improperly filled in and so cannot be counted in the final tally. If an eligible voter does not attend a polling place he or she may be punished by methods such as a fine or community service.

Why should we use our right to vote?

Our right to vote is important and we should use it because:

- it will ensure that Scotland and the UK stay democratic
- it ensures that people are represented democratically at local, national and European level
- it allows us to hold representatives to account
- if we do not vote then unpopular parties may pass laws which we do not want
- it allows the government to gain an understanding of what the public want
- if representatives do not do what voters want, voters can elect someone else the next time
- people have fought and died in the past to win us the right to vote
- people in dictatorships do not have the right to vote; we should appreciate our rights
- if you don't vote you don't have the right to criticise what the government does
- if the turnout is very low those elected may not represent the views of the electorate

? Questions

1. Make a list of those who have the right to vote in elections.
2. Make a list of those who do not have the right to vote in elections.
3. **Describe** the responsibilities associated with the right to vote.
4. What is voter turnout?
5. **Explain** what is meant by compulsory voting.

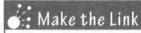

6. Copy and complete the following spider diagram.

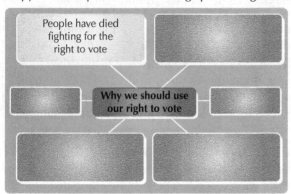

Activity

Homework
Conduct a survey among eligible citizens, such as family members, teachers etc, to find out the reasons why they did or did not vote in the 2016 Scottish Parliament election. Display your results in a suitable way, such as in a bar graph or pie chart.

7. In your opinion, do think it is important that people use their right to vote? Give reasons to **support** your answer.

8. Voter apathy is when there is lack of concern, enthusiasm or interest by voters at election time. Can you think of any reasons why voters might be apathetic? Give examples to **support** your point.

Political parties in Scotland

A political party is a group of people who have the same ideas about running the country. They join together to try to win elections. The party that wins the most seats during an election usually becomes the government and they will work to make their policies the laws that the people of the country have to live by. Political parties are always working to gain support so that when the next election takes place voters are more likely to vote for them.

The main political parties in Scotland are:

- The SNP
- The Labour Party
- The Scottish Conservative Party
- The Liberal Democrat Party
- The Scottish Green Party
- Independent candidates

Each political party has their own ideology (ideas and ideals) based on how they think about the world.

Make the Link

More information about conducting a survey can be found on page 219.

In Maths you will have learned how to report findings in different ways.

Word bank

• Independent candidates
Those candidates for election who are not linked to any political party.

• Ideology
A body of ideas or beliefs that determine the aims of an organisation.

N5 A political spectrum is used to classify ideologies in terms of their position on a scale.

Left wing	Centre	Right wing

Political parties on the left wing have beliefs that are usually progressive in nature, they look to the future, aim to support those who cannot support themselves, are idealist and believe in equality. Left wing supporters believe in taxation to redistribute wealth and are also in support of things like the National Health Service (NHS) and social security. In Scotland and the UK the main left wing parties are the SNP and the Labour Party.

Political parties on the right wing have beliefs that value tradition, they believe in equity, survival of the fittest and economic freedom. They typically believe that businesses shouldn't be regulated (controlled) and that we should all look after ourselves. Right wing supporters believe they shouldn't have to pay for someone else's education or health service. In Scotland and the UK the main right wing party is the Conservative Party.

At the centre of the political spectrum there is the belief that tradition is important but change should be supported if most people want it; the government should play a role only in that it improves the lives of citizens. The Liberal Democrats are the political party most commonly seen as holding the centre ground.

Nowadays, political parties have moved either to the 'centre-left' or 'centre-right', meaning most mainstream parties are neither very left wing, nor very right wing. This may be because there is not mass public support for a political change resulting in a significant shift of society either strongly to the left or the right.

Figure 4.4: *Political parties often align themselves to the left or right of the political spectrum*

📖 Word bank

• Social democratic

The use of 'democratic' means to achieve socialism. Socialism involves the means of production (the facilities and resources for producing goods) and distribution of goods being owned collectively or by a centralised government that often plans and controls the economy.

Beliefs of Scotland's main political parties

Scottish National Party (SNP) **SNP✕**	The SNP is a left of centre social democratic political party that has gained considerable support across Scotland. The party is committed to achieving independence for Scotland and has campaigned for many decades on this issue. In the 2016 election the SNP was elected to a third term in the Scottish Parliament.

The Scottish Conservative Party Scottish Conservatives	The Scottish Conservative Party is a centre-right political party that traditionally gains most of its support from middle- and upper-class voters. The party says it 'stands for freedom, enterprise, community and equality of opportunity as it is a party of choice, responsibility, localism, low taxation and strong but limited government'. The party won 31 seats in the 2016 Scottish Parliament election making it the official opposition party.
The Scottish Labour Party Scottish Labour	The Scottish Labour Party is a centre-left political party that traditionally gains most of its support from working-class voters. The party has links with many trade unions in Scotland. The party stands for 'social justice, strong community and strong values, reward for hard work, decency and rights matched by responsibilities'. The party came third in the 2016 Scottish Parliament election. This was very unusual as historically Labour has been the first or second party in parliament.
The Scottish Liberal Democrat Party SCOTTISH LIBERAL DEMOCRATS www.scotlibdems.org.uk	The Scottish Liberal Democrat Party is a centre-left political party. The party says it 'exists to build and safeguard a fair, free and open society, in which we seek to balance the fundamental values of liberty, equality and community and in which no-one shall be enslaved by poverty, ignorance or conformity'. In the 2016 Scottish Parliament election the party won five seats, keeping the same number of seats as in 2011.

? Questions

1. Name the main political parties in Scotland.
2. **Explain** what is meant by an ideology.
3. **Describe** what politics parties on the left wing, right wing and centre believe in.

What is a manifesto?

Before an election, political parties produce a document called a manifesto. This is an outline of the policies (plan or course of action) they promise to introduce if they are elected to form the government. These promises can be outlined under specific policy areas, such as education, health, justice etc.

Below you will find a table giving the key points from each of the main parties' manifestos from the 2016 election.

SNP
- Increase the NHS revenue budget by £500 million more than inflation by the end of the parliament – an increase of almost £2 billion in total.
- Almost double the number of hours of free nursery education for all three- and four-year-olds – from 16 hours a week to 30 hours a week by 2021.
- Invest in infrastructure to ensure all of Scotland has access to superfast broadband, build 50,000 affordable new homes and continually improve transport links.
- Protect free university education.
- Campaign for Scotland and the UK to remain in the EU.

Scottish Conservative Party
- Fight against any attempts to 'drag our country back to a second independence referendum'.
- Focus on a Scottish welfare system with three basic principles at its heart:
  ○ It should primarily support the most vulnerable.
  ○ It should be flexible and personalised.
  ○ It should give those who can and want to work the opportunities and support to do so.
- Introduce a 'graduate contribution' to further and higher education – graduates pay back £1,500 for every year of their course once they are earning more than £20,000 a year.
- Protect health spending in Scotland by ensuring the health budget rises annually – an increase of £1.5 billion over five years.
- Support rural businesses across Scotland.
- End the right of prisoners to apply for parole in the case of the worst crimes committed – life should mean life.

Scottish Labour Party
- Use the new powers of the Scottish Parliament to protect the NHS budget.
- Keep university tuition free and reverse cuts to student grants.
- Scrap the Council Tax and replace it with a new property tax that the party says would leave 80% of households better off.
- Deliver a publicly owned 'People's ScotRail'.
- Make clear Scottish Labour's support for the UK remaining a member of the EU.
- Help first-time buyers save for a deposit.

Scottish Liberal Democrats
- Introduce a 'pupil premium' for schools to put towards closing the attainment gap between wealthy and more deprived pupils.
- Change the law to put mental health on the same statutory footing as physical health.
- Fund the NHS so that it stays ahead of inflation and keeps pace with funding in the rest of the UK.
- Remove the bedroom tax from the Scottish system.
- Increase the number of affordable homes by 50,000 over the next parliament.
- Increase the funding for Police Scotland by £20 million and protect it in real terms in order to preserve staff numbers.

Scottish Green Party
- Use the new devolved powers to cut income tax for lower earners.
- Provide funding for an additional 4,000 full-time equivalent teachers.
- Support the development of more community greenspaces throughout the country.
- Enforce a permanent ban on fracking and unconventional fossil fuel extraction.
- Put an end to discrimination and tackle hate crime against lesbian, gay, bisexual, transgender and intersex (LGBTI+) people.
- Campaign for a written constitution, produced by the Scottish people in a citizen-led process.

> **GO! Activity**
>
> **Group work**
>
> Select one of the political parties in Scotland from the list below:
>
> - SNP
> - Scottish Conservatives
> - Scottish Labour
> - Scottish Liberal Democrats
> - Scottish Greens
>
> Use the manifesto proposals above and the internet to make notes on the key policies of one of these parties. Once you have done this you should take part in 'political speed dating' with your classmates:
>
> - divide a double page into four and in each corner write down the names of the main parties
> - the class should be split into two groups
> - Group One students should stay in their seats and Group Two should rotate as many times as possible so that each Group Two student spends time with each Group One student
> - in the time allocated by your teacher you should share as many policies with each other as you can. You should write these policies on your page so that by the end you are more informed about the views of different political parties

How do you become a candidate in an election?

Standing as a candidate in an election is another way that individuals can participate in politics in Scotland. To become a candidate an individual must be aged over 18 years old and be a British citizen. A nomination form needs to be signed by 10 voters from that constituency. The papers must be returned along with a £500 deposit to the Returning Officer (who manages the election in the constituency). Candidates do not need to be a member of a political party.

The main parties have their own selection methods, usually involving local party members voting for a candidate to stand for election. Once the candidate has been chosen, 10 party members sign the candidate's nomination papers and the political party usually pays the deposit. The deposit is refunded provided that the candidate gains 5% or more of the total valid votes cast in the constituency.

The election campaign

Before an election can take place, an election campaign is rolled out. An election campaign is when candidates and their parties try to persuade voters to choose them on election day. During the election campaign candidates are competing against each other to win votes.

Becoming a member of a political party is another way to participate in politics. Many people pay annual membership fees or make donations to the political party that they feel closely represents their views and beliefs. Party members can attend local meetings and

Figure 4.5: *Senior members of the SNP join a candidate on the campaign trail*

Hint

If your school holds Pupil Council elections, think about the ways the candidates tried to persuade you to vote for them.

Word bank

• **Canvassing**

Speaking to voters to try and convince them to support a particular candidate or idea.

sometimes national conferences. In addition to this, party members offer assistance to candidates by canvassing voters on the campaign trail. The major political parties will have many supporters to help do this – if you look on each of the main political parties' websites you will notice that you can sign up to volunteer for the next election campaign.

These parties also have a large campaign budget to help them get elected. Each candidate and their supporters need to get their message across to as many people as they possibly can. They try to persuade voters that their party's policies would be the best for their area and for Scotland as a whole.

Hint

There are strict limits on what is spent once the campaign begins. Each candidate has to account for their election expenses after the poll. Candidates can spend up to a certain amount depending upon whether they are standing in an urban or rural constituency (candidates are able to spend more per voter when standing for election in rural areas due to the geographical spread of voters and the costs associated with campaigning in these areas).

Figure 4.6: *An election candidate canvassing door-to-door*

The methods used by candidates and their supporters include:

- putting up posters around the constituency with party promises, candidate's name and picture on them
- canvassing voters by talking to people in the street and knocking on the doors of houses of constituents
- handing out leaflets containing manifesto policies
- putting a loud speaker on a car and driving around the constituency talking about policy
- holding public meetings to discuss policies and meet voters
- attending debates with other prospective candidates
- visiting local businesses, schools etc.
- organising media events – TV, radio and newspaper interviews
- political parties can create Party Election Broadcasts which can be shown on TV during the election campaign
- keeping a blog and/or updating social networking sites while on the campaign trail
- organising transport to take people to the polling station on election day
- trying to persuade people at the last minute at the entrance to the polling station

> **Hint**
>
> Positive publicity in the media can help a candidate gain votes.

Figure 4.7: *Party leaders attending a televised debate*

> **Make the Link**
>
> You may have taken part in a short performance in Drama or Media Studies.

Activity

Group work

In small groups, choose a political party and create a Party Election Broadcast. To be successful in this task your group must:

- refer to the name of the political party you have chosen throughout
- mention policies from the party's manifesto
- the party's policies should be compared to those from other political parties
- use persuasive language throughout to persuade voters to choose your party

📖 Word bank

• Polling card

A card sent to all registered voters shortly before an election. The card gives information about the election and the voter such as the date of the election, the location of the polling station, opening and closing times and the name, address and electoral number of the voter.

• Polling clerk

A person who checks the electoral register to confirm that the voter is eligible to vote in a certain polling station.

• Verified

Confirmed as correct.

Figure 4.10: *Locked ballot boxes being taken away for counting*

❓ Questions

1. **Explain** what a manifesto is.
2. Using the manifesto promises decide which party you would vote for. Give reasons to **justify** your choice of party. **Explain** why you did not choose the other parties.
3. Briefly **explain** the process involved in standing as a candidate for election.
4. Make a spider diagram to show the various methods a candidate and their supporters may use during an election campaign.
5. Which method of campaigning **do you think** is the most effective and why?

Election day

- Scottish elections usually take place on the first Thursday in May of a specific year.
- Voting normally takes place at a polling station between the hours of 7am and 10pm. Polling stations are usually primary schools or community centres which are easy for local constituents to access.
- Those who are eligible to vote are listed on the electoral register and receive their polling card in advance of election day (see page 62 for more information about registering to vote).
- Voters should take their polling card to the polling station, where their name will be checked on the electoral register by the polling clerk (though taking the card is not mandatory, it can help speed up the process).
- The polling clerk gives the voter their ballot paper(s). You cast your vote in secret in a polling booth.
- Voters go into the polling booth and mark their preference(s) on the ballot paper.
- Ballot papers should then be placed in a locked ballot box.
- Once the polling stations have closed the ballot boxes are taken to the town hall where they are opened and counted.
- Once all the votes have been counted and verified the winner is announced.

🔵 Activity

Show your knowledge

Create a story board showing a step-by-step guide to what happens on election day. You should include words and pictures to show that you fully understand the process.

Referenda

Voting in a referendum is another way to participate in politics in Scotland. A referendum is a vote that is held when the government wants to find out what the electorate thinks about a particular subject. Voters are usually asked to respond either 'yes' or 'no' to the question being asked. The outcome of the referendum will depend upon how the majority of voters voted.

On 23rd June 2016, the UK electorate voted in the 'United Kingdom European Union Membership Referendum', also known as the 'EU referendum' and the 'Brexit referendum'. The referendum was to gauge support for the country either remaining a member of the European Union (EU) or leaving the EU. The result was a simple majority of 51.9% in favour of leaving the EU. Although the referendum was non-binding, the government promised to implement the result, and it initiated the official EU withdrawal process on 29th March 2017, which put the UK on course to leave the EU by 30th March 2019, after a period of Brexit negotiations.

📖 Word bank

- **Non-binding**

Where there is no legal obligation to act on the result of a vote or agreement – in this case the government did not have to go ahead with the process of leaving the EU but it promised the electorate that it would follow the result of the referendum.

Summary

In this chapter you have learned:

- the meaning of participation
- the rights and responsibilities associated with taking part in elections
- the main political parties in Scotland
- how to stand as a candidate for election
- about election campaigns in Scotland
- how to vote in elections

Learning Summary

Now that you have finished the **Participation** chapter, complete a self-evaluation of your knowledge and skills to assess what you have understood. Use the checklist below and its traffic lights to draw up a revision plan to help you improve in the areas you identified as red or amber.

- I can explain what participation means.
- I can state the various ways people can participate in a democracy.
- I can list those who do and do not have the right to vote in elections.
- I can describe the rights associated with voting in elections.

- I can explain what is meant by voter turnout.

- I can suggest why voter turnout is not as high as it was in the past.

- I can state the arguments for and against compulsory voting.

- I can outline why people should use their right to vote.

- I can explain what a political party is.

- I can list the main political parties in Scotland.

- I can explain what an ideology is.

- I can describe the political spectrum that exists in Scotland.

- I can explain what a manifesto is.

- I can describe the manifesto policies of the main political parties during the 2016 Scottish Parliament election.

- I can explain the process involved when standing as a candidate for election.

- I can describe the methods used by candidates and their supporters during an election campaign.

- I can outline the process that takes place on election day.

- I can explain what a referendum is.

Examples

In Modern Studies it is essential that you are able to back up any point you make with relevant evidence. When you are considering the statements above try to think of relevant examples for each response. You may wish to note these examples under each statement in your revision notes.

5 Influence

What you will learn in this chapter

In this section students will make a choice of a group which influences decision makers on a Scottish basis. They will cover the media and then choose either trade unions OR pressure groups.

- The purpose of pressure groups, trade unions and the media.
- The aims of pressure groups, trade unions and the media.
- The methods pressure groups, trade unions and the media use to influence decision-making in Scotland.

Pressure groups

A pressure group is a group of individuals working together in pursuit of a common cause. Pressure groups try to influence public policy through their actions in support of that cause.

 Make the Link

You may have studied pressure groups in Business Management and/or History.

 Activity

Discuss
With your shoulder partner, create a list of the different pressure groups you have heard of, e.g. the World Wide Fund for Nature (WWF).

Members of pressure groups join together because they have similar views on a specific issue or a range of issues linked to a theme. Pressure groups are not political parties and do not want to become the government. It can be difficult for individuals on their own to influence policy and political decisions and a group of like-minded people working together can have more impact and can be more successful in getting their concerns heard by the government, the general public and the mass media.

There has been a dramatic increase in the number and range of pressure groups in recent years. There are many reasons why this happened; one main reason may be because more people have chosen to become politically active through their membership of groups, organisations and associations of various kinds rather than through voting and joining political parties. Pressure groups include registered charities, trade unions, faith-based organisations, professional and business associations, and community groups.

Figure 5.1: *The World Wide Fund for Nature (WWF) logo*

Types of pressure groups

Pressure groups can differ greatly from one to another; one way is that they can be local, national or even international in their focus. As a result of this, pressure groups vary in size from very small groups with only a handful of members who want to deal with a local issue, to very large organisations with millions of members all over the world.

Figure 5.2: *Pressure groups can focus locally or globally*

Local pressure groups

Group	Aims
Aberdeen Wildlife Trust	Inform the citizens of Aberdeen on wildlife topics or particular species through workshops and events.
Dual the A75	Encourage the Scottish government to improve the A75 road in Dumfries and Galloway. It is over 90 miles long and mostly single carriageway.
Friends of the River Kelvin (FORK)	Build public awareness and commitment to the care and maintenance of the Kelvin and its tributaries.

Communities Opposed to New Coal at Hunterston (CONCH)

Communities Opposed to New Coal at Hunterston (CONCH) had been campaigning since 2009. 22,000 people lodged objections to Ayrshire Power's plans for a coal-fired station at Hunterston making it the most unpopular proposal in Scottish planning history. The group used various methods to draw attention to their cause: they contacted MSPs and used the mass media and local events such as Sand Art to create giant sand drawings in support of the campaign. In June 2013, Ayrshire Power formally withdrew their plans for a coal-fired power station at Hunterston.

Figure 5.3: *Sand Art created to support the CONCH campaign*

National pressure groups

Group	Aims
Shelter Scotland	A charity that works to alleviate the distress caused by homelessness and bad housing.
Scottish Society for the Prevention of Cruelty to Animals (SSPCA)	Scotland's animal welfare charity encourages kindness to animals. Their aim is to prevent cruelty through education, investigate abuse, rescue animals in distress and find animals new homes.
Scottish Campaign for Nuclear Disarmament (SCND)	The SCND works for the abolition of all nuclear weapons in Britain as a step toward the global elimination of these weapons of mass destruction.

Figure 5.4: *The Scottish Campaign for Nuclear Disarmament logo, also used internationally as a peace sign*

International pressure groups

Group	Aims
Greenpeace	Aims to defend the natural world and promote peace by investigating, exposing and confronting environmental abuse, and championing environmentally responsible solutions.
Amnesty International	A campaigning organisation whose purpose it is to protect people wherever justice, fairness, freedom and truth are denied.
Save the Children	The organisation works in 120 countries to save children's lives. They fight for children's rights and to help them fulfil their potential.

Figure 5.5: *Amnesty International supporters marching for their cause*

Hint

There are many pressure groups in Scotland who aim to influence political decision-making (especially because the Scottish Parliament has a number of devolved powers). Therefore, UK-based national pressure groups will often have a designated Scottish section that deals with issues in Scotland.

Make the Link

In Geography you may have looked at these international pressure groups, or ones similar to them.

Activity

Research
Use the internet to research examples of other local, national and international pressure groups.

Insider and outsider groups

Insider groups are regularly consulted by the government and operate inside the decision-making process. The degree of how regularly they are consulted, on what matters and how seriously their opinions are taken varies depending on the group. For example, MENCAP Scotland – a group representing people with mental health disabilities – works closely with the Scottish government to make an impact on mental health issues or policies.

Outsider groups have to work outside the governmental decision-making process and, therefore, have fewer opportunities to determine the direction of policy. For example, PETA Scotland – People for the Ethical Treatment of Animals (Scotland) – aims to protect the rights of all animals. Through public education, research, special events, celebrity involvement and protest campaigns, the group tries to get the Scottish government to create new legislation.

Figure 5.6: *PETA logo*

Insider groups	Outsider groups
Access to policymakers	No/limited access to policymakers
Usually have a high profile	May have a low profile
Have mainstream goals	Radical goals
Tend to have financial stability	Tend to have a lack of financial stability
Strong leadership	Strong grassroots support

Cause and interest groups

Cause (also known as promotional) groups are made up of individuals who share similar concerns about particular issues with the aim of changing opinions and attitudes. For example, ASH Scotland – Action on Smoking and Health (Scotland) – work to eliminate the harm caused by tobacco.

Interest (also known as sectional) groups are concerned with the interests of a particular section of society and usually represent the interests of their members, such as professional organisations and trade unions. For example, the FBU Scotland – Fire Brigades Union (Scotland) – is the voice of firefighters and the fire and rescue service in Scotland.

Think point

Some pressure groups prefer to be outsider rather than insider groups. Why do you think this is the case?

Cause groups	Interest groups
Promote a cause	Defend interests
Open membership	Closed membership
Focus on concerns that affect the masses – a group for the people	Focus on concerns that affect specific groups – a group for certain individuals
Benefit others or wider society	Benefits members only
Members usually make donations	Members usually pay fees

❓ Questions

1. **Explain** what a pressure group is and why they exist.
2. Outline the reasons why people might join a pressure group.
3. Create a spider diagram to show examples of the pressure groups you know of. Divide the diagram into three focus areas: local, national and international.
4. **Describe** what an insider pressure group is. Include an **example** of a Scottish insider pressure group in your answer.
5. **Describe** what an outsider pressure group is. Include an **example** of a Scottish outsider pressure group in your answer.
6. Create a table to show the main differences between insider and outsider groups.
7. **Explain** what a cause group is. Include an **example** of a Scottish cause pressure group in your answer.
8. **Explain** what an interest group is. Include an **example** of a Scottish interest pressure group in your answer.
9. Create a table to show the main differences between cause and interest groups.

Hint

Not all groups fit neatly into these categories, and some groups fit into more than one category.

Activity

Show your knowledge
Using the pressure groups you have researched, identify whether they are insider or outsider groups, and whether they are cause or interest groups.

Methods used by pressure groups

The methods pressure groups use tend to reflect the area they are interested in. A pressure group generally tries to gain as much publicity as possible for its cause. Attention from the mass media can encourage more people to join and provide the pressure group with the ability to draw direct attention to their cause.

Make the Link

You may have learned about the mass media in Media Studies.

Figure 5.7: *Attracting TV and other media to a cause helps it to reach a wider audience*

Demonstration

Pressure groups can make direct contact with the public by inviting members to march through the streets holding signs and banners, handing out leaflets and using loudspeakers publicising their aims. If lots of people attend the event this normally attracts widespread media coverage and can influence the government.

Figure 5.8: *Pro-independence campaigners in Edinburgh*

Make the Link

Pressure groups use emotive and persuasive language to gain public support. You may have learned about this in English.

Figure 5.9: *There are various forms of mass media available to pressure groups*

Figure 5.10: *Petitions are a useful tool in showing public feelings*

For example, in May 2018 thousands of pro-independence campaigners marched through the streets of Edinburgh in support of an independent Scotland.

Using the mass media

Due to developments in the mass media such as the internet, social networking and 24/7 news, pressure groups have the opportunity to use the mass media to great advantage. Increasingly, pressure groups are using social networking sites such as Facebook and Twitter to build support for their cause and put pressure on decision makers. Using a hashtag when campaigning on Twitter makes it easier for people who might be interested in the cause to find information about it. Pressure groups may even use a well-known celebrity to publicise their cause.

For example, Sir Ian McKellen frequently shares his support for gay rights on Twitter and the Stonewall website.

Pressure groups that have the support of the media and the wider public have more chance of pressurising the government into taking the pressure group's advice. If the government is seen to be responding to public opinion they may gain support from the media.

For example, Citizens Advice Scotland was allocated additional funding from the Scottish government to help them cope with the increasing demand for help from hard-hit families as a result of Westminster's cuts. Some Scottish newspapers supported the government's decision.

Petitions

Pressure groups will try to convince the relevant policymaker about the strength of public feeling on an issue by collecting as many signatures as possible from people who support their cause. The Scottish Parliament encourages responsible participation in the democratic process and the use of the Public Petitions Committee in the Scottish Parliament has been very popular. In Scotland, you only need one signature to introduce a petition, whereas in Westminster, you need 100,000. E-petitions are carried out entirely online.

Leaflets and posters

The creation of promotional materials draws attention to a campaign and can persuade ordinary people to take action themselves, e.g. by writing to the relevant representative. For example, groups such as the SSPCA and Sense Over Sectarianism use controversial and powerful images on their posters to get attention for their cause.

Contact or lobby representatives

Representatives, such as MSPs or MPs, meet with members of the pressure group and listen to the arguments being put forward. The representative may be able to influence decision makers. They could also attempt to introduce laws that support the aims of the pressure group.

Shelter Scotland's 'Banish the Bedroom Tax Monster' Campaign involves lobbying the Scottish government to express their opposition of the under-occupancy charges applied to those who claim housing benefit and have a spare bedroom(s).

Professional lobbyists

Professional lobbyists are people whose job it is to contact government decision makers and persuade them to change the law. For example, wealthy pressure groups like the British Dental Association (Scotland) can employ people to do this. The lobbyist does not have to necessarily agree with the cause for which they are lobbying.

Public meetings

Groups attempt to get as many people as possible to attend meetings publicising the aims of the pressure group. Pressure groups can invite influential people to speak in support of their cause at the meeting.

Both the 'Vote leave' and 'Remain' campaigns organised public meetings across the UK in the build-up to the referendum on membership of the EU.

Figure 5.11: *Professional lobbyist*

Figure 5.12: *Pressure groups use public meetings to voice their opinions*

Direct action

This is action that affects the government or the running of the country. Direct action is often (but not necessarily) illegal. Stunts, strikes, blockades, boycotts and sit-ins are all examples of direct action.

The Scottish Campaign for Nuclear Disarmament (SCND) often holds blockades at Faslane naval base.

 **Activity**

Show your knowledge
Create a mind map to show the various types of action that pressure groups can take. You should research further **examples** of pressure group actions in order to exemplify each of the methods.

Figure 5.13: *Protests are common at Faslane*

 Activity

Research
Use the internet to research a pressure group you are interested in. Create a poster/leaflet/social networking page that can be used to inform the general public about the group. Include information about the following:

1. The pressure group's name.
2. When the group was formed.
3. Why it was set up.
4. What it aims to achieve and whether it has been successful.
5. Real **examples** of the methods the pressure group uses.

 Hint

The founding principles of the Scottish Parliament were discussed on page 21.

Figure 5.14: *Freedom of expression*

Rights and responsibilities of pressure groups

The founding principles of the Scottish Parliament give pressure groups the opportunity to directly influence government policy; this is because the Scottish Parliament encourages responsible participation in the democratic process.

Pressure groups have rights and responsibilities when participating in the democratic process. Their rights allow them to use certain methods to make the public and government aware of their views, but these rights are also balanced by responsibilities. The responsibilities pressure groups have usually determine the way they can behave in particular situations.

The right to freedom of expression is regarded as one of the most important human rights. Many of the rights that pressure groups have are based on the principle of freedom of expression.

Rights	Responsibilities
The right to free assembly (protest) allows group members to meet to discuss and promote their views.	The organiser needs to tell the police in writing six days before a protest is held. The police must be informed of the date and time of the protest, the route, and the names and addresses of the organisers. Protesters must behave within the law.
The right to criticise (comment on negatively) the government or other organisations.	Not to tell lies about people or organisations. If the group is slanderous (tells lies that will harm the reputation of another) it is going against defamation laws and could be sued.
The right to promote their cause using methods such as the mass media, leaflets, posters etc.	To give accurate information. If the laws of libel are broken then the pressure group can find itself in trouble. Misrepresenting their cause can damage a pressure group's reputation.

📖 Word bank

• **Defamation**

The action of damaging the good reputation of someone.

• **Libel**

A false publication, as in writing, print, signs or pictures, that damages a person's reputation.

❓ Questions

1. **Explain, in detail,** four methods used by pressure groups to influence the Scottish government. Include **examples** of Scottish pressure groups in your answer.

2. Which method **do you think** is the most effective way to influence the Scottish government? Give reasons to **support** your answer.

3. Which method **do you think** is the least effective way to influence the Scottish government? Give reasons to **support** your answer.

4. **Describe, in detail,** the rights and responsibilities that pressure groups have.

5. 'Pressure groups are good for democracy.'

    Give one reason to **support** and one reason to **oppose** this statement.

GO! Activity

Show your knowledge

Choose a pressure group that you are interested in. Write a letter to a person of power and influence, asking them to support the pressure group. For example you could write to:

- the head of the local council or a relevant local councillor if your issue is a local matter
- the First Minister or a relevant MSP if your issue is a devolved matter
- the Prime Minister or a relevant MP if your issue is a reserved matter

Remember the different powers that each representative has. You could ask them to introduce a Members' Bill, ask a question at Question Time or simply post a Tweet in support of the pressure group.

Before you start writing, plan the organisation of your letter and ensure you use the correct layout. Use the table below to help you.

Technique	Purpose	Aim of writing
To persuade	To give reasons to persuade others to think again/change their actions.	To persuade the government to stop taking a particular action.
To argue	To weigh up what's fair and unfair in different situations.	To explain your reasons for wanting the government to end a particular action: do this through the use of counter-arguments.
To advise	To suggest what others should do.	To offer sympathy, explaining that you want to stop others from feeling the way they do; to advise them on how they might use their experiences to help others.

Make the Link

You may have learned about trade unions in History.

Trade unions

Trade unions are organisations that aim to represent employees by helping them to achieve common goals and to protect themselves against employers. Trade unions communicate with employers about a large range of issues such as pay, health and safety, pensions and discrimination. Around 30% of workers in Scotland (and the UK) belong to a trade union and this covers a wide array of professions from cleaners to footballers.

Figure 5.15: *Trade unions allow common goals to be met*

GO! Activity

Discuss

With your shoulder partner, create a list of the different trade unions you know of. An example might be the National Union of Rail, Maritime and Transport Workers (RMT).

Examples of trade unions include:

- Unison Scotland is Scotland's largest public service union. It represents staff who provide public services, such as NHS workers etc.
- Scottish Unite represents members from every type of workplace, such as construction and IT
- The Educational Institute of Scotland (EIS) is the largest teaching union in Scotland
- Equity Scotland is a trade union for professional performers and creative practitioners in Scotland

To participate in trade union activities workers need to join a union appropriate to their profession and pay a membership subscription. Members can then:

- attend union meetings in the workplace and discuss issues such as pay and working conditions. Collective bargaining may then take place
- ask the union advice when they have a problem in the workplace, e.g. if they are being asked to do a job they are not trained for
- promote equal rights and fight discrimination that may exist for some members, such as women and ethnic minorities
- vote in ballots held by the union. Sometimes these ballots will be to decide whether or not the union should take industrial action. At other times the ballot may be to elect a new representative within the union such as a shop steward
- stand as a candidate in an election to become a union representative, also known as a shop steward
- take part in a form of industrial action, such as a strike
- receive legal advice and representation on professional matters and benefits such as discounts from specific companies

Why do some people decide not to join a union?

- An individual might be self-employed or work for their family business and have no need to join a union.
- Some employers have non-union agreements forbidding workers from joining a union.
- The cost of joining and remaining a member could be too high, especially for low-paid or part-time workers.
- Some well-paid workers do not see the point as they are happy with their conditions of employment.
- Employees who are not members can enjoy the benefits of pay rises and better working conditions negotiated by the unions without joining.

GO! Activity

Homework
Conduct a survey of adults who work to find out how many of them are a member of a trade union. You should also find out what union they are a member of and their reason for being part/ not part of a union. Display your results in a suitable way, such as a table or bar graph.

📖 Word bank

- **Collective bargaining**
A process of negotiations (talks) between employers and the union aimed at reaching agreements on pay and working conditions.

Figure 5.16: *RMT logo*

Figure 5.17: *UNISON logo*

Incorporating the Variety Artistes' Federation
Figure 5.18: *Equity logo*

Figure 5.19: *Striking is one option open to union members*

✦ Make the Link

In Maths/Numeracy you should have learned how to display information in graphs.

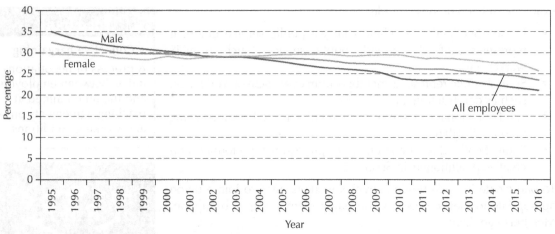

Figure 5.20: *Trade union membership by gender, 1995–2016*

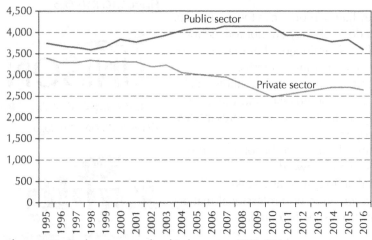

Figure 5.21: *Trade union membership by sector, 1995–2016*

📖 Word bank

• **Public sector**

The part of the economy concerned with providing basic government services, such as the police, teachers etc.

• **Private sector**

The part of the economy run by private individuals or groups, usually as a means of enterprise for profit.

🔵 Activity

Use your skills

Trade union membership has changed over the years. Using the information in Figures 5.20 and 5.21, make **conclusions** about each of the following:

• trade union membership levels in the public sector between 1995 and 2016

• trade union membership levels in the private sector between 1995 and 2016

• the gender of trade union members between 1995 and 2016

What is industrial action?

If a trade union believes that its members are not being treated fairly and negotiations with employers are not working then it might decide to take industrial action. Industrial action is any action taken by employees to put pressure on employers. Trade union members have the right to vote on whether or not to take industrial action. If a majority of members agree then action is usually taken by all members. However, if an individual member decides they do not want to take part in industrial action then they do not have to. Taking industrial action shows the general public that a dispute (disagreement) is going on between the employer and the trade union.

Actions taken by trade unions

Type of industrial action	Description
Go slow	Employees perform their duties, but at a slower pace. By doing this they aim to reduce productivity and cost the employer money. This is one of the least disruptive forms of industrial action but it may lead to further action being taken. In 2009 thousands of postal workers deliberately took their time in sorting the mountain of mail that had built up following strikes.
Overtime ban	Employees limit their working time to the hours specified in their contracts, refusing to work any overtime. Because there is no breach of contract by the employees there is less chance of disciplinary action by the employer. An overtime ban can have a significant impact on industries that normally operate outside of regular office hours, such as emergency services, public transport or retail. The trade union Unite conducted an overtime ban on First Aberdeen buses in March 2018 due to a dispute over contracts. The industrial action was agreed when members were balloted. The aim was to cause maximum problems for the employer unless they agreed to negotiations with the union.
Work to rule	Employees do no more than the minimum required by the rules of their contract, which has the effect of slowing down production. This action is less susceptible to disciplinary action as employees are simply obeying the rules. For example, a teacher who is working to rule may refuse to supervise the canteen at lunchtime if it is not written into their contract that they have to do this.
Strike	This involves a work stoppage caused by the mass refusal of employees to perform their duties. Strike action can be short term, usually one day; selective, only one group within an organisation is taking part; or long term, until the end of the dispute. The longer a strike goes on the more damaging effect it has on employers. A strike is the most serious form of industrial action. Workers usually form a picket line outside of their workplace during the strike in order to persuade fellow employees and the public to support them by not crossing the picket line. During an official strike employees are not paid. For example, in 2018 members of Unite, Unison and the GMB undertook a strike in East Dunbartonshire Council due to changes to terms and conditions. The strike forced schools, libraries, leisure centres and council offices to close. See the newspaper article on page 89 for further information on this strike.

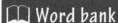

📖 Word bank

• **Picket line**

A boundary established by workers on strike, especially at the entrance to the place of work, which others are asked not to cross.

Figure 5.22: *Striking workers form a picket line outside their workplace*

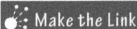

☄️ Make the Link

The Police Act, 1919 outlawed police membership of unions and industrial action. You will learn more about the police in Section 2.

📖 Word bank

• **Keynote speech**

A speech addressing the main issues.

Trade unions need to be able to influence decision makers in order to achieve their aims and represent their members. They can do this in a number of ways which can be similar to the methods used by pressure groups:

• trade unions can lobby politicians. This is when they directly try to persuade MSPs to make decisions in their members' favour. Trade unions such as the EIS can sometimes achieve success for their members by lobbying the government. Additionally, trade unions can sponsor an MSP. This is when they donate money to a politician they think is favourable to their cause. This can help an MSP in an election and aid the trade union's cause

• trade unions can also organise demonstrations where keynote speeches are made to rally support. For example, teaching unions such as the EIS and Scottish Secondary Teachers Association (SSTA) have organised large demonstrations to show their opposition to government budget cuts

• trade unions can create petitions, including e-petitions, and submit them to the Petitions Committee. Ultimately, actions taken by trade unions are aimed at attracting media attention in support of their cause

❓ Questions

1. What is a trade union?
2. Why do employees join trade unions?
3. Why do some employees choose not to join a trade union?
4. **Explain** what is meant by industrial action.
5. Create a spider diagram to show the main types of industrial action.
6. **Describe, in detail,** the main types of industrial action that can be taken by trade unions. Include some **examples** of Scottish trade unions in your answer.

DAILY NEWS

world - business - finance - lifestyle - travel - sport

Mass workers protest as 'summer of discontent' four-day strike shuts East Dunbartonshire schools

Workers have been holding a mass protest and lobby outside council offices in East Dunbartonshire as a four-day strike which forms part of a 'summer of discontent' has shut all schools and nurseries.

The dispute over terms and conditions cuts including slashing staff holidays has meant some end of term church services cancelled and end of year events and balls postponed including end of primary school P7 celebrations.

Some parents have complained about the timing of the strike as they make urgent child care arrangements.

Protesters have been gathering at East Dunbartonshire Council headquarters where there is a meeting of the full council on the first day of four 24-hour strikes.

Members of the Unison, Unite and GMB trade unions will strike on June 21, 22, 25 and 26 over proposed cuts to workers' terms and conditions.

That would mean three days cut from holiday entitlement; scrapping of enhanced overtime rates; reducing the time when unsocial hours payments apply and slashing the payments to employees who volunteer for redundancy.

The strike has meant that the community hubs at Bearsden, Bishopbriggs, Kirkintilloch and Lennoxtown would be closed along with the council's customer contact centre.

All East Dunbartonshire libraries will be closed on strike days along with the Auld Kirk Museum and Lillie Art Gallery.

Green waste collections have been suspended from June 21 through to the morning of June 29.

Food waste bins and dry recycling will be collected on the next scheduled collection day after the industrial action.

East Dunbartonshire Council said: 'In an effort to avoid strike action, the council made a further offer to the trades unions to allow further time for negotiation on the areas being identified as of most concern. To enable those further negotiations the strike would need to be suspended.'

Simon Macfarlane, UNISON's regional organiser, said: 'There has been an overwhelming response today from UNISON members. We had hoped that the council would see sense and we continued talking in good faith.'

[Source: http://www.heraldscotland.com/news/ 16306298.mass-workers-protest-as-summer- of-discontent-four-day-strike-shuts-east-dunbartonshire- schools/]

Figure 5.23: *Rights are only guaranteed if the trade union fulfils its responsibilities*

? Questions

1. What type of industrial action was taken in East Dunbartonshire in 2018?
2. Why did union members take industrial action?
3. What facilities were affected by the strike?

Rights and responsibilities of trade unions

Trade unions have rights that they are entitled to but they also have responsibilities which they must adhere to. Trade unions and their members have a responsibility to act within the law at all times.

Rights	Responsibilities
To ballot members to see if the majority of members are in favour of taking industrial action.	To hold a secret ballot and inform members of the outcome. Once the decision is confirmed the union must inform the employer. Advance notice must be given in the outcome of a strike being held.
To take industrial action in order to protect the rights of the workers.	To ensure that all forms of industrial action are peaceful and within the law.
To form a picket line outside the workplace. The Code of Practice on picketing says usually there should be no more than six people outside an entrance to a workplace.	Must not break the rule around lawful picketing. For example, pickets must not prevent people from going to work or doing their usual work if they want to do so.
To try to attract new trade union members.	Not to pressurise anyone into joining a trade union. No employer or employment agency may require an employee to join a trade union or be a member of a specific trade union.
Trade unions can ask employers to make changes to employees' conditions of employment.	Trade unions must not make unreasonable demands, e.g. they should not ask for a 100% pay rise for employees.

The work of a shop steward

One of the most important people in a trade union is the shop steward (sometimes called union representative). The shop steward is an employee who has been elected by the union members to represent them. The shop steward is elected by a secret ballot. He/she is the first person a member will go to in order to seek help or advice about a problem at work.

Shops stewards represent members by helping to find solutions to their problems. When union members have a problem it is the shop steward they turn to. Shop stewards might need to help sort out problems with issues such as equality in the workplace. The shop steward will take the problem up with the employer on behalf of the members or the shop steward will advise members on how to take the matter further.

The shop steward can represent the member during meetings with the employer. This could involve dealing with worker disciplinary hearings, accompanying workers during management interviews, negotiating with employers over worker concerns such as pay, overtime, holidays and health and safety, and finally raising issues with management formally or informally. The member can request that their shop steward be present to aid them. If a member needs legal advice they can receive this by contacting the union.

Figure 5.24: *The shop steward can accompany the employee to meetings with management*

The shop steward will attend union meetings and share information with members. Meetings are usually held at the union headquarters where union matters are discussed and voted on. He/she will let members know what was discussed by holding a meeting, distributing leaflets and newsletters, sending emails, or by maintaining the union notice board, e.g. putting up posters etc. Members have the right to approach the shop steward to discuss union meetings.

Shop stewards continually try to recruit new members. Increasing and maintaining trade union membership is important to ensure the union continues to support its members. A shop steward can do this by actively persuading people to join the union, distributing leaflets and putting up posters, and encouraging membership around the workplace.

❓ Questions

1. **Explain, in detail,** the rights and responsibilities of trade unions.
2. **Describe** the ways in which employees can participate in how their trade union is run.
3. What is a shop steward?
4. How do union members choose their shop steward?
5. What problems might a member go to a shop steward with?
6. How can the shop steward represent the members of the union?

🟢 Activity

Research
Use the internet to research a trade union you are interested in. Create a poster/leaflet/social networking page that can be used to inform the general public about the group. It should include the following information:

1. The trade union's name.
2. When the group was formed.
3. Who the group represents.
4. The aims of the trade union.
5. Real examples of the industrial action the trade union has used.
6. An overall **conclusion** as to how well the trade union represents its members.

The media

Scotland has a strong media history, with its own local and national newspaper titles, television and radio channels, in addition to UK-wide media sources. The media's role is to inform the public on important issues that affect people, whether these issues are local, national or international.

Newspapers

Many people in Scotland get their political news from newspapers but people are now more likely to access online rather than print editions to read the news. Newspapers aim to educate and inform people on current events as well as provide entertainment. In Scotland, the most widely read tabloid newspapers are the *Scottish Sun* and the *Daily Record*. The most widely read 'quality' newspapers are the *Herald* and the *Scotsman*.

Newspapers can choose how they report the news and different newspapers can present the same story in different ways. Through their choice of stories, pictures and headlines, newspapers often present a one-sided approach to news reporting.

Most newspapers are politically biased and often make it very clear to their readers which political party they support by urging their readers to vote for that party. However, this does not mean that voters are always persuaded by the newspaper they read. Many people buy a newspaper for other reasons, such as to read the sport section, or are not influenced by what they read. It has also been suggested that the people who are likely to read the paper might actually influence what the paper writes because the newspaper editors will want to make their paper appeal to as wide an audience as possible in order to maximise sales.

People tend to consume news online

⚬⋰ Make the Link

You might have watched clips of party political broadcasts in English as examples of persuasive language.

TV and radio

While newspapers can present a biased view of events, the law requires television news to be fair and balanced. Television companies are expected to report the facts and to be balanced in their analysis. For example, representatives from different political parties must be given proportionately equal time to present their views on important issues.

In recent election campaigns, there have been a number of television debates involving the leaders of different political parties. These debates were watched by millions of voters all over the UK. Post-debate analysis has generally suggested that most people who watched the debates had already decided who they were going to vote for and were not influenced by what they heard. Therefore although one party leader may have appeared to have 'won' the debate, overall the debates actually had little impact on the way people voted.

Online

Increasingly, people in Scotland use the internet, and social media in particular, as a source of information. The internet allows people almost unlimited access to information, which means people are better informed than ever before. However, it also allows people to post almost anything they choose and as a result some information is not accurate. The term 'fake news' describes news stories which gain a lot of attention and 'shares' on social media platforms but aren't actually true.

For political parties in Scotland, the internet offers the chance to connect directly with voters. Many political parties have social media accounts and the SNP encourages all of the party's MSPs to have a Twitter account. However, recent research suggests that people use the internet to seek out information about political parties that they already support, which suggests that the information they encounter doesn't actually change their opinion and therefore doesn't alter election results.

? Question

Copy and complete the table. The first row has been done for you.

Type of media	Role/purpose	Effective at influencing?
Newspaper	To inform, to educate, can be biased.	Can reach thousands of people. Also available online. Level of influence is unclear because people may read the newspaper for other reasons, such as the sport section.
Television and radio		
Internet (including social media)		

Summary

In this chapter you have learned:

- the purpose of pressure groups, trade unions and the media
- the aims of pressure groups, trade unions and the media
- the methods pressure groups, trade unions and the media use to influence decision-making in Scotland

Learning Summary

Now that you have finished the **Influence** chapter, complete a self-evaluation of your knowledge and skills to assess what you have understood. Use the checklist below and its traffic lights to draw up a revision plan to help you improve in the areas you identified as red or amber.

- I can outline the purpose of pressure groups. ⬭ ⬭ ⬭

- I can explain the aims of different pressure groups. ⬭ ⬭ ⬭

- I can describe the different methods pressure groups can use to achieve their aims and influence the Scottish government. ⬭ ⬭ ⬭

- I can describe the rights and responsibilities of pressure groups when trying to influence decision-making in Scotland. ⬭ ⬭ ⬭

- I can outline the purpose of trade unions. ⬭ ⬭ ⬭

- I can explain the aims of different trade unions. ⬭ ⬭ ⬭

- I can describe the different methods trade unions can use to achieve their aims and influence the Scottish government. ⬭ ⬭ ⬭

- I can describe the rights and responsibilities of trade unions when trying to influence decision-making in Scotland. ⬭ ⬭ ⬭

- I can explain the ways shop stewards can represent their members.

- I can describe the role of the media.

- I can describe the different types of media.

- I can explain the effectiveness of the media in influencing the public.

Examples

In Modern Studies it is essential that you are able to back up any point you make with relevant evidence. When you are considering the statements above try to think of relevant examples for each response. You may wish to note these examples under each statement in your revision notes.

Crime and the law in the United Kingdom

In Section 2 there is a choice of topic; you can study **either** social inequality **or** crime and the law. In this book we will be looking at **Crime and the Law**.

Course and Assessment Specifications

National 4 *(Social Issues in the United Kingdom)*

Outcome 1

1 Use a limited range of sources of information to make and justify decisions about social issues in the United Kingdom, focusing on either social inequality or crime and the law by:

1.1 Making a decision using up to three sources of information.

1.2 Briefly justifying a decision using evidence from up to three sources of information.

Outcome 2

2 Draw on a straightforward knowledge and understanding of social issues in the United Kingdom, focusing on either social inequality or crime and the law by:

2.1 Giving straightforward descriptions of the main features of a social issue which draw on a factual knowledge of either social inequality or crime and the law.

2.2 Giving straightforward explanations relating to a social issue in the United Kingdom.

National 5 *(Social Issues in the UK)*

Option 1: Social Inequality

Nature of social inequality
- nature and extent of inequality in Scotland and/or the UK
- evidence of social inequalities in Scotland and/or the UK, such as official reports and academic research

Causes of social and economic inequality
- employment/unemployment
- income
- educational attainment
- discrimination

Consequences of social and economic inequality
- on individuals
- on families
- on communities
- on wider society

Option 2: Crime and the Law

Nature of crime
- nature and extent of crime in Scotland and/or the UK
- evidence of crime in Scotland and/or the UK, such as official reports and academic research

Causes of crime
- social causes and explanations of crime
- economic causes and explanations of crime
- biological causes and explanations of crime

Consequences of crime
- on perpetrators
- on victims
- on families
- on communities
- on wider society

Social Issues in the United Kingdom

Level 3 and 4 experiences and outcomes relevant to this topic

The Social Issues in the United Kingdom topic naturally builds upon the knowledge already secured in the third and fourth level experiences and outcomes, and in particular:

❖ I can gather information and use it to investigate. **SOC 4-16b**

❖ I can understand how the media affects attitudes. You may have covered how the media affects what people think of crime and criminals. **SOC 3-17b**

❖ I can understand the rights and responsibilities of people in society. **SOC 3-17a**

❖ I can understand how decision-making bodies (like the government) make laws. **SOC 4-18a**

6 The nature of crime

What you will learn in this chapter

- What crime is.
- Types of crime.

What is crime?

A crime is any action that breaks the law of the land. Laws are currently passed by the UK Parliament in Westminster, the Scottish Parliament in Holyrood and the European Parliament in Brussels. This will change after Brexit in 2019 when laws passed by the EU will no longer apply to the UK. However, many of the laws passed by the EU have already been adopted into UK law. Any individual who does something that a law forbids has committed a crime. Anyone who commits a crime may be punished for this action.

The figures published by the Scottish government in July 2018 show that the total number of crimes recorded by the police decreased by 3% in the period between 2015–16 and 2016–17 – a drop of more than 7,500 crimes. Crime has been on a downward trend in Scotland since 2006–07, with an overall decrease of 43%. This continues a generally decreasing trend in recorded crime in Scotland, from a peak in 1991 when crime reached a record high of 572,921. Recorded crime is now at its lowest level since 1974.

Figure 6.1: *The scales of justice*

📖 Word bank

- **Law of the land**

Historically the rules of the kingdom, but today the principles of justice in a given place.

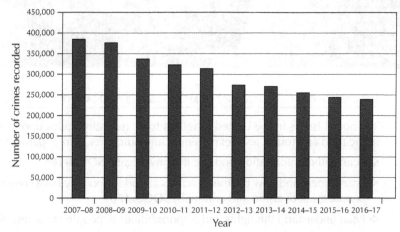

Figure 6.2: *Crimes recorded by the police in Scotland, between 2007–08 and 2016–17*

In terms of violent crime in 2016–17, there were 61 cases of homicide (murder) involving 64 victims. This is an increase of six victims from 2015–16. There were 77 persons accused of homicide in Scotland in 2016–17.

The overall decrease in recorded crime between 2015–16 and 2016–17 was replicated in 20 of the 32 local authorities, with 11 experiencing an increase and one with little change from the previous year. Since 2007–08, all local authorities have shown a decrease in recorded crime, varying from a drop of 13% in Midlothian to a drop of 61% in Na h-Eileanan Siar (Western Isles).

Clear-up rates (the percentage of crimes that are solved) for total recorded crimes decreased by 1.6% from 51.6% to 50.0% in 2016–17. This clear-up rate is the lowest since 2011–12. The clear-up rate in 2016–17 for sexual crimes is the lowest since 1981.

Activity

Research

Working individually, use the information above and the internet to research the crime levels in Scotland for the last ten years. Provide a written one-page report to your teacher: you may wish to include graphs and other visual ways of presenting the information. In your report you may wish to consider:

- have crime levels increased or decreased overall?
- have violent crime levels increased or decreased?
- what percentage of crimes are solved?
- are crime levels higher in certain areas in Scotland?
- any other information you think is relevant

The Scottish government website has an area dedicated to crime and justice which may help you with this (QR code below).

 Make the Link

You will have learned about how laws are made in Section 1. The area of law and order is mostly devolved to the Scottish Parliament, however Westminster can make laws on some criminal activity, for example drug use.

Figure 6.3: *Police officers on duty*

 Make the Link

In Maths you may look at how statistics can be used to give information and how they are sometimes used to make information look more negative or positive than it actually is.

Laws

Laws are necessary in society to ensure that everyone's rights are protected and their safety is ensured. This means that laws alter over time to keep up with changes in society – something that may have been illegal in the past may now be considered acceptable by law; for example, abortion and same-sex marriages were both once illegal but today they are not.

Word bank

• **Prosecuted**
When a person is formally charged with a crime and legal proceedings begin.

 Think point

Do you think eight is old enough to be criminally responsible? Is it better to increase the age to 12? Do you think 12 is old enough to be prosecuted for a crime? Your teacher may ask you to debate the criminal age of responsibility.

 Activity

Research
Research the legal age for the activities listed in the table in other countries. Are they different in England? Or in the United States?

? Questions

1. What is a crime?
2. Using **evidence** from the written information above, make a **conclusion** about crime in Scotland.
3. Name any laws that have changed recently. You may be able to think up some recent **examples** of your own.

As laws are designed to protect everyone's rights, different laws apply to different age groups. It was previously the case that you could be held responsible for a crime as young as age eight in Scotland (although you could not be prosecuted until age 12) but a bill is currently being passed to increase the criminal age to 12. It is very important to know which laws apply to you.

The table below shows the legal age for some activities in Scotland. You can get a proof-of-age card issued under the UK's national PASS scheme. These cards use photo identification and carry the PASS logo in a hologram.

Alcohol
• At 16, you can buy and consume beer, wine or cider with a meal in a restaurant, at the manager's discretion.
• At 18, you can buy alcohol in licensed premises and consume alcohol in a bar.
• If you are under 18, the police can confiscate alcohol from you if you possess alcohol in a public place.
Babysitting
• At 16, you can be held legally responsible for babysitting.
Contract
• At 16, you can enter into a legally binding contract. If you are under 16, you can also do this if the contract is usual for someone of your age and its terms are not unreasonable (like a Young Scot card).
Crime
• At 12, you can be held responsible for any criminal actions.
○ You would normally be dealt with through the Children's Hearings System until you reach the age of 16.
○ If you were charged with murder, manslaughter or rape, you would likely be dealt with through the court system.
• At 16, you can be prosecuted in the District Court, Sheriff Court or High Court.
○ Under 16, you can be prosecuted in either the Sheriff Court or High Court, but only on the instructions of the Lord Advocate.
• At 16, you can be detained in a Young Offenders' Institution.
• At 21, you can be sent to an adult prison for detention.

Fireworks
- At 18, you can buy or possess fireworks.

Passports
- You can apply for a UK Passport from birth.
  - A parent with parental responsibilities and rights generally has to sign an application for a UK Passport by a child under the age of 16.
  - If you are under 16, you can only apply for a five-year passport.
- At 16, you can apply for a UK Passport on your own behalf.
- At 16, you can apply for a 10-year passport.

Pets
- At 16, you can buy a pet.

Smoking
- At 18, you can buy cigarettes.

Standing for election
- At 14, you can stand for election as:
  - a Member of the Scottish Youth Parliament
- At 16, you can stand for election as:
  - a Community Councillor
- At 18, you can stand for election as:
  - a Member of your local council
  - an MP (UK Parliament)
  - an MSP (Scottish Parliament)
- At 21, you can stand for election as:
  - an MEP (European Parliament) (this will no longer be a position following Brexit in 2019)

Types of crime

The Scottish government divides crime into three main categories:

- crimes against the person
- crimes against property
- other crimes

Within these categories there are many types of crime.

Crimes against the person – violent crimes and sexual offences

Murder

Murder is the unlawful premeditated killing of one human being by another. Premeditated means the murder was planned in advance. People found guilty of murder face the most serious of punishments and will have to spend time in prison. If the murder is found to be motivated by racism, homophobia or religious beliefs then the sentence is often even more severe.

📖 Word bank

- **Motivation**
A reason for doing something.

- **Homophobia**
Negative feelings and actions towards homosexual (gay) people.

☄ Make the Link

In the USA many states have the death penalty, which was abolished in the UK in 1965. You may study the death penalty in RMPS.

Figure 6.4: *The punishment for assault is often very serious*

Assault

When someone is hit or beaten this is called assault. Individuals found guilty of assault will face serious punishment, including possible stays in prison or a young offenders' institution. As with murder, if the attack is found to be motivated by racism, homophobia or religious beliefs the punishment is likely to be more severe.

DAILY NEWS

world - business - finance - lifestyle - travel - sport

Shabaz Ali and his family came to Scotland seeking safety from war-torn Syria, but he almost died in a drug-fuelled racist attack in Edinburgh

When Shabaz Ali opened his eyes, after fighting for his life in hospital for three days, he didn't know where he was.

After his father answered his questions, Shabaz told him he had no future in Scotland. 'We ran away from war in Syria, I do not want to die here. This country is not safe for me,' he said.

Shabaz, 25, had been stabbed repeatedly in a racist attack by teenager Sean Gorman, in an Edinburgh homeless hostel after asking a friend of Gorman's to turn down his music.

The 18-year-old will be sentenced next month after admitting the racially aggravated attempted murder, at the High Court in Edinburgh yesterday. In court, it emerged that he had previously been jailed in January 2017 for charges of assault to severe injury and endangering life. Although he received a 26-month jail sentence he was released early, in September last year.

Mr Ali came to Scotland after his father Sivan fled Syria in 2000 fearing his life was in danger because of increasing persecution over his work as a Kurdish political activist.

Sivan became a British citizen, and had brought his family over to what they believed was safety in Edinburgh.

In June 2015, Sivan and his son lost nine members of their family after an attack by

Islamic State on their home town of Kobani in northern Syria.

The court heard that Mr Ali's mother returned to Syria to be with her own mother, her only surviving relative. But Shabaz and his father remained in Scotland, where Mr Ali was working as a manager in a barber's shop and hoping to attend university. They became homeless in April this year, however, and ended up staying, along with Mr Ali's cousin, Malak, in a homeless hostel in Upper Gilmour Place, in Edinburgh.

It was here, on May 3 this year, that Mr Ali, who had to work in the morning, complained to Gorman's friend about loud music coming from their room.

However, Gorman, who had drunk almost a litre of vodka and had taken drugs, confronted Mr Ali and told him 'Go back to your country,' before stabbing him six times with a lock knife he had bought on Ebay for £50.

The court heard Mr Ali's cousin was attempting to film the confrontation on her phone, but Gorman was undeterred, warning chillingly: 'I will end your life... I will end your life on camera' while pointing at Malak.

The prosecutor told the court about the devastating impact the attack had had on the family. Although doctors managed to save Mr Ali's life, he suffered life changing injuries. His father has also had to stop working, Mr Prentice said.

He added, of Mr Ali: 'He can barely walk. Between them, they have no income. They have applied for benefits but do not meet the criteria for any form of financial support. Sivan also supports his niece Malak Alahmad. She is still going through a visa application process and has no form of income.'

He said the family had complained about Mr Ali being placed at the hostel because they felt he was unsafe there, the last occasion just days before the attack.

Mr Ali's father was present in court to hear Mr Prentice's narration along with the family's lawyer Mr Anwar. Lord Woolman deferred sentence so the court could obtain reports about Gorman's character. He will be sentenced at the High Court in Edinburgh on August 17 2018.

[Source: http://www.heraldscotland.com/news/16366406.shabaz-ali-and-his-family-came-to-scotland-seeking-safety-from-war-torn-syria-but-he-almost-died-in-a-drug-fuelled-racist-attack-in-edinburgh/]

 Activity

Research
Research assault cases in Scotland. Try to find at least three different cases where different punishments have been given. **Do you think** prison should be an automatic sentence for racist attacks?

📖 Word bank

- **Lenient**

  Not harsh or strict enough.

- **Repeat offender**

  A person who has been convicted of breaking the same law two or more times.

- **Fire raising**

  The crime of deliberately setting fire to someone else's property.

Figure 6.5: *It is illegal to carry a knife in Scotland*

Rape and sexual assault

Rape is when someone forces another person to have sex against their will. A large proportion of rape victims are women but men can be victims of rape too. Sexual assault is any sexual contact that is not wanted by any individual. Punishments given out for rape are sometimes considered to be too lenient.

Knife crime

Knife crime is mentioned regularly in the media, perhaps due to the devastating effects injury caused by it can have. It is often portrayed as a type of crime usually committed by young people. Laws have been made stricter recently to try and clamp down on knife crime; for example, the maximum sentence in Scotland for anyone found guilty of carrying a knife is now five years, up from four years previously.

Domestic violence

Domestic violence applies to violent or aggressive behaviour in the context of a family or relationship. This can also include child abuse. Domestic violence may include emotional and/or physical abuse and may have long lasting impacts on an individual's life. Research has shown that on days when there are Old Firm (Celtic v Rangers) football matches there is a spike in domestic violence; often a lot of alcohol is drunk at these matches, and this suggests that there is a link between alcohol and domestic violence.

Crimes against property

Housebreaking

Housebreaking is when an individual has had to break locks or another secure device in order to access the property; the offender may then proceed to steal items from the household.

Theft

This can include anything from theft from an individual in the street or on public transport, to shoplifting. People convicted of theft face various consequences depending on the value of the goods stolen and whether the individual is a repeat offender or not.

Damage to property

Damage to property is often referred to as vandalism. Vandalism is deliberately causing damage to property or deliberately causing fires. Vandalism and anti-social behaviour can often go hand in hand.

Other crimes

Anti-social behaviour

Anti-social behaviour incorporates many elements of vandalism and fire raising. Anti-social behaviour refers to crimes that affect local communities and make people feel unsafe in their own local area, or even their homes.

White-collar crime

White-collar jobs are defined as those carried out by individuals working in office environments. Sociologist Edwin Sutherland defined white-collar crime as 'a crime committed by a person of respectability and high social status in the course of his occupation'. These are crimes

Figure 6.6: *White-collar crime*

such as bribery, corruption, fraud and embezzlement (embezzlement is when an individual uses someone else's money that has been entrusted to them to meet their own needs).

Blue-collar crime

Blue-collar jobs are defined as manual jobs that often involve labouring or unskilled work, and that are usually low paid. People who work in blue-collar jobs are often from deprived inner city areas that lack opportunities. Blue-collar crimes are likely to be those described above, e.g. crimes against property or crimes against the person.

Figure 6.7: *Car crimes can include vandalism and theft*

Traffic crime

Crimes such as speeding or driving without insurance are common types of traffic crime. Although some people might think these crimes are less serious than others mentioned above, they can often lead to more serious offences like death by dangerous driving. Driving while under the influence of alcohol or drugs is also a traffic crime.

Alcohol crime

Alcohol crimes are actions committed while under the influence of alcohol. Alcohol can lower inhibitions and people may do things they wouldn't normally do when sober. Drunkenness, breach of the peace or drinking underage can all be punished by police.

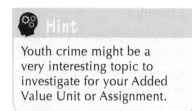

Figure 6.8: *Speeding is driving faster than the speed limit*

Drug crime

All illegal drugs are put into one of three categories, according to how dangerous they are. Different drugs affect people in different ways; if a drug is not Class A that does not mean it is safe and it can still have severe consequences.

What crimes are most/least common?

Serious crimes, such as rape, assault and murder, make up only 8% of all crimes recorded. White-collar crimes are also uncommon.

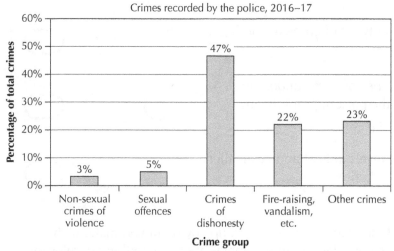

Figure 6.10: *Crimes recorded by the police by percentage*

Crimes recorded by the police, 2016–17

Non-sexual crimes of violence: 3%
Sexual offences: 5%
Crimes of dishonesty: 47%
Fire-raising, vandalism, etc.: 22%
Other crimes: 23%

Percentage of total crimes / Crime group

Figure 6.9: *Graffiti is one kind of vandalism*

> **Hint**
>
> Youth crime might be a very interesting topic to investigate for your Added Value Unit or Assignment.

The most common types of crime are those of dishonesty (i.e. offences such as burglary or robbery) with acts that damage property, such as vandalism, coming second. Young people are most likely to be involved in these types of crime due to boredom and peer pressure.

? Questions

1. Create a spider diagram showing the types of crime and give **examples** of each.
2. What is the difference between blue-collar crime and white-collar crime?
3. Using the **evidence** in Figure 6.10 make a **conclusion** about the most common category of crime.
4. Use Figure 6.10 to create a pie chart of crime in Scotland.

Summary

In this chapter you have learned:

*   the different types of crime

Learning Summary

Now that you have finished **The nature of crime** chapter, complete a self-evaluation of your knowledge and skills to assess what you have understood. Use the checklist below and its traffic lights to draw up a revision plan to help you improve in the areas you identified as red or amber.

*   I can understand that crime is any action that breaks the law of the land.

*   I can understand that the laws in Scotland are made by the UK Parliament in Westminster and the Scottish Parliament in Holyrood.

*   I can list the many different types of crime according to the government statistics.

*   I can group the different types of crime under the headings: crimes against the person, property and other crimes.

*   I can describe how crime levels in Scotland have fallen in recent years for almost all crimes.

Examples

In Modern Studies it is essential that you are able to back up any point you make with relevant evidence. When you are considering the statements above try to think of relevant examples for each response. You may wish to note these examples under each statement in your revision notes.

7 Causes of crime

What makes people commit crime?

People are responsible for their own behaviour. However, some factors in life may increase the chances of people acting irresponsibly. This relates to the way in which people are socialised and depends upon the way they are brought up, the peer group they belong to and the role models they may or may not have. Some groups in society are, however, statistically more likely to break the law than others. Those most likely to break the law and commit crime are white, working-class males under the age of 25.

Peer pressure/gang culture

The need to follow what everyone else in your group of friends is doing can be very powerful. If a person does not do what the rest of the group does they can face threats or even exclusion from the group and the fear of 'not fitting in' often encourages people to commit acts they wouldn't otherwise. For example, if an individual is involved with underage drinkers or other criminals there is a danger of giving in to the pressure of this group. In many communities there are groups of young males at the lower end of the social scale who live in areas with very high crime rates. Some youngsters will commit crime to draw attention to themselves and to win popularity within a group. Frequently, rival gangs can form and this can increase levels of crime. It is also often the case that young males in these gangs may be labelled as 'trouble-makers'; sociologists argue that treating people as criminals means that they will continue to behave like criminals because no one expects anything different. Gang-related behaviour can often be linked to poverty and geographical location.

📖 **Word bank**

- **Socialised**

The way someone learns to behave in order to fit in with their group.

- **Social scale**

The structure of a society, usually with the richest people at the top and the poorest at the bottom.

Make the Link

If you study Sociology you may have learned about the causes of crime and the arguments of nature versus nurture.

Figure 7.1: *Peer pressure can lead to disruptive behaviour*

Figure 7.2: *Abandoned and burnt-out cars littering the landscape*

Make the Link

You may cover absolute poverty in developing countries in Geography.

Word bank

• **Persistent poverty**

Being in relative poverty for three or more out of four years.

Poverty

Poverty remains a substantial problem in Scotland, and when this book was published in 2018 the continuing effects of the recent recession had made this worse. In each year between 2014 and 2017, one million people in Scotland were living in poverty, which was a slight increase on previous years. The 2018 statistics also show 8% of people are in persistent poverty. These figures represent the highest levels of poverty since 2011.

Most people living in poverty do not break the law, but some do. Poverty can lead to boredom; this may encourage some people to commit crimes to give them something to do. Poorer families may not be able to afford activities and basic material goods, meaning crime becomes more attractive as a means to meet these needs.

Some people in poverty see a future of low pay or unemployment and know this will never allow them to have a fancy car, a big house or designer clothes. This is often linked to the type of communities poorer families and individuals live in – with few amenities nearby and cut off from the areas of wealth that might offer better paid jobs, better schools and a route out of poverty. As a result poorer families often feel frustrated and trapped in their environment. One way to solve this is to turn to crime in order to pay for the lifestyle they cannot afford legally. This is an economic cause of crime.

Many in poverty also feel socially excluded.

Biological theories

Biological explanations of crime assume that some people are 'born criminals' and are visibly and mentally distinct from non-criminals, which means that some people are more psychologically predisposed to committing criminal acts.

Research shows people who commit crimes are more likely to get angry or have no empathy or understanding of another person's feelings, as in the case of a psychopath. Research of this kind has focused on the way the brain works in people who commit crime – the psychological make-up of the criminal.

Other research suggests that people who commit crimes are more likely to look a certain way and have different physical characteristics. Cesare Lombroso (1835–1909) was an Italian criminologist. He observed the physical characteristics of Italian prisoners and compared them to those of Italian soldiers. He concluded that the criminals were physically different. He compiled a list of physical characteristics which he said criminals were more likely to possess than non-criminals. Five of these characteristics in a man indicated they were more likely to commit a crime. For women it was only three.

- a proportioned face-to-head ratio
- large monkey-like ears
- large lips, jaw or chin
- a twisted nose
- excessive cheekbones
- long arms
- excessive wrinkles on the skin
- tattoos

Figure 7.3: *Cesare Lombroso*

Some research has suggested that criminals have an extra Y chromosome that gives them an XYY chromosomal make-up rather than an XY make-up. Normally, males have 46 chromosomes including one X and one Y chromosome. Males with XYY syndrome have 47 chromosomes, two of which are Y chromosomes. This is said to link to crime as some of the complications can be low IQ and social and emotional difficulties which have both been linked to causing crime, especially violent crime. Researchers in Finland found that prisoners there are at least 5–10% more likely to commit violent crime because of their genetic make-up.

However, many of the biological theories of crime have been disproved and are not very relevant to our current understanding of why people commit crime.

Social exclusion

The government describes social exclusion as what 'happens when people or places suffer from a series of problems such as unemployment, discrimination, poor skills, low incomes, poor housing, high crime, ill health and family breakdown'. As a result, individuals do not feel like they are part of society. This may be due to a lack of education leading to an inability to secure well-paid employment and may also be linked to poor facilities in certain areas.

People who feel excluded may then turn to crime as a way of dealing with their situation or as a way of being able to take part in society. Many feel that we live in a very materialistic society where status is measured by what people 'own'; it is often the case that individuals feel they need to have certain possessions such as the latest tablet computer or smartphone in order to 'fit in'. People may feel that they have to steal or commit other crimes in order to feel as good as their friends or the people around them.

Social exclusion is often linked to geographical location and poverty.

Word bank

• Facilities
Places provided for a useful purpose like schools, leisure facilities, other recreational activities and housing.

• Materialistic
Caring about things more than people.

Figure 7.4: *Lack of money and greed for money can lead to crime*

📖 Word bank

• Organised crime

Widespread criminal activities controlled by a structured hierarchy of people.

• Lucrative

Producing a great deal of profit.

• Sink estates

A council housing estate, often on the edge of town, with high levels of poverty.

• Deprivation

The damaging lack of the basic necessities in life.

• Poverty cycle

A set of factors or events by which poverty will continue without help from outside.

Figure 7.5: *Kids can escape poverty through education*

👤 Hint

The best descriptions of causes of crime show the links *between* the causes.

Poor role models

'How young people learn what is acceptable and normal behaviour' is referred to as socialisation. If this process breaks down then young people may turn to criminal behaviour and this can be passed down through generations, from parents to children, through learned behaviour.

Learned behaviour such as family break-ups, absent parents (particularly fathers) and criminal friends can lead to skewed values of what is right and wrong, and crime can become 'normal' behaviour.

Children require good role models who hold good moral values and do not advocate crime in order to cope in the wider world and, when these are lacking, children may require support from social services and mental health services. Statistics show that children who access these services are more vulnerable to becoming involved in crime.

The lack of role models can often be linked to geographical location.

Greed

In order to 'fit in' individuals may feel the pressure to steal the latest gadgets or become involved in other criminal activity. Although they may not be doing it entirely to survive, some may feel that theft is the only way to 'fit in' with the rest of society.

Some people are career criminals who make their living from organised crime. The drug trade (the importing, manufacturing and selling of drugs) can often be a very lucrative trade where some can make vast amounts of money, far more than is necessary to survive. This can be described as greed and is an economic cause of crime.

Geographical location

Rural areas and suburbs have a lower crime rate than inner city areas and 'sink estates'. The wealth of an area is an important factor in crime levels; the highest levels of violent crime occur in the poorest areas. Drug and alcohol abuse is more common in these areas, which often see crimes being committed while under the influence or to fund a habit.

Due to the high levels of unemployment in inner city areas, many young people in poorer areas find themselves with time on their hands but nothing to do due to the lack of facilities in the area. When hanging around with no real purpose the opportunity to get involved in a crime such as vandalism, fighting or joyriding can be difficult to resist.

The culture and values in many inner city communities or 'sink estates' can also contribute to crime levels as many may see criminal behaviour as 'acceptable' because of the role models they are surrounded by.

The geographical location that an individual finds themselves in may also be linked to poverty.

Lack of education

In areas of deprivation some people experience a low level of education. In areas of high poverty, often formal education is not valued and is not seen as a route by which young people can escape from the poverty cycle. People may not do well at school, possibly due to truancy or underachievement. As a result they cannot get a good job that will give them good pay, leaving them unable to escape the cycle of poverty. This can then lead to status frustration, where individuals feel they are stuck in a certain 'rut' in society and unable to escape the poverty cycle. This may encourage individuals to turn to crime.

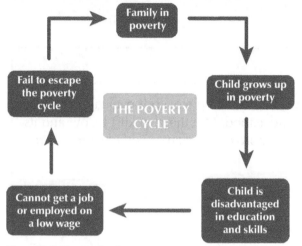

Figure 7.6: *The cycle of poverty*

Alcohol and drugs

The British Crime Survey (2015) reported that the perpetrator was believed to be under the influence of alcohol in 47% of violent offences. The Scottish Crime and Justice Survey (2016) reported that 60% of young offenders were under the influence of alcohol at the time of their offence. Researchers also suggest that around one-third to half of all thefts are related to drug use. Alcohol and drugs can lower inhibitions and encourage people to make decisions they wouldn't when sober.

Those who are addicted to Class A drugs, such as heroin or cocaine, find that their habit becomes very expensive – sometimes running into hundreds of pounds a week. Many addicts are therefore forced to turn to crimes such as robbery or prostitution in order to get money to pay for their drugs.

There are often higher levels of drug and alcohol abuse in poverty-stricken areas.

? Questions

1. 'People are responsible for their own actions, their circumstances do not matter. If someone commits a crime it is their own responsibility.'
    Do you agree with the statement? Give reasons for you answer.

2. **Explain, in detail,** why alcohol and drugs can cause criminal behaviour.

3. Why do some people suggest that higher crime levels are linked to poverty?

4. 'Everybody has the opportunity to escape the cycle of crime.' why the person who made this statement may be accused of being **selective in the use of facts**.

GO! **Activity**

Show your knowledge
Create a mind map of the different causes of crime. Try to show the links between the causes. Use each of the different bold headings to create a different point of information. It may be useful to use different colours to show the different reasons and the links between the causes.

GO! **Activity**

Show your knowledge
Imagine you have to summarise the causes of crime in a Tweet to a friend. This means you can only use 280 characters, what would you say?

Make the Link

In Social Education you may examine the causes of youth crime in your area.

Summary

In this chapter you have learned:

- the causes of crime

Learning Summary

Now that you have finished the **Causes of crime** chapter, complete a self-evaluation of your knowledge and skills to assess what you have understood. Use the checklist below and its traffic lights to draw up a revision plan to help you improve in the areas you identified as red or amber.

- I can describe the role of gang culture in causing someone to commit a crime.
- I can describe how poverty can lead to criminal behaviour.
- I can explain the biological causes of crime.
- I can explain social exclusion.
- I can explain how social factors can lead to crime.
- I can describe how greed can lead someone to commit a crime.
- I can explain how economic factors can lead to crime.
- I can describe the impact of geographical location on criminal behaviour.
- I can explain the impact of poor role models on criminal behaviour.
- I can describe the contribution of alcohol and drugs to crime.

Examples

In Modern Studies it is essential that you are able to back up any point you make with relevant evidence. When you are considering the statements above try to think of relevant examples for each response. You may wish to note these examples under each statement in your revision notes.

8 Consequences of crime

Impact of crime

Crime impacts on victims, perpetrators, families, communities and wider society.

Victims of crime suffer the immediate impacts such as physical harm and loss of or damage to property. The 'aftermath' (fear of crime) often far exceeds the immediate impact. The prevalence of crime can also cause distress to the wider society through the fear of crime.

A criminal record may mean that criminals face the consequences of their actions for the rest of their lives. Businesses affected by crime may experience a negative impact on their profits or even ability to continue trading. All criminal activity represents a cost to the Scottish government ranging from police wages to the cost of prison.

Figure 8.1: *The impact of crime can have a shattering effect on lives*

Victims

The chance of being a victim of a crime is not the same for everybody in society and some groups are more likely to be victims of a crime than others. For example, statistically, young people face higher risks of crime than older people. The Scottish Crime and Justice Survey 2017 showed that 24% of 16–24-year-olds were victims of crime compared to only 9% of those aged 60 or older. This could be because young males are much more likely to be involved in criminal behaviour such as gang culture. The risk of being a victim of any crime was slightly higher for males than for females. Again, this could be because males are more likely to commit crimes. The risk of being a victim of crime was much greater for people from ethnic minority backgrounds. This may be linked to the higher levels of poverty for ethnic minorities as areas in poverty experience more crime, this could also be due to racism in society.

We are all different and crime affects victims in different ways. The effects of crime can last for a long time, irrespective of the seriousness of the crime. Some people cope very well with the most horrific crimes while others can be very distressed by a minor incident. Victims may feel angry, upset or experience other strong emotions, and this may impact on their job, relationships and mental health. These feelings may develop into long-term problems such as depression or anxiety-related illness.

Make the Link

We use a lot of statistics in Modern Studies; you will probably cover how statistics can be misleading in Maths.

Victims may also have to deal with physical changes. For example, a victim of a serious assault may have broken bones which may restrict their movement, their job and their standard of living.

Perpetrators

Any individual who commits a crime has to accept the consequences of their actions. If convicted, a criminal will have a criminal record which may have to be declared when applying for jobs and may decrease the number of employment opportunities available to them. A lot of employers will not hire individuals who have a criminal record and those with convictions may end up trapped in low-paid, temporary, part-time or zero-hour contract work.

Individuals may then be trapped in the cycle of poverty and therefore feel forced to commit more criminal acts in order to survive. Criminals may also have to spend time in prison away from their friends and family and, while this may be necessary for punishment, it may also impact negatively on friends and family as they are separated from their loved one.

Families

Families of both the perpetrator(s) and the victim(s) may be affected by crime. A victim of crime may react in a number of different ways: they may become withdrawn, they may lose their job and may lash out at those close to them. For the families of victims this may mean that they live with somebody who has completely changed. They may feel uneasy in their own home and not want to upset the victim. There may also be a financial burden on the family of the victim if they are no longer able to work. The family of murder victims may also feel the emotional impact of having a loved one missing from key events in life such as birthdays, weddings, grandchildren etc.

The families of perpetrators of crime may also experience similar problems. If the offender is sentenced to a community protection order they may have to move house, stay in their house at certain times of the day or stay away from certain areas, all of which would also impact on their family. This impact could be financial, such as the cost of moving house or paying bills if the perpetrator is unable to work. There could also be an emotional impact, such as having to move to a new, unfamiliar place. If the perpetrator is given a jail sentence their family may have to travel hundreds of miles to visit them in prison. This could be expensive and time-consuming. The family may also have to deal with the emotional impact of that person not being there for special events such as birthdays. Some argue that the family of the perpetrator has not committed a crime and shouldn't have to miss out on family moments.

Communities

Communities which experience high levels of crime are often adversely affected. People may be frightened inside or outside their own home. High levels of crime keep property prices low and homeowners can

Figure 8.2: *A criminal record can make life very difficult*

find it more difficult to sell their property. Crime has an impact on home insurance premiums – it makes it more expensive to insure a property and in extreme cases an insurance company may decline to insure someone because of where they live. New businesses may avoid opening in the area and existing businesses may close down if they suffer repeated theft or vandalism, or if they lose customers as a result of crime in the area. This can lead to poverty, social exclusion and the ghettoising of that community, which in turn may cause more crime.

Wider society

Crimes such as shoplifting and fraud cost businesses in the UK billions of pounds each year. According to research done by the Scottish Business Resilience Centre in 2017, the cost of business crime in Scotland was over £8 billion. To try and prevent crimes such as shoplifting, many companies employ security guards, others attach 'anti-theft tags' to expensive goods and many increasingly use recording devices such as CCTV. All of these added security methods cost a business money.

A third of all crime related to business is now committed using the internet. Internet crime mainly involves thieves stealing highly confidential business data such as customers' personal information. Gaining access to this type of information can result in thieves getting rich very quickly. UK companies such as banks, insurance companies and energy suppliers have recently been the victims of internet crime. Again, installing extra internet security can cost businesses greatly.

The Scottish and UK governments have tried to combat the increase in internet crime by setting up special internet crime units. The Scottish Business Crime Centre works with businesses and aims to use the latest security technology to catch internet thieves.

The cost of crime in Scotland and the UK as a whole is very large. The cost of putting criminals through courts and punishing them has to be supplied from taxes which otherwise could have been spent on other public services.

Often losses due to theft are passed on to customers as businesses have to increase their prices to make up the loss. Insurance payments increase for businesses and individuals, impacting negatively on the economy as people have to spend more money on insurance and therefore have less money to spend on other things.

When crime rates are high, countries look unstable to the rest of the world and their currency can decrease in value.

In addition to this we must consider the cost of treating victims of violence through the NHS and Victim Support services. Victim Support spent £42.9 million treating victims of crime in the UK in 2017.

Figure 8.3: *Criminals can operate online to steal customers' private, often financial, details*

> ### 📖 Word bank
>
> • **Ghettoise**
> To restrict to an isolated or segregated place, group or situation.

> ### Make the Link
>
> You may cover the cost of criminal activity to businesses in Business Management.

> ### Make the Link
>
> In Section 3 you will learn about the cost of crime to the international community.

> ### GO! Activity
>
> **Discuss**
> With your shoulder partner, create a bullet pointed list of the impact of crime on victims, perpetrators, families, communities and wider society. You should use the information above to help you.

Summary

In this chapter you have learned:

- the impact of crime on society

Learning Summary

Now that you have finished the **Consequences of crime** chapter, complete a self-evaluation of your knowledge and skills to assess what you have understood. Use the checklist below and its traffic lights to draw up a revision plan to help you improve in the areas you identified as red or amber.

- I can explain that crime has short and long-term consequences.

- I can explain that victims of crime may suffer emotional, physical and financial consequences.

- I can explain that crime can impact negatively on families of victims.

- I can explain that perpetrators' families can be affected negatively by crime.

- I can explain that perpetrators' lives may be ruined by crime.

- I can explain that wider society is impacted financially by crime.

- I can explain that communities can be destroyed by crime.

Examples

In Modern Studies it is essential that you are able to back up any point you make with relevant evidence. When you are considering the statements above try to think of relevant examples for each response. You may wish to note these examples under each statement in your revision notes.

9 Criminal justice system

What you will learn in this chapter

- The court system in Scotland.
- The youth justice system in Scotland.

Convicting criminals

Scotland has long had a unique court and criminal justice system that is very different to that within the rest of the UK. The main difference is that Scottish courts allow the 'not proven' verdict. This is used when there is not sufficient evidence to prove a person guilty but there remains suspicion that they are not entirely innocent. Some people think the not proven verdict is unfair as it leaves the accused without the label of 'innocent'.

The **Criminal Proceedings etc. (Reform) (Scotland) Act 2007** created six sheriffdoms in Scotland:

- Glasgow and Strathkelvin
- Grampian, Highlands and Islands
- Lothian and Borders
- North Strathclyde
- South Strathclyde, Dumfries and Galloway
- Tayside, Central and Fife

Court system

Each sheriffdom contains one or more Sheriff Courts and a number of Justice of the Peace Courts. The High Court of Justiciary is based in Edinburgh but travels around major towns and cities.

When a crime is committed, and the police have charged someone with a criminal offence, the details are sent to the Procurator Fiscal who looks at the evidence and decides whether or not to go ahead with prosecution. If the Procurator Fiscal decides that the case should proceed then those accused will appear before one of three courts: the Justice of the Peace Court, the Sheriff Court, or the High Court of the Justiciary (known as the High Court). In these courts it is decided whether the accused is guilty, not guilty or not proven. Then, if necessary, a sentence will be handed out. Each court deals with different offences depending on the seriousness of the crime, and either solemn or summary procedure can be used.

Figure 9.1: *The entrance to the Sheriff and Justice of the Peace Courts in Edinburgh*

📖 Word bank

- **Solemn procedure**
Trial before a Sheriff or judge and a jury of 15 people.

- **Summary procedure**
Trial before a Sheriff or Justice of the Peace and no jury.

Justice of the Peace Courts

Justice of the Peace Courts were created by the **Criminal Proceedings etc. (Reform) (Scotland) Act 2007** to replace District Courts. The process brought all the courts under the control of the Scottish Court

Figure 9.2: *Paisley Sheriff Court*

📖 Word bank

- **Custodial**

A sentence consisting of containing the offender, usually in a prison.

- **Sheriff Principle**

The senior legal authority for the local area.

- **Ineligible**

Legally or officially unable to be considered for a position.

☄ Make the Link

You may have taken part in a mock trial using solemn procedure in English, or other subjects.

Figure 9.3: *Entrance to the High Court of Justiciary building in Glasgow*

System rather than local authorities, and this was intended to streamline the system.

Justice of the Peace Courts are the lowest level of criminal court and therefore handle relatively minor crimes such as breach of the peace, minor assaults, minor road traffic offences and animal cruelty. Justice of the Peace Courts operate a summary procedure which consists of a lay magistrate (Justice of the Peace) and no jury. A lay magistrate (Justice of the Peace) is appointed from within the local community and is not usually a legally qualified judge, however they will have been trained in criminal law and procedure. When the court is in session lay magistrates have access to lawyers who can advise them on law and procedure. The maximum sentences that a lay magistrate can impose in a Justice of the Peace Court are custodial sentences of up to 60 days, and fines of up to £2,500.

Sheriff Courts

Each sheriffdom has a Sheriff Principal who is in charge of all of the Sheriff Courts in the area and of ensuring that all 'court business is carried our efficiently'. For example, the current (2018) Sheriff Principle of North Strathclyde is Sheriff Principal Duncan Law Murray.

The Sheriff Court deals with more serious offences committed within the sheriffdom. As the crimes tend to be more serious, the Sheriff Court may use summary procedure or solemn procedure depending on the case. Under summary procedure, the sentencing powers are limited to three months imprisonment, unless there are previous convictions, or a fine of £5,000. Under solemn procedure, the Sheriff can impose a prison sentence of up to three years or an unlimited fine, unless previous laws define a maximum fine for the offence. If a Sheriff ever feels that a harsher punishment is called for then they can refer the case to the High Court for sentencing, where a more severe punishment may be handed out.

The High Court of the Justiciary

The High Court is Scotland's highest criminal court. This court only conducts trials under solemn procedure with a legally trained judge and a jury of 15 men and women. A jury is chosen from the list of people on the electoral register; anyone who is over 18, has lived in the UK for at least five years since the age of 13, and is not currently ineligible can be summoned for jury duty.

The High Court usually sits in Edinburgh but also travels to different parts of Scotland; it has permanent buildings in Glasgow and Aberdeen and uses the Sheriff Court buildings in Stirling, Oban, Inverness, Dundee, Perth, Dumfries, Jedburgh and Ayr. The High Court deals with the most serious of crimes such as treason, murder, rape, armed robbery, drug trafficking, sexual offences involving children and certain offences under the **Official Secrets Act**. In difficult cases, such as a highly public murder trial, there may be three judges sitting. The High Court has unlimited sentencing powers in terms of imprisonment and fines.

GO! Activity

Show your knowledge

Complete simple diagrams showing the crimes, procedures and sentencing of the three criminal courts. The High Court has been done for you below.

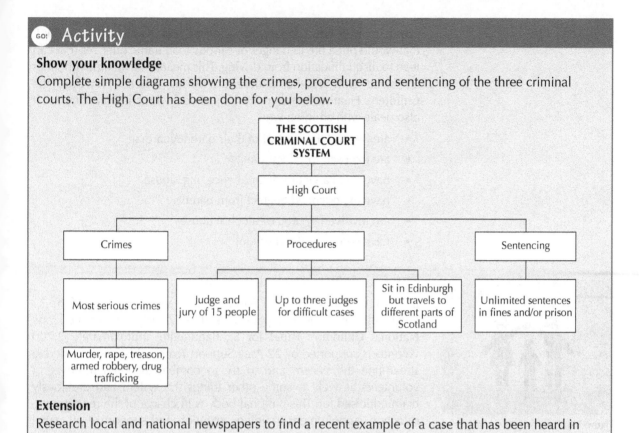

Extension

Research local and national newspapers to find a recent example of a case that has been heard in each of the courts. Summarise the procedure followed, the verdict and the sentence given.

Civil courts and the right to appeal

The civil court settles disputes between people about non-criminal matters. This court sits in Parliament House in Edinburgh and acts as a Court of Session. In some cases, convicted criminals may have the opportunity to appeal their conviction or their sentence and the Court of Session deals with appeals from any of the other three courts in Scotland. Any appeal heard here can be referred on to the House of Lords in London, where the case may be heard and the decision overturned.

📖 Word bank

• **Court of Session**

The highest civil (as opposed to criminal) court.

• **Appeal**

When someone who has been convicted of a crime asks for the decision to be reviewed. This is only allowed in certain cases.

❓ Questions

1. What is solemn procedure?
2. What is summary procedure?
3. If a criminal is unhappy with their conviction, which court may they appeal to?

Scottish youth justice system

Scotland has a unique Children's Hearing system that is very different from juvenile justice systems elsewhere in the UK and the rest of the world. Children (those under 16 years old) are only considered for prosecution in court for serious offences such as murder, an assault that would put a life in danger or serious road traffic offences that can lead to disqualification from driving. This means that all other offences are dealt with by the Children's Hearing system. However, the Children's Hearing system does not just deal with criminal offences, it also deals with children who:

- are beyond the control of their parent/guardian
- are exposed to 'moral danger'
- have been a victim of an offence, e.g. abuse
- have experienced neglect from parents
- are involved in drug or alcohol abuse
- have failed to attend school

The Children's Hearing system

In 2013, Children's Hearing Scotland took over the running of the 32 local authority (council) panels used previously and created one National Children's Panel for Scotland with approximately 2,700 volunteers supported by 22 Area Support Teams. This was intended to streamline the system and to try to combat the high turnover of volunteers as well as some other things the system had previously been criticised for. This national body is in charge of the recruitment, selection, appointment, training, retention and support of all panel members.

Figure 9.4: *Protecting the child*

How the Children's Hearing system works	
Step 1	Referral to the Children's Reporter.
Step 2	Initial investigation is carried out – three possible outcomes.
Step 3	Referred to a hearing in front of the Children's Panel – one of three decisions will then be made.

A referral may be made to the Children's Reporter by the police in criminal cases, or by a social worker, health or education services, a member of the public or the child themselves. When the reporter receives the original referral they will carry out an initial investigation, which would involve things like collecting witness statements from teachers, police, social workers etc. Once this initial investigation has been carried out the reporter has three options:

1. If they think the problem is under control by the family they will take no further action.

2. They may refer to the local authority who can offer extra support such as counselling, usually involving the support of a social worker.

3. Or, if it is decided that compulsory supervision methods are needed, they may arrange a hearing of the Children's Panel.

📖 Word bank

• Moral danger

When a child is in need of protection from parents or guardians who behave in an immoral or wrong way.

• Children's Reporter

The person who is employed to make decisions about a young person to help them sort their problems out.

• Compulsory supervision methods

The social worker assigned to the child, along with others (e.g. the child's school), will work out a plan to improve the child's situation.

The Children's Hearing

The purpose of a hearing of the Children's Panel is to decide on the measures of care that are in the best interests of the child. In cases where a crime has been committed the hearing is not usually about deciding on a 'punishment', it is more often about helping the child move away from the criminal behaviour.

The people who sit on Children's Hearings are known as the Children's Panel. They are volunteers and come from a wide range of occupations and backgrounds and they all have experience of, and an interest in, helping and supporting children. Members are trained for their role with the Children's Panel and all panels must contain a mix of men and women.

Figure 9.5: *Supporting the child*

The hearing is designed to support the child. The young person must always be present during the meeting, along with a person of their choosing. The parents/carers will attend and there are also three panel members present at the meeting who have to discuss and decide the next steps that should be taken. The meeting takes place in the young person's local area in order to encourage the young person to feel comfortable. The panel receives reports from the young person's social worker and sometimes the school. Everyone has the opportunity to look at the reports and discussion will be centred around the 'grounds for referral'. The young person has to agree to the grounds they have been given during the hearing; if they do not agree then they may be referred to one of the adult courts.

> 📖 **Word bank**
>
> • **Grounds for referral**
>
> Reasons to send the child on to the next stage of the process, e.g. lack of parental care.

The hearing normally lasts around an hour and then a decision has to be made by the three panel members about the next steps. The panel can make three decisions:

1. Firstly, that they don't need to do anything about the grounds for referral and decide not to take it any further. This is called 'discharging the case'. This might be because things have improved for the young person at home or school and the panel members don't feel that the young person needs to come back to another hearing.

2. Secondly, they may decide that more information is needed to help them make a decision about what is best for the young person, and they can decide to continue the hearing at a later date. They would then ask the reporter to carry out further investigations.

3. Thirdly, they may agree that compulsory measures of supervision are needed to help the young person, and can make a Compulsory Supervision Order.

A Compulsory Supervision Order is a legal document that means that the local authority is responsible for looking after and helping the young person. It can state where the young person must live and other conditions that must be followed. It may be necessary to put the young person into secure accommodation (a place they cannot leave) because there is suspicion that they could hurt themselves or others if they are left in their own home. They may also be fitted with an electronic tag to stop them from entering certain areas. To place a child on a Compulsory Supervision Order is a very serious decision and is not taken lightly by the Panel Members. A Compulsory Supervision Order must be reviewed at another hearing within a year.

Figure 9.6: *The people who would attend a Children's Hearing*

GO! Activity

Discuss
Discuss with your shoulder partner how the Children's Hearing system helped Craig. Write a short summary of the positive changes Craig made.

Craig's story

CASE STUDY

Craig was 15 when he first got into trouble with the police. He had become involved with a local gang and in a short space of time had committed 15 offences. He had been vandalising the local area, and had started drinking and smoking cannabis.

Craig was living with his mum and her new boyfriend. His mum's boyfriend had a criminal record and a history of drug misuse.

The police caught Craig and referred him to the Reporter. His mum was very upset and angry with him. The Reporter decided it was important that Craig went to a Children's Hearing.

At his hearing, Craig said he was really sorry for getting involved with the gang. He said he had been showing off and trying to impress them. He also stated he was unhappy at home.

The Panel Members made a Compulsory Supervision Order. His mum was happy as she wanted him to stay away from the gang and she later left her boyfriend. They also put in a condition that he attend a special drugs awareness programme for teenagers.

As part of his Compulsory Supervision Order, Craig was placed on a work experience programme which then offered him the opportunity to train to become a mechanic. Craig has not been in trouble with the police since.

Proposals for change

The Children's Hearing system is sometimes criticised because 60% of cases are to do with the welfare and care of children, which some argue would be better dealt with elsewhere. Some critics see the hearing system as a 'soft' way of dealing with criminal behaviour and they believe it does not prevent crime in later life. There are also a lot of changes in staff members on the Children's Panel and some children feel intimidated by having to appear in front of one, so the truth is not always uncovered. Because of these criticisms the Scottish Prisons Commission has recommended 'Youth Hearings' for16- and 17-year-olds. Under proposals these would deal exclusively with criminal cases of 16- and 17-year-olds. They would be structured more like an adult court rather than a supportive panel and the focus would be on giving the appropriate punishment. However there would also be support to tackle the causes of crime and prevent youngsters from reoffending.

 Activity

Group work
With your shoulder partner, make up a quiz on the youth justice system in Scotland. Then test your classmates to see how much they've learned. Your quiz should have at least 10 questions; you might wish to make them multiple choice. Your teacher will want to see that you also have answers to the questions to show your understanding.

? Questions

1. Why might a young person be referred to the Children's Hearing system?
2. **Describe** the steps of the Children's Hearing system. Include the possible options available at each stage.
3. What is a Compulsory Supervision Order?
4. **Explain** how the Compulsory Supervision Order benefitted Craig.
5. What changes have the Scottish Prisons Commission recommended to the current Children's Hearing system?

Sentencing

Scottish courts have a range of sentencing powers available to them. In 2017, 49% of all convictions resulted in a financial penalty. Most of these are fines, however those convicted can also be ordered to pay a compensation order to the victim. The traditional way of dealing with criminals is by placing people in prison where they are physically confined and usually deprived of a range of personal freedoms. In 2017, the number of convictions resulting in a custodial sentence increased to 14% of all convictions. This is still lower than in previous years.

Figure 9.7: *A judge's gavel and soundboard for use in court*

A custodial sentence is most frequently used for crimes involving violence, including rape and sexual assault. The average length of a custodial sentence in 2016–17 was around 10 months (313 days), which was 7% (20 days) longer than in 2015–16. These figures reflect the Scottish government's advice to remove sentences of less than three months.

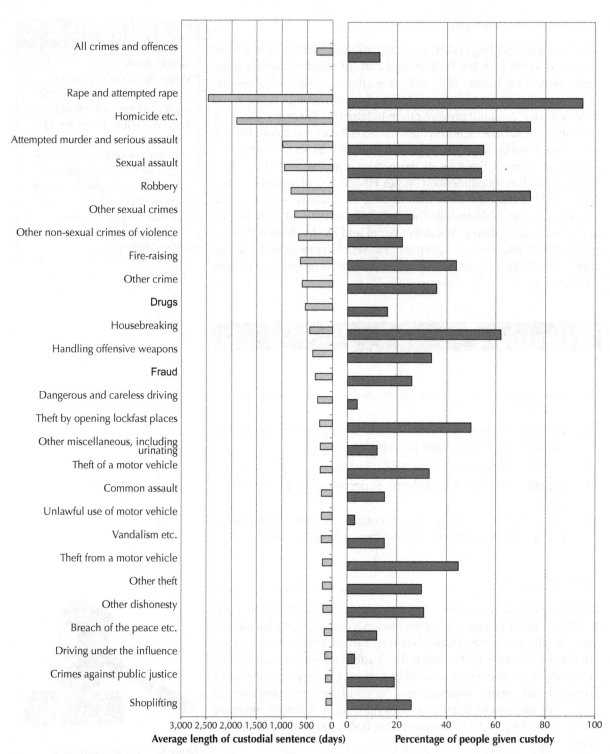

Figure 9.8: *Crimes and sentences (excludes crime types where the number of people sentenced to prison is fewer than 30)*

Effectiveness of Scottish courts

There are arguments on both sides as to the effectiveness of the Scottish court system. The system can be considered effective because there are low (and decreasing) levels of crime in Scotland, the public are generally happy that the justice system is effective and, to a certain extent, judges have individual freedom on sentencing. However, the system can also be considered ineffective because short sentences are ineffective, reoffending rates are high and some people believe the not proven verdict is ineffective and unclear.

Low (and decreasing) levels of crime

The levels of crime in Scotland have decreased by 4% since 2014–15 and have decreased by 41% since 2006–07. This suggests that the sentences issued by the courts are acting as a deterrent and therefore reducing crime. It also suggests that the court system is able to identify perpetrators who would benefit from a rehabilitation order.

Public confidence

The Scottish Crime and Justice Survey 2016–17 found that the majority of the public has confidence in the criminal justice system. This suggests the court system is doing a good job.

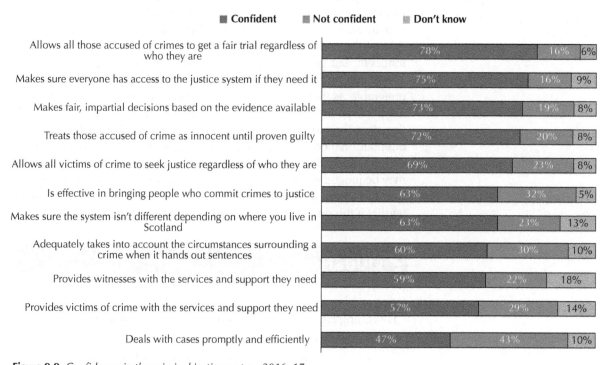

Figure 9.9: *Confidence in the criminal justice system 2016–17*

Individual freedom of judges

The Scottish courts have a range of sentencing powers available to them and it is possible to argue that they are effective in tackling crime because sheriffs and judges have the opportunity to assess each case. They can issue a sentence that they think is appropriate to the crime.

Sentences such as Drug Treatment and Testing Orders (DTTOs) can be given to help offenders rehabilitate (see page 144), and prison can be used as a last resort or as a deterrent.

Short sentences are ineffective

David Strang, the Chief Inspector of Prisons, has called for an end to jail terms of less than 12 months. He states that over half of people who are released from a sentence of less than 12 months reoffend within one year. The length of these sentences means that prisoners don't have the opportunity to access the full range of the rehabilitation services available within prison and some argue that the prison environment is not harsh enough to be seen as a deterrent in such a short period of time. However, the fact that the courts continue to issue short sentences suggests the system is ineffective at tackling crime. Chapter 10 looks at custodial sentences in more detail.

High rates of reoffending

One-third of offenders reoffend within one year of being released from prison. This may suggest that the courts are not issuing the most appropriate sentence in every case.

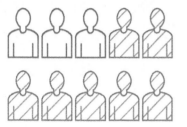

Figure 9.10: *Reconvictions within one year of release*

Not proven verdict is ineffective

The 'not proven' verdict is an acquittal verdict used when the judge or jury does not have enough evidence to convict the accused but is not convinced of their innocence in order to bring a 'not guilty' verdict. Essentially, the judge or jury is unconvinced that the suspect is innocent, but guilt has not been proven 'beyond reasonable doubt'. The main criticisms of this verdict are that the main two verdicts are preferable as they direct the jury to look at the evidence and to find the accused innocent if there is any doubt, meaning there is a solid decision. The 'not proven' verdict carries with it an implication of guilt but no formal conviction, and so the accused is often seen to be guilty without the option of a retrial to clear their name. This means people may be judged negatively by the public. Critics argue that where there is evidence to suggest guilt, a jury would be likely to pass a guilty verdict if the option of 'not proven' wasn't available to them.

? Questions

1. Using Figure 9.8, make **conclusions, with evidence,** about:
    *   the crime that received the longest sentences
    *   the crime where most people received custodial sentences

2. Give three arguments **with evidence** to suggest the Scottish court system is effective in tackling crime.

3. Give three arguments **with evidence** to suggest the Scottish court system is ineffective in tackling crime.

4. Explain the not proven verdict.

5. Why could it be argued that the not proven verdict is ineffective in tackling crime?

Summary

In this chapter you have learned:

- how the court system in Scotland works
- about the unique youth justice system in Scotland

Learning Summary

Now that you have finished the **Criminal justice system** chapter, complete a self-evaluation of your knowledge and skills to assess what you have understood. Use the checklist below and its traffic lights to draw up a revision plan to help you improve in the areas you identified as red or amber.

- I can outline the three different levels of criminal courts in Scotland.

- I can describe summary and solemn procedure and the role of the Procurator Fiscal.

- I can describe the Children's Hearing system, what it allows young people to experience and what decisions it can take.

- I can comment on the effectiveness of the Scottish court system.

Examples

In Modern Studies it is essential that you are able to back up any point you make with relevant evidence. When you are considering the statements above try to think of relevant examples for each response. You may wish to note these examples under each statement in your revision notes.

10 Responses to crime

Figure 10.1: *An illuminated sign outside a police station*

SEMPER VIGILO

POLICE SCOTLAND
Keeping people safe

Figure 10.2: *The Police Scotland logo*

The role of the police

Police Scotland is the national police force of Scotland. It was formed on 1st April 2013 when the eight territorial police forces and the Scottish Crime and Drug Enforcement Agency joined together to produce one force. By bringing together expertise from across the country Police Scotland aims 'to improve service delivery to individuals and local communities in Scotland', by combining resources to work more efficiently and save money.

Scotland's police force has faced a number of controversies since 2013, prompting a number of changes and the launch of 'Policing 2026: Serving a Changing Scotland'. The strategy includes:

- investing £3.6m in expanding specialist technological provision with new offices in the North and West and rolling out mobile technology units around the country so that local officers can examine devices instantly
- purchasing unmanned aerial vehicles, primarily for remote and rural use to aid searches for missing people
- piloting a range of mobile devices for operational use, enabling officers to access core systems and applications away from base
- a public consultation on the use of body worn video
- increasing automatic number plate recognition coverage, intelligence and capabilities
- investing in our workforce wellbeing, modernising staff pay and reward, and introduction of a new leadership strategy

[Source: http://www.scotland.police.uk/about-us/policing-2026/]

Police Scotland is led by a Chief Constable and is made up of police officers, police staff and special constables. The Chief Constable is supported by a team of Deputy Chief Constables, Assistant Chief Constables and Directors. Police Scotland's focus is on 'Keeping People Safe', which it says is at the heart of everything that it does.

There are 13 local policing divisions, each headed by a Local Police Commander. Each division has response officers and community officers, as well as teams for local crime investigation, road policing, public protection and local intelligence.

Alongside the local policing divisions, there are a number of national specialist divisions. The Specialist Crime Division (SCD) provides specialist investigative and intelligence functions such as major crime investigation, public protection, organised crime, counter-terrorism, intelligence and safer communities.

What do the police do?

The **Police (Scotland) Act 1967** lays down the general functions of the police. These duties did not change with the introduction of Police Scotland.

The roles of the police

- maintain law and order
- detect crime
- prevent crime
- protect the public

Police Scotland state they will uphold these duties by continuing with the values of integrity, fairness and respect. In order to carry out these duties the police have a number of powers.

Powers of the police

Stop and question a suspect or witness

The police can stop any individual to ask what they are doing and where they are going. They can ask questions about a particular incident or general questions.

Search a person suspected of having an offensive weapon, stolen property or drugs, or of being a terrorist

Although police can question anyone they can only search a person if they have good reason, for example if they suspect them of carrying an illegal weapon. After the September 11th terrorist attacks on the USA in 2001, the police are also allowed to search anyone suspected of being a terrorist.

Detain a person at a police station for 24 hours for questioning without charging them

Police can keep people at a police station and question them for 24 hours, although a single 'session' of questioning cannot go on for more than six hours. If all questions are not answered then the police can apply for an extension of 12 hours. For a terrorist offence police can apply for a maximum of 14 days extension without charge.

Arrest a person and charge them with a crime that they have seen them committing or for which they have reliable witness and evidence

Usually the police will have a warrant to arrest a suspect but there are circumstances where an arrest is made on the spot. This would include someone caught committing a crime, running away from a crime scene or carrying out dangerous or threatening behaviour.

Hint

Many local initiatives are continuing under Police Scotland; your teacher may encourage you to investigate initiatives in your local area.

Make the Link

In Section 3 of this textbook you will study terrorism and the impact it has had on the world in more detail.

Figure 10.3: *A person can be detained by the police for up to 24 hours*

📖 Word bank

- **Charge**

An official statement by the police that they believe someone guilty of a crime.

- **Warrant**

A document that allows the police to enter premises or arrest a suspect.

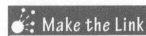

Figure 10.4: *Littering can result in an on-the-spot fine*

Enter a building with a warrant, **or without one if they hear a disturbance, are pursuing a criminal or suspect it is a drug den**

In order to enter a building the police must have reasonable grounds to believe a suspect or evidence is on the premises. If you are arrested the police have the right to enter any premises where you were during or immediately before the arrest. The police obtain a warrant by asking the courts to issue one.

Use reasonable force in pursuit of their duties

Police have the duty to use persuasion wherever possible, but when that is not successful they can use force. Police have batons and pepper spray as part of their regular issue kit. They are able to use force in pursuit of arrest, to protect themselves, or to protect other members of the public.

Issue fixed penalty notices (fines)

Police have the power to issue fines for certain offences, for example driving without a seatbelt or littering. The police issue these fines on the spot rather than going through the court system, which would take much longer.

Other police bodies

There are a number of other police bodies who operate in Scotland, including:

• British Transport Police – police force of the railways providing a service for rail operators, their staff and passengers

• Ministry of Defence Police – provide security within Ministry of Defence property across Britain (e.g. the nuclear submarine base at Faslane)

• Civil Nuclear Constabulary – provides protection for nuclear materials on designated UK nuclear licensed sites and in transit

• United Kingdom Border Agency – an agency of the Home Office tasked with protecting the UK's border, also in charge of immigration

Approaches to policing

Proactive policing

Police will target known criminals, especially those involved in organised crime, using informants and local intelligence to try and prevent any serious crimes from happening in the first instance. Proactive policing is likely to involve the use of modern technology such as phone bugging, CCTV and email hacking.

Zero tolerance

All crimes will be dealt with by a high-profile police presence. Sometimes surveillance will be carried out in order to target crime hot-spots (places where a crime often takes place) in advance of a police presence being deployed; often this tactic is used to combat alcohol-related crimes in city centre areas. Under a zero tolerance initiative, any individuals caught carrying out the crime in question will often be given the most severe punishment available rather than a police warning.

Police: zero tolerance for parade louts   `CASE STUDY`

Police have warned marchers in today's Orange Order parade through Glasgow city centre that officers will take a 'zero tolerance' approach to sectarian behaviour and drinking in public.

Some 8,000 marchers from 182 lodges marched from George Square to Glasgow Green, accompanied for the first time by 800 professionally trained stewards paid for by the Orange Order.

Police arrested 32 people – six for sectarian offences.

[Source: http://www.heraldscotland.com/news/home-news/ police-zero-tolerance-for-parade-louts.14244612]

Figure 10.5: *Community support officers*

Community policing

Police attempt to build a relationship with the local area through education, neighbourhood watch schemes and 'bobbies on the beat'. A recent initiative saw all schools have a campus police officer employed, at least on a temporary basis. Community policing is designed to build trust and therefore to help solve problems more easily or prevent problems from arising in the first place.

Police Scotland uses a combination of approaches to policing in order to achieve the best possible outcome. Recently they have increased their use of CCTV and community policing in order to try and increase police presence in local communities.

Figure 10.6: *CCTV cameras are seen more and more around our towns and cities*

Police initiatives

Initiative on violence

One of the first initiatives launched by Police Scotland is designed to fight violence, disorder and anti-social behaviour. Despite overall levels of violence decreasing, Police Scotland is concerned that violence in the home is increasing. To combat this, Police Scotland is implementing a national campaign against violence and is working with partner agencies to tackle such crimes. They will encourage people to reduce their alcohol intake in an attempt to decrease alcohol-related violence. The initiative also aims to target well-known offenders and problem locations in order to try to reduce both alcohol-related violence and domestic violence. Police Scotland plans to use intelligence to prevent violent crime by removing weapons, drugs and alcohol from well-known violent crime hot-spots.

 Word bank

• **Partner agencies**
Other organisations working to meet the same goal.

Hint

Some people think 'bobbies on the beat' are more effective than CCTV cameras because an actual police presence may make people think about their actions more than a camera.

Firearms Surrender Campaign

Police Scotland launched the Firearms Surrender Campaign in 2018. Over a two-week period in the summer, illegally held firearms and ammunition could be handed over to the police without risk of prosecution (unless investigations showed that the weapon had been used in a crime). The campaign was part of a drive to reduce the number of illegal weapons in the public domain and make communities safer.

? Questions

1. **Describe** Police Scotland. How is it different from the previous system?
2. What are the main duties of the police?
3. Choose the three most important powers of the police. **Explain** why you think they are important.
4. Write a paragraph on the different approaches to policing.
5. Which approach(es) to policing does the 'initiative on violence' use? **Justify** your answer.
6. Explain the aim of the Firearms Surrender Campaign.
7. Which other police bodies operate in Scotland?

 Activity

Research
Use the website of Police Scotland http://www.scotland.police.uk/ to research current initiatives.

 Activity

Discuss
With your shoulder partner, discuss the advantages and disadvantages of CCTV for police use in Scotland.

CCTV

CCTV is used to detect crime as it is happening, to try and deter the public from committing crimes in the first place and in the hope that the public will feel safer in their communities. It is thought that if someone can see a CCTV camera they are less likely to carry out a crime, such as theft or assault, as they know the film of the incident could be used to prove their guilt.

CCTV footage of a crime can be used as evidence in court. CCTV camera operators can also report crimes as they are happening, allowing the police to intervene. Police officers and local councils believe that CCTV is an effective way of preventing crime; this can be seen in the widespread network of CCTV surveillance monitoring Scotland's towns and cities which has trebled in the past 10 years to comprise more than 4,000 cameras monitored by local councils and Police Scotland.

Some people think CCTV is an invasion of privacy and that it does not actually help the police to do their job; they believe that more police officers on the street would make people feel safer and prevent crime from occurring in the first place. However, others think CCTV is crucial in fighting crime; they argue that the police can't be everywhere and CCTV can be the eyes and ears of police officers: in Edinburgh, figures show CCTV resulted in 1,816 camera-assisted arrests in 2017. Others would suggest that CCTV doesn't work on its own but can work in partnership with other methods.

? Questions

1. Give one advantage of CCTV **using evidence** from the information above.

2. Give one disadvantage of CCTV **using evidence** from the information above.

3. 'CCTV is useless, it has not helped the police solve any crimes and the public hate it.'

   Explain why the person who made this statement may be accused of being **selective in the use of facts**.

4. Give at least one advantage of using an internet search engine as a source of information for an investigation into CCTV.

5. Give at least one disadvantage of using an internet search engine as a source of information for an investigation into CCTV.

6. Suggest another research method that you could use to investigate CCTV. **Explain** why it would be a good method.

Effectiveness of Police Scotland in tackling crime

Police have to abide by the law just like everyone else. Police are regulated by a special set of guidelines and the public can make a complaint against the police if they feel they have overstepped their powers, for example if they feel a false statement has been made against them. Complaints against the police are followed up by the Scottish Police Complaints Commissioner. Police are required to be fair and legal and this should ensure effectiveness.

Critics believe Police Scotland is too big and that links with local communities have been lost. They say that law and order issues in Glasgow or Edinburgh are very different from those in, for example, Elgin, Stornoway or the Hebrides. Police Scotland has been accused of being unresponsive to local community needs and not dealing effectively with local issues. In 2015, there were calls for change following the failure to investigate a car crash on the M9 motorway which led to the deaths of two people.

The overall job of the police is to protect the community, prevent crime if possible and once a crime has been committed, apprehend those responsible. In general, most would agree that Police Scotland carries out this job effectively.

CASE STUDY

DAILY NEWS

world - business - finance - lifestyle - travel - sport

M9 fatal car crash: Police apologise to families of couple left dying

Relatives of car crash victims who were not found for three days have received an apology from police who said they had 'failed' the families.

Driver John Yuill, 28, died and his 25-year-old girlfriend Lamara Bell was left in a critical condition after their hatchback came off the motorway.

Officers were called out at 10am on Wednesday when the crashed blue Renault Clio was spotted by a farmer in his field off the M9 near Bannockburn in Scotland.

The couple were last seen with friends on the south shore of Loch Earn, Stirlingshire, in the early hours of Sunday.

Police Scotland confirmed it had actually received a call later the same day to say a car had left the road – but the report was not followed up.

It means Mr Yuill and Ms Bell could have been lying there dying for up to three days.

Police Scotland's Chief Constable Sir Stephen House said today: 'I completely understand the level of concern being raised about the circumstances surrounding the handling of the incident of the crash near the M9 slip road at Bannockburn, and in particular, Police Scotland's response to information received.

'That we failed both families involved is without doubt.

'However, I want to make clear to members of the public, and all those who have rightly expressed concern, that the mistakes made in not responding to the call from a member of the public on Sunday July 5 arose because the information received was not entered on to our systems.

'We know that just prior to 11.30am on Sunday July 5 2015 a member of the public contacted Police Scotland via the 101 system to report that they could see a vehicle down an embankment near the M9 slip road at Bannockburn.

'All callers to 101 receive an electronic options menu. This call was answered within six seconds following that message by an experienced officer and the relevant details were given by the caller.

'For reasons yet to be established this call was not entered on to our police systems and not actioned out to operational teams in the Stirling area to respond and trace the vehicle.'

Mr Yuill was declared dead at the scene while Ms Bell was taken to Glasgow's Queen Elizabeth University Hospital where her condition is described as 'very serious'. The Police Investigations and Review Commissioner (Pirc) has begun an independent investigation into the circumstances of the incident.

[Source: https://www.dailystar.co.uk/news/latest-news/453182/couple-left-dying-car-crash-m9-bannockburn-stirling-police-scotland-apology]

GO! **Activity**

Discuss
The case study with a partner, take notes on how this shows a failure by police Scotland. Can you link it to the aims of the police?

Custodial sentences

For anyone over the age of 21 a custodial sentence means a stay in prison. If a young person between the ages of 16 and 21 is given a custodial sentence then they will attend a young offenders' institution such as Polmont Young Offenders.

Figure 10.7: *What purpose should being behind bars serve?*

- The Scottish Prison Service (SPS) manages prisons in Scotland.
- The SPS is an agency of the Scottish government and was established in 1993.
- The SPS has 13 publicly managed prisons and two privately managed prisons with over 7,500 prisoners in total.
- The purpose of the SPS is to:
  ○ ensure criminals are kept in secure custody
  ○ care for prisoners
  ○ deliver opportunities that attempt to reduce reoffending once a prisoner returns to their community. They aim to do this by offering education programmes, training and drug rehabilitations

There is debate over what the role of prisons should be; some feel it should only be to punish, and to protect society from criminals. They would argue that the reduction of civil liberties will deter criminals from committing crimes again as they will not want to go back to prison. Others suggest that prisons should help criminals to prevent future reoffending. Short prison sentences are shown to be least effective: in 2011 offenders who were released from a custodial sentence of three months or less had the highest reconviction frequency rate compared to those who were released from longer sentences.

Due to the ineffectiveness of these short sentences, the Scottish government put in place a 'presumption against short sentences of three months or less'. This means that the courts still have the option to use short sentences if they wish but the Scottish government advises against it.

David Strang, Chief Inspector of Prisons, said he would like to see an end to all sentences of less than a year in Scotland, arguing that people are more likely to reoffend after serving short periods in jail for minor offences. It is claimed that short sentences cause major upheaval in a perpetrator's life, with the potential to result in the loss of a job, home and family support, and therefore encourage the person to continue to commit crime when they are released in order to survive.

> ### 📖 Word bank
>
> - **Civil liberties**
> Rights and freedoms of the individual.

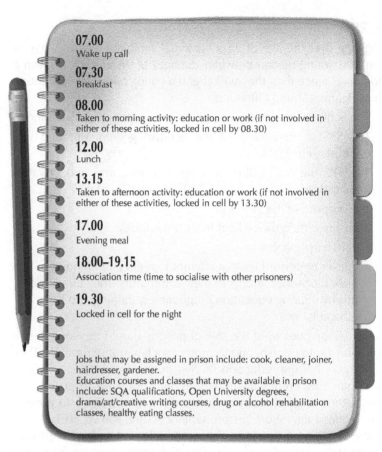

07.00
Wake up call

07.30
Breakfast

08.00
Taken to morning activity: education or work (if not involved in either of these activities, locked in cell by 08.30)

12.00
Lunch

13.15
Taken to afternoon activity: education or work (if not involved in either of these activities, locked in cell by 13.30)

17.00
Evening meal

18.00–19.15
Association time (time to socialise with other prisoners)

19.30
Locked in cell for the night

Jobs that may be assigned in prison include: cook, cleaner, joiner, hairdresser, gardener.
Education courses and classes that may be available in prison include: SQA qualifications, Open University degrees, drama/art/creative writing courses, drug or alcohol rehabilitation classes, healthy eating classes.

Figure 10.8: *Daily life in prison for a category B prisoner. Category B is for serious offenders – the possibility of escape must be made very difficult for them*

The below table shows the arguments surrounding whether prisons work or not.

Prisons work:	Prisons don't work:
Retribution: crime needs to be punished, people should know society will punish serious offences.	**Overcrowding:** too many people are sentenced to six months or less. Many people are in prison for non-payment of fines. In June 2013 prison numbers reached a record high with nearly 8,154 people in jail in Scotland.
Protection: society must be protected from murderers, rapists, terrorists, persistent offenders.	**Expense:** it costs over £34,000 per year per inmate to keep people in prison. Alternatives to prison such as electronic tagging are much cheaper.
Deterrence: shows that society has rules that should not be broken. Fear of punishment stops more crimes happening.	**Unjust:** most people in prison are working-class. Middle- and upper-class people are less likely to go to jail, perhaps because people with a higher income can afford better legal representation.
When in prison offenders will be removed from their normal surroundings. This may give them a **chance to change**.	Three out of four prisoners reoffend. 90% of Barlinnie Prison inmates are **repeat offenders**, usually committing the same type of crime. First-time offenders are exposed to habitual criminals; people in prison may learn how to commit more serious crimes.

Effectiveness of prisons

Prisons have been criticised for apparently being 'too easy'. A survey carried out by researcher Gary McArthur, from the University of Portsmouth, in 2015 showed many prison staff believe inmates have it 'too easy' behind bars and that prisons do not act as a deterrent. The research found that 70% of officers either agreed or strongly agreed that 'life is too easy for prisoners in Scotland' with 'luxuries' like games consoles, multiple TV channels, sweets and chocolate plus pool and snooker tables too readily available.

Undercover television programmes and other research have also found that drugs are readily available in prisons. Prisoners have smuggled mobile phones into prison and have shared videos of illegal drugs in prison on social media. This behaviour fuels criticism of prisons and requests for reform.

The Scottish Prison Service states that historically prisons were a place for punishment but they now focus more on education and rehabilitation. Modern prisons allow outside visitors and encourage offenders to educate themselves. For example, the prison may offer creative writing classes where writers come in to help inmates to develop their talents. Artists may also attend to encourage prisoners to use art to help with their rehabilitation. The aim of these classes is to ensure that, on their release, offenders will have the knowledge and skills to enable them to find work outside and therefore reduce the chances of them reoffending.

📖 Word bank

• **Rehabilitation**
Programmes within the prison that prepare the prisoner for returning to life outside in a productive way.

Non-custodial sentences

One of the key challenges for the Scottish justice system is dealing with low-level offenders who commit crimes that cause havoc, disturbance, upset and fear in communities, such as vandalism and arson. For many that are convicted the punishment is a short prison sentence; however, if the aim is to prevent repeated offending the evidence shows that prison is not working for these types of offenders. In order to try to reduce reoffending, alternatives to prison have been used by the courts.

Figure 10.9: *Reducing the number of custodial sentences will mean a saving for the taxpayer*

Fine

A fine is a sum of money paid by the convicted person to the court. This could be paid in one lump sum or paid in instalments over a longer period of time. If the convicted person fails to pay the fine they may be sentenced to a prison stay as an alternative. Fines allow individuals to continue living their lives and do not have the same stigma attached to them as a stay in prison.

Figure 10.10: *Paying a fine is a common non-custodial sentence*

Community Payback Orders (CPOs)

The new Community Payback Order came into effect on 1st February 2011. Courts can impose one or more of a range of requirements, depending on the nature of the crime and the issues that need to be addressed in order to stop reoffending. When sentencing the offender to a CPO, the court could require them to:

- carry out hours of unpaid manual work in the community
- be subject to periods of supervision where they would have to report to a local police station or probation officer
- comply with specific conduct requirements, such as not attending certain areas or associating with certain individuals
- pay compensation to the victim(s)
- participate in alcohol, drug or mental health treatment interventions

At the same time, tougher punishments have been introduced to deal with those who do not carry out their order properly, for example a prison sentence.

CPOs mean offenders are being punished by being sent out to improve streets and neighbourhoods to repay communities for the damage caused by their crimes; at the same time, CPOs address the issues that can influence repeat offending behaviour, such as drug or alcohol addiction. The work they carry out may also help the offenders gain valuable experience that they can use in order to apply for a job. Some examples of unpaid work being carried out by offenders across Scotland include:

- clearing pathways of snow or ice
- building eco-plant areas for school children
- repainting community centres or churches
- cleaning beaches
- growing vegetables and distributing the produce to care homes and local charities

Figure 10.11: *Working in a vegetable garden or allotment to grow produce for the community: paying it back*

DAILY NEWS

world - business - finance - lifestyle - travel - sport

Poster girl for community payback plan sent back to jail

A woman who posed with [the then] justice minister Kenny MacAskill to promote the government's policy on alternatives to custody has been sent back to prison.

Cheryl Ferguson admitted breaching the terms of her community service order by repeatedly failing to turn up for appointments or carry out unpaid work.

The 29-year-old from Dundee was given the original order last March after she admitted stealing sweets, hair accessories and a children's craft kit from an Asda store.

Ferguson was hailed as a model reformed offender thanks to community sentences, but at Dundee Sheriff Court it emerged she had committed two further crimes since the order was made.

A spokesman for Dundee City Council, which runs the women's project that Ferguson helped front, insisted the scheme does have a positive effect.

He said: 'The project has had success in breaking a cycle of repeat offending.

'Given the level of offending this individual had before, there has been a positive impact through the project.'

[Source: http://news.stv.tv/tayside/223064-community-payback-poster-girl-cheryl-ferguson-back-behind-bars/]

 Activity

Discuss

Discuss with your shoulder partner the cases of Cheryl Ferguson and North Lanarkshire Council. Discuss why some people may argue that CPOs work, and why others may argue they don't. Come to an overall **conclusion** as to whether CPOs have been successful or not. You should then produce a written report for your teacher that has two structured paragraphs which use the 'Point, Explain, Example' structure (see page 236). They should provide **explanations of your decision** on CPOs. You should then produce a final paragraph as a conclusion.

DAILY NEWS

world - business - finance - lifestyle - travel - sport

Community benefits from offenders' payback scheme

Removing 65,000 illegally dumped tyres, spending over 3,700 hours clearing snow during severe winter and gardening for over 20,000 hours to provide fresh fruit and vegetables to local elderly residents ...

These are just some of the ways offenders have paid back the community for crimes they committed.

North Lanarkshire Council hosted an event focussing on the new Community Payback Orders. Father Kelly of St Brigid's RC Church in Newmains said: 'The service has transformed the grounds of the parish. It's continuing and is going from strength to strength. I'm delighted with the work being carried out.'

'People don't always fully recognise the benefits that projects involving offenders bring,' explained Mary Fegan, head of social work services. 'We've got a range of fantastic projects on the go, ranging from decoration and furniture building, to providing vegetable gardens and pavilions for schools.

'Statistics show that three out of five people on schemes like these don't reoffend. These orders in turn bring environmental benefits to local areas, local businesses benefit from placements and ex-offenders feel they are making amends for crimes.'

Robert Lees, from North Lanarkshire, told how he carried out his community service in a local workshop. With over 20 years' of joinery experience, Robert was given a range of projects to work on.

He said: 'I'm a qualified joiner and was able to use my skills in the workshop. I also worked closely with other young people and taught them basic joinery skills. I helped make sandpits for nurseries, a school pavilion and benches for memorial gardens.

'I really enjoyed the work and the experience. It was good to give something back.'

[Source: http://www.dailyrecord.co.uk/news/local-news/community-benefits-offenders-payback-scheme-2571764/]

Restriction of Liberty Order (electronic tagging)

A Restriction of Liberty Order requires an offender to be restricted to a specific place for a maximum period of 12 hours per day for up to a maximum of 12 months, for example their own home or a temporary residence. The offender may also be restricted from a specified place or places for up to 24 hours a day for up to 12 months. There are three main situations when the court tends to use this sentence:

1. For offenders whose behaviour outside their home is dangerous to themselves or others.

2. As an alternative for offenders who could otherwise have been imprisoned; a tag may be used as an effective part-time home imprisonment.

3. To restrict the offender from going to a certain area, for example to reduce the risk of the offender either carrying out or being the victim of an assault.

Figure 10.12: *An electronic tag to be worn by an offender*

A person wearing an electronic tag is expected to:

- stay at the restriction place during the times specified, and not arrive there late
- not attempt to remove the tag
- not move address without permission

Drug Treatment and Testing Order (DTTO)

DTTOs are aimed at breaking the link between drug use and crime. Courts can make an order requiring offenders to undergo treatments either as part of another community order or as a sentence in its own right. It is a high-level, demanding treatment that can last from six months to three years. Offenders are forced to confront their addictions and also take part in therapy to encourage them to confront the issues that made them drug users in the first place. Although DTTOs do work for some offenders, those given a DTTO have the highest reconviction frequency rate, with around 70% of those given DTTOs reoffending within a year.

The number of non-custodial sentences imposed (excluding fines) during 2016–17 was 18,943. In addition to this, 5,000 people were given Community Payback Orders instead of a custodial sentence. Nearly 70% of DTTOs, other CPOs and tagging orders that finished in 2016–17 resulted in successful completion. During this period there has been a decline in the one-year reconviction rate (the number of offenders who receive another conviction within a year of the end of their previous sentence). Some say that this proves that non-custodial sentences are more effective, however others would still argue that non-custodial sentences are not harsh enough and do not provide an effective deterrent to committing crime.

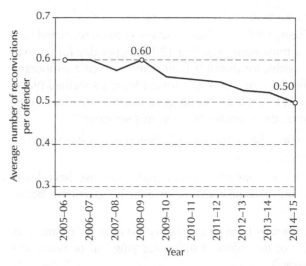

Figure 10.13: *Average number of reconvictions per offender, 2005–06 to 2014–15. These figures from the Scottish government show a 17% decrease in reconvictions since 2005–06*

? Questions

1. What is the difference between custodial and non-custodial sentences?
2. Why have some people criticised prisons as a method of punishment?
3. Choose the three strongest arguments that support the use of prison sentences. **Explain** why you consider them to be the best arguments.
4. What are the main non-custodial sentences available to Scottish courts?
5. Humza Yousaf, the Cabinet Secretary for Justice in Scotland in 2018, says 'community sentences are proven to be more effective than prison at reducing reoffending'.

   Give one reason to **support** his statement.
6. 'Reoffending rates have been falling since 2005.'

   Using Figure 10.13, give one piece of **evidence to support** this statement.

Government responses to crime

Alcohol laws

Minimum pricing

One way the government attempts to reduce crime is by introducing laws to help prevent crime from happening in the first place. An example of this is the **Alcohol (Minimum Pricing) (Scotland) Act 2012**. It is estimated that alcohol is the root cause of around 75% of crimes in Scotland so by attempting to tackle excessive drinking, the

Scottish government is attempting to reduce levels of crime. It is difficult to comment on the success of the policy because the law has only been recently introduced but the statistics below illustrate some of the problems that the new law is seeking to address.

- It is estimated that in 2016, 240 people were killed, 1,260 were seriously injured and in total there were over 9,000 casualties in drink-drive accidents.

- Drunkenness and other disorderly conduct accounted for 10% of miscellaneous offences in 2016–17. This equates to 15,796 offences.

- The Scottish Crime and Justice Survey 2016–17 found that in 42% of violent crime, the victim said the offender was under the influence of alcohol.

- A report by the Scottish Prison Service found that 60% of young offenders were drunk at the time of their offence (Prisoners Survey 2015 – Young People in Custody).

Arguments for minimum pricing	Arguments against minimum pricing
A higher minimum price will mean that the government will collect more tax from alcohol sales; this could help the NHS pay the bills that come about as a result of alcohol abuse, like liver disease.	The minimum price will affect those on low incomes the most. There is already a lot of tax on alcohol.
It may discourage younger drinkers from drinking too much.	A higher minimum price could encourage people to switch to dangerous illegal 'home brews' and replacement alcohol.
People may go out to a pub and spend money there, rather than drinking cheap alcohol from supermarkets in their house, meaning local businesses will profit.	It will be an easy way for supermarkets to increase their profits by increasing their prices more than the tax demands.

Discount deals

Discount deals have already been banned in supermarkets. A provision of the **Licensing (Scotland) Act 2005**, introduced in October 2011, placed restrictions on how alcohol could be displayed and promoted. Sales of alcohol have dropped in Scottish supermarkets since the ban; many argue this will improve the health of the Scottish public and will reduce crime levels. If this ban was introduced in pubs and clubs this may also decrease sales and reduce drunk and disorderly behaviour.

Drink-driving

Another example of action the Scottish government has taken in order to reduce crime is lowering the drink-drive alcohol limit. In 2014, the legal alcohol limit was reduced from 80 mg to 50 mg in every 100 ml of blood. The government believes this will reduce the number of people who drink any alcohol at all before driving and ultimately reduce the number of accidents and cases of death by drink-driving. The case study below shows how government policy translates into police initiatives.

Police Scotland stop 195 drivers over drink-drive limit in two-week-long crackdown

Some 195 drivers have been stopped for drink/drug offences during a two-week-long Police Scotland crackdown.

The Scotland-wide campaign meant that 4,500 people were tested between June 29 and July 13.

Out of almost 200 over the limit, 10 of them were caught 'the morning after'.

Another eight drivers had previous convictions for drink/drug driving.

Chief Superintendent Stewart Carle, Head of Road Policing for Police Scotland, said: 'The high number of drivers detected remains a great concern – one person over the limit is one too many.

'Drink/drug drivers are making very bad decisions, putting themselves, their passengers and other road users at grave risk when the options of abstinence or alternative travel arrangements are always available.'

[Source: https://www.glasgowlive.co.uk/news/glasgow-news/police-scotland-stop-195-drivers-14933613]

Football violence

The Scottish government has attempted to reduce crime in Scotland by introducing the **Offensive Behaviour at Football Act 2012**. There is a history of rivalry between fans of Celtic and Rangers football clubs. This rivalry is often focused on the Catholic/Protestant historical associations of the clubs. There is evidence of a similar rivalry between fans of Hibs and Hearts football clubs. This rivalry can sometimes spill over into violence and religious intolerance. The 2012 act gives police more powers to arrest fans who sing bigoted or sectarian songs either while travelling to football matches or while there. Fans who are convicted face up to five years in prison. The Scottish government claims that there has been a reduction in sectarian-related crime but others suggest that violence remains a big problem in Scottish football. In 2018 this act was repealed due to criticisms that it restricted freedom of speech.

DAILY NEWS

world - business - finance - lifestyle - travel - sport

Two men stabbed in Ibrox football violence

Two men have been seriously injured in violent clashes before Rangers' Europa League game against Osijek in Glasgow.

The trouble occurred near Ibrox before the second leg of the second qualifying round tie with the Croatian side.

Police said they had been called to Edmiston Drive at its junction with Paisley Road West just after 19:00.

The injured men, aged 24 and 40, are being treated for stab wounds at the Queen Elizabeth University Hospital. Both are in a stable condition.

Police Scotland officers have appealed for witnesses to contact them.

Det Insp Steven Wallace said: 'This type of violent behaviour will not be tolerated and it is absolutely vital anyone with information that could assist with our investigation comes forward.'

[Source: https://www.bbc.co.uk/news/uk-scotland-glasgow-west-45052342]

? Questions

1. **Describe** how the Scottish government has tried to reduce alcohol-related crimes.

2. Use the **evidence to explain** why it is necessary to tackle alcohol-related crime in Scotland.

3. 'Alcohol is not a major factor in criminal behaviour.'

   Explain fully why the person who made this statement could be accused of being **selective in the use of facts**.

4. What has the Scottish government done to try to reduce football violence?

5. What evidence is there to suggest that the Offensive Behaviour at Football Act 2012 has not been successful?

 Hint

Information on how to answer 'selective in the use of facts' questions can be found on page 239.

Summary

In this chapter you have learned:

- what the role of the police is
- what the role of prisons is
- what the role of the government is

Learning Summary

Now that you have finished the **Responses to crime** chapter, complete a self-evaluation of your knowledge and skills to assess what you have understood. Use the checklist below and its traffic lights to draw up a revision plan to help you improve in the areas you identified as red or amber.

- I can identify when Police Scotland was formed and what geographical areas it covers, both nationally and in its divisions.

- I can outline the duties and powers laid out by the Police (Scotland) Act 1967.

- I can list the ways police approach crime fighting and what resources they have to help combat crime.

- I can give evidence to support the argument that Police Scotland is effective and evidence to support the argument that it is ineffective.

- I can give examples of non-custodial punishments that courts can give out and argue why they are thought of as both effective and not effective.

- I can give examples of the advantages and disadvantages of custodial sentences.

- I can describe how the government attempts to reduce crime.

- I can comment on the effectiveness of the government in reducing crime.

Examples

In Modern Studies it is essential that you are able to back up any point you make with relevant evidence. When you are considering the statements above try to think of relevant examples for each response. You may wish to note these examples under each statement in your revision notes.

Terrorism

In Section 3 there is a choice of topic; you can study **either** a major world power **or** a significant world issue. In this book we will be looking at the significant world issue of **terrorism**.

Course Assessment Specification

National 4 (*International Issues*)

Outcome 1

1 **Use a limited range of sources of information to draw and support conclusions about international issues, focusing on either a major world power or a significant world issue by:**

1.1 Drawing a conclusion using up to two sources of information.

1.2 Briefly supporting a conclusion using evidence from up to two sources of information.

Outcome 2

2 **Draw on a straightforward knowledge and understanding of international issues, focusing on either a major world power or a significant world issue by:**

2.1 Giving straightforward descriptions of the main features of an international issue that draws on a factual knowledge of either a major world power or a significant world issue.

2.2 Giving straightforward explanations relating to an international issue.

National 5 (*International Issues*)

Option 1: World Power

Political system

- political system
- participation
- representation

Influence on other countries

- political influence
- economic influence
- military influence

Social and economic issues

A minimum of *three issues* should be studied. At least one issue covered should be a social issue and one an economic issue.

- employment
- poverty/inequality
- population movement
- health
- education
- crime and the law

Effectiveness in tackling social and economic issues

A minimum of *three issues* should be studied. At least one issue covered should be a social issue and one an economic issue.

Option 2: World Issue

Nature and causes of the conflict/issue

- political causes
- social causes
- economic causes

Consequences of the conflict/issue

- impact on those immediately affected
- impact on other countries and their governments (including the UK)
- regional and/or wider international consequences

Attempts to resolve the conflict/issue

- bilateral, regional and/or international organisations – role and motivation
- military attempts to resolve conflict/issue
- non-military attempts to resolve conflict/issue

Evaluation of international organisation(s) in tackling the conflict/issue

- evidence of success/failure
- reasons for success/failure
- consequences of success/failure

International Issues

Level 3 and 4 experiences and outcomes relevant to this topic

The International Issues Section naturally builds upon the knowledge already secured in the third and fourth level experiences and outcomes, and in particular:

❖ By examining the role and actions of selected international organisations, I can evaluate how effective they are in meeting their aims. **SOC 4-19b**

❖ I can contribute to a discussion on the actions and motives of a group or organisation that seeks to achieve its aims by non-democratic means. **SOC 4-18c**

❖ I can present an informed view on how the expansion of power and influence of countries or organisations may impact on the cultures, attitudes and experiences of those involved. **SOC 4-19a**

❖ I can use my knowledge of current social, political or economic issues to interpret evidence and present an informed view. **SOC 3-15a**

❖ I can explain why a group I have identified might experience inequality and can suggest ways in which this inequality might be addressed. **SOC 3-16a**

❖ I have compared the rights and responsibilities of citizens in Scotland with a contrasting society and can describe and begin to understand reasons for differences. **SOC 3-17a**

11 Terrorism as an international issue

What you will learn in this chapter

- Understand and identify terrorist behaviour.
- Understand why terrorist organisations exist.
- Explain the differences between domestic and international terrorism.
- Understand how terrorism has affected Scotland.

The origins of terrorism

International terrorism has arguably become the biggest threat to global security in recent years. In fact, according to the Global Terrorism Index 2017, more countries experienced at least one death from terrorism than at any other time in the previous 17 years. Of the 163 countries included in the index, 106 of them experienced at least one terrorist attack.

Figure 11.1: *More than 50 people were killed in the 2013 Reyhanll car bombings in Turkey*

Make the Link

In History you may learn that the French Revolution was also known as the 'reign of terror'.

Figure 11.2: *Global terrorism incidents, injuries and fatalities, 1970–2016*

The word 'terrorism' itself originally comes from the French word 'terrorisme' and dates from the time of the French Revolution. Causing 'terror' or 'fear' hasn't changed much in the intervening years. Terrorist organisations and individuals sympathetic to their actions continue to exist today.

What is 'terrorism'?

Terrorism is the use of violence to achieve a stated political goal. Organisations and individuals who are members of terrorist organisations want to achieve a political aim; this might be a greater say in how their country is run, or they might disagree with a foreign government's ideology.

It is important to remember when studying this global issue that some members of terrorist groups would not consider themselves to be so; they might consider themselves to be members of a pressure group and might even consider action taken in defence of their beliefs as justifiable.

Both pressure groups and terrorist organisations seek to make political gains through their actions. The difference between them, however, is that terrorist organisations use violence and other illegal actions to further their cause. This could be in the form of a mass killing, for example as was the case in May 2017 when an Islamic fundamentalist suicide bomber detonated a shrapnel-laden homemade bomb, killing 23 and injuring over 800 people at the end of a music concert at Manchester Arena. Terrorism can be identified, therefore, by the way in which violence is used to try to achieve stated aims.

Figure 11.3: *The French Revolution was characterised by the use of the guillotine*

Figure 11.4: *Crime scene investigators work the scene after the Manchester bombing*

Defining terrorism

In November 2004, a United Nations Secretary General report described terrorism as any act 'intended to cause death or serious bodily harm to civilians or non-combatants with the purpose of intimidating a population or compelling a government or an international organisation to do or abstain from doing any act'.

📖 Word bank

- **Justifiable**
Able to be shown to be right, reasonable or defensible.

- **Fundamentalist**
A person who believes in the strict and literal interpretation of their religion's holy texts.

⁍ Make the Link

In History you may have studied groups such as the suffragettes and the Bolsheviks; do you think that these groups were 'terrorists'?

📖 Word bank

- **United Nations**
An organisation of independent states formed in 1945 to promote international peace and security. There is more information about the UN on page 191.

Activity

Discuss

Discuss the UN definition of terrorism with your shoulder partner and decide upon your own definition. Try to limit your definition to 280 characters (the length of a Tweet) so that it may be shared and discussed with your classmates.

Today the term 'terrorism' remains a hotly debated concept. Those in terrorist organisations, such as the IRA or al-Qaeda, often would not consider themselves to be 'terrorists'. Equally, there are many people who sympathise with the beliefs of terrorist organisations but who do not support the way they try to gain political support. In 2002, for example, the then UK Prime Minister's wife, Cherie Blair, commented that many young Palestinians felt they had 'no hope' but to resort to blowing themselves up. Mrs Blair was referring to suicide bombings that had taken place hours before in Jerusalem, killing 19 Israelis and injuring 40 others. While Mrs Blair was forced to apologise for her comments, it nevertheless shows that people can be sympathetic to terrorist organisations' aims without necessarily supporting their behaviour.

It is even more controversial to be seen as a terrorist sympathiser and in 2018 Jeremy Corbyn, the leader of the Labour party, has faced serious backlash due to admitting that he was present as a wreath laying ceremony in memory of Palestinian terrorist suspected of carrying out the 1992 bombing in Paris.

Figure 11.5: *Aftermath of a Palestinian suicide bomb attack in Dimona, 2008*

 Make the Link

You will have learned in Section 1 how pressure groups can work legitimately to affect government and make change happen.

 **Questions**

1. **Describe** what you understand by the term 'political goal'.
2. **Explain** the type of behaviour that terrorist organisations and supporters use in order to achieve their goals.
3. Outline the differences between terrorist organisations and pressure groups.

Domestic terrorism

Historically, terrorist organisations have focused on domestic struggles. You may already know of groups such as the Irish Republican Army (IRA) and the Spanish group Euskadi Ta Askatasuna (ETA). These organisations have tried to achieve their political goals by carrying out terrorist attacks.

 **Word bank**

• **Domestic**

Within your own country.

The IRA

The IRA's historical goal was to create a united Ireland. Members of this terrorist group believed that the only way to achieve this goal was to carry out terrorist attacks in order to make their position heard. While the IRA has split into various different groups since its beginnings, those sympathetic and supportive of the cause remain active. In 1998 one of these groups, 'The Real IRA', was responsible for the Omagh bombing in which 29 people were killed and another 220 people injured.

ETA

Similarly in Spain, ETA have existed since the 1950s, and were founded with the stated aim of creating a 'homeland' for the Basque regions of Spain. While ETA, like the IRA, have declared many ceasefires over the years, the group are responsible for the deaths of 829 people in total since their emergence. Both ETA and the IRA operated at a relatively local level and their attacks were rarely carried out outside the country they operated in. This is what is meant by *domestic terrorism*.

Figure 11.6: *Northern Ireland was formed in 1921, following the end of British rule in the Republic of Ireland*

📖 Word bank

- **Ceasefire**
A truce; a temporary stopping of fighting.

Figure 11.7: *Memorial to the victims of the IRA's bombing in Omagh*

🧠 Hint

You might be part of your school council and try to bring about change in school through having meetings with your teachers, for example.

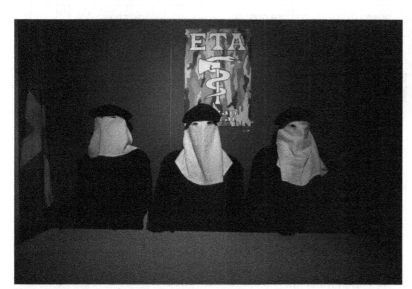

Figure 11.8: *ETA regularly tried to negotiate with the Spanish government via anonymous video broadcasts like the one shown*

Global terrorism

Today, the modern face of terrorism is global and terrorist organisations are no longer limited in terms of how they can cause terror, fear and intimidation in the actions that they carry out. Global terrorism affects us all – from travelling on a plane to entering a public building, and even using the internet, security measures across the world are now much stricter than they were before 2001. The Global Terrorism Index study shows how the threat of terrorism to global security has increased in recent years.

September the 11th

Modern-day terrorism has changed significantly since the events of September 11th 2001. On that day four planes were hijacked by Islamic terrorists. Two of the planes were flown into the World Trade Center towers in New York. The towers collapsed killing thousands of people. Another plane was crashed into the Pentagon, the centre of America's military headquarters in Washington D.C., and a fourth plane crashed nearby in the state of Pennsylvania. It is thought that this fourth plane was bound for the White House and that the passengers on board managed to overpower the terrorists.

Al-Qaeda, a terrorist organisation headed by an individual named Osama bin Laden, was quickly linked by American intelligence to the attacks.

In total, almost 3,000 people died in the attacks, including 227 civilians and the 19 hijackers aboard the four planes; 67 British people were also killed that day.

Word bank

- **Intelligence**
Information gathered by national security organisations.

Figure 11.9: *The World Trade Center shortly after the first hijacked plane hit*

Year	Terrorism incidents	Terrorism deaths
2002	1,332	4,799
2012	8,500	15,436
2017	10,900	26,502

[Source: Global Terrorism Database https://www.start.umd.edu/gtd/]

Questions

1. **Explain** where the word 'terrorism' originates from.
2. **Describe, in detail,** what has changed about the focus of terrorist attacks in recent years. In your answer you should refer to the IRA and to ETA.
3. Outline the events of September 11th 2001.
4. 'Terrorism isn't a global threat today. After September the 11th the number of incidents decreased. More people were dying because of terrorism in 2002, but that isn't the case anymore.' Helen McLean.

   Using only the information in the above table, give two reasons to **oppose** the view of Helen McLean.

The Scottish connection

Scotland has its own experience of the effects of international terrorism. In 1988 a bomb exploded on Pan Am 103, a flight from London Heathrow destined for New York. The bomb killed all 243 passengers on board and 11 people on the ground as the aircraft crashed into the town of Lockerbie in the Scottish Borders.

Figure 11.10: *Aftermath of the Lockerbie bombing*

The Glasgow airport attack

In June 2007, on the first Saturday of the school summer holidays, Glasgow airport was attacked by two Islamic extremists. Bilal Abdullah was born in England and was a qualified doctor working in the Royal Alexandria Hospital in Paisley. His accomplice in the attack was Kafeel Ahmed, born in India, a qualified engineer who was studying for a PhD.

At approximately 3pm on the 30th of June, a green Jeep Cherokee that was loaded with propane was driven into the front doors of Glasgow International Airport and set on fire. Security bollards outside the airport prevented the car from actually entering the airport itself where it could have caused serious destruction. Ahmed, the driver, was badly burned in the incident and five members of the public were also injured.

The suspects were both arrested, but Ahmed later died of his injuries in hospital. Abdullah was found guilty of conspiracy to commit murder and was sentenced to 32 years in prison. Police later linked the attack to a foiled car bomb explosion in London.

Asked of his motivations for the attacks while on trial, Dr Bilal said the destruction of Iraq was the main driving force behind his actions.

Figure 11.11: *Partial view of the damaged Jeep used in the Glasgow airport attack*

? Question

Make notes on the Glasgow airport attack of 2007. In your notes you must detail the names of the individuals responsible, the cause of the attack and any damage that occurred as a result.

Summary

In this chapter you have learned:

- how to identify terrorist behaviour
- why terrorist organisations exist
- the differences between domestic and international terrorism
- how terrorism has affected Scotland

Learning Summary

Now that you have finished the **Terrorism as an international issue** chapter, complete a self-evaluation of your knowledge and skills to assess what you have understood. Use the checklist below and its traffic lights to draw up a revision plan to help you improve in the areas you identified as red or amber.

- I can explain what 'domestic terrorism' is.
- I can explain what 'global terrorism' is.
- I understand why terrorism has become a 'global issue'.
- I can explain what has changed about the focus of terrorist attacks in recent years.
- I can outline what happened on September 11th 2001.
- I understand how the events of September 11th have changed the role of terrorism.
- I can explain what happened in the Glasgow airport attack in 2007.
- I understand how the global issue of terrorism is relevant to me as a student in Scotland.

Examples

In Modern Studies it is essential that you are able to back up any point you make with relevant evidence. When you are considering the statements above try to think of relevant examples for each response. You may wish to note these examples under each statement in your revision notes.

12 The nature and causes of terrorism

What you will learn in this chapter

- How to identify the political, social and economic factors that make individuals become involved in terrorism.
- How to identify the factors that make terrorist groups most likely to attack.
- How to explain the different tactics used by terrorists.

The causes of terrorism

The actions individuals and groups take are very rarely without reason or cause. While many people might disagree with that reason entirely, others believe that they have no option but to engage in terrorist activity in order to achieve their aims. Even when unsuccessful, terrorists may consider the activity worthwhile as it draws attention to their cause.

There are many different factors that can drive someone to become a terrorist. Sometimes people can become radicalised because of their beliefs or because of their distrust in others. For others, political decisions can mean that they feel so disempowered that they view violent terrorist activities as a last resort.

The ideology which informs a terrorist organisation is very important when analysing the causes of terrorism. An ideology is a body of ideas or beliefs that determines the aims of an organisation. It can be social, economic or political in nature.

Social and economic causes

Identity

Some people feel that they have no identity or belonging. This means that they may feel frustrated with the government of their country or another, and they might view violence as the only way to express this. When people feel cut off from society they may also become less engaged with democratic participation, for example through protest.

In July 2011, the Norwegian Anders Behring Breivik was responsible for the deaths of 77 people after he planted a car bomb in Oslo and then opened fire at a youth camp outside the city. Breivik, an anti-Islamic extremist, claimed that the attacks were justified in order to stop the 'Islamisation of Norway'.

 Activity

Discuss
Discuss with your shoulder partner the reasons why you believe people become involved in terrorist organisations or terrorist behaviour.

 Hint

Peer pressure is often used in school to make people do things they might not ordinarily be inclined to do.

Word bank

- **Radicalisation**
When a person or a group become extreme in their belief system.

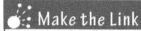 **Make the Link**

You may learn about radicalisation in RMPS.

Figure 12.1: *Flowers laid around Oslo cathedral following the attacks of July 2011*

Figure 12.2: *A sign for Huntingdon Life Sciences outside the facility*

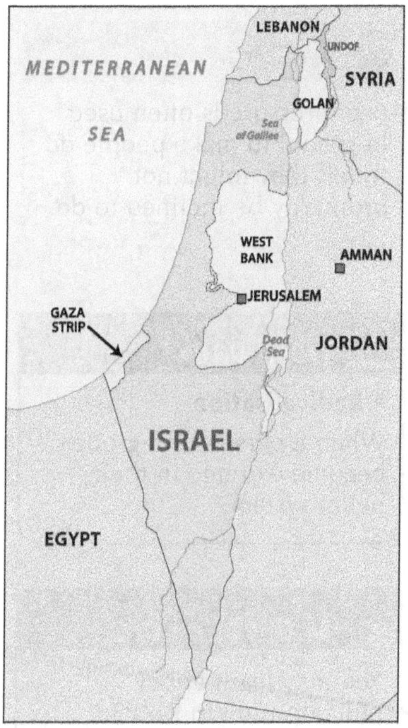

Figure 12.3: *The disputed Gaza Strip highlighted by the arrow*

Beliefs

Some individuals feel that their beliefs are not properly represented by the country in which they live. As such, they feel that making a political statement through terrorist activity is the only way to have their beliefs heard.

In 2009 a judge in England branded seven animal rights extremists 'urban terrorists' and jailed them for a total of 50 years. The group worked to intimidate workers at Huntingdon Life Sciences, which carries out animal testing for medical research. They sent hoax bombs allegedly contaminated with the AIDS virus to employees' homes, poured paint stripper on cars and wrote things like 'murderer' or 'puppy killer' on the walls of employees' houses.

Retaliation

Others may retaliate against what they see as the unjust actions of individuals or groups. In May 2013 Palestinian resistance fighters in the Gaza Strip sent a mortar shell into southern Israel, a day after an air strike by Israeli forces.

The conflict in the Middle East continues and focuses on the recognition of borders. Estimates claim that since the year 2000 at least 1,253 Israelis and 9,733 Palestinians have been killed in the conflict.

Religious ideology

Religious extremism continues to be the most likely cause of a terrorist attack. People who commit terrorist attacks in the name of their religion are referred to as 'religious extremists'. While organisations such as al-Qaeda and the Taliban often dominate the news headlines, it is important to understand that extremism happens in many different religions.

In April 2013 the American government listed evangelical Christianity as the highest terrorist threat to its national security. The Christian Patriot movement believes that the American government is involved in a conspiracy to deny its citizens their 'constitutional rights'. Their ideology is associated with White Supremacy – the belief that white people are superior to all other racial backgrounds.

> ### 📖 Word bank
>
> • **Evangelical**
> Belonging to a Christian group that stresses the authority of the Bible.

What is Islamic State (IS)?

CASE STUDY

Islamic State, often referred to as IS, ISIS or ISIL, is a militant group that carries out international terrorist attacks and has been active since 2014. IS has claimed responsibility for numerous terror attacks in the Middle East, Europe and the USA. These attacks have resulted in multiple deaths and numerous injuries. IS developed from al-Qaeda, the group responsible for the terrorist attacks in the United States on 11th September 2001. Since then, IS has grown in size and strength and is now considered the most dangerous terrorist group in the world.

Between 2015 and 2018, IS claimed responsibility for a number of high-profile terrorist attacks, including:

- shooting at Tunisian National Museum (24 foreign tourists and Tunisians killed), March 2015

- suicide attack at Sana'a mosque, Yemen (142 Shia civilians killed), March 2015

- shooting at Tunisian tourist resort (38 European tourists killed), June 2015

- suicide attack at Suruç, Turkey (33 leftist and pro-Kurdish activists killed), July 2015

- bombing of Metrojet Flight 9268 over Sinai (224 killed, mostly Russian tourists), October 2015

- bombings in Ankara, Turkey (there are reports of between 102 and 109 pro-Kurdish and leftist activists killed), October 2015

- suicide bombings in Beirut, Lebanon (43 Shia civilians killed), November 2015

- co-ordinated attacks in Paris, France (130 civilians killed), November 2015

- car bomb attack in Aden, Yemen (Jaafar Mohammed Saad, the governor of Aden, plus six others killed), December 2015

- suicide bombing in Istanbul, Turkey (11 foreign tourists killed), January 2016

- three co-ordinated suicide bombings in Brussels, Belgium (32 civilians killed), March 2016

- shootings and suicide bombings at Atatürk Airport, Turkey (48 foreign and Turkish civilians killed), June 2016

- truck attack in Nice, France (86 civilians killed), July 2016

- double bombing in Kabul, Afghanistan (at least 80 civilians killed, mostly Shia Hazaras), July 2016
- truck attack in Berlin, Germany (12 civilians killed), December 2016
- shooting at nightclub in Istanbul, Turkey (39 foreigners and Turks killed), January 2017
- bombing on Saint Petersburg Metro, Russia (15 civilians killed), April 2017
- suicide attack at Manchester Arena (22 civilians killed), May 2017
- co-ordinated suicide bombings in Tehran, Iran (18 civilians killed), June 2017
- bombing and suicide bombing in Pakistan (at least 131 killed), July 2018

GO! Activity

Extension
Use the internet to research one or more of the incidents listed in the case study in more detail.

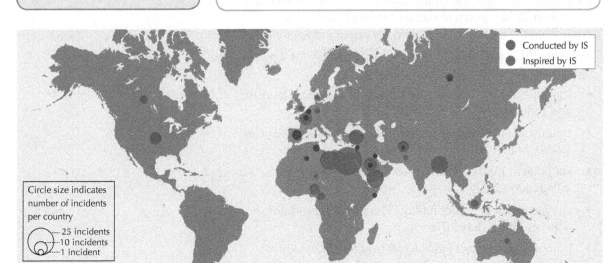

Figure 12.4: *The location of terrorist attacks by IS, June 2014 to February 2018*

Poverty and deprivation

Terrorists may also be driven by a sense of poverty and deprivation within their group or country. This can be seen in Somalia and Nigeria, where many individuals have grown up with no education and a lack of employment prospects. This environment has led some people to turn to groups such as Al-Shabaab (Somalia) and Boko Haram (Nigeria). Extremist groups attract those in poverty as they may see the group as a 'family' who will provide for them. They may also see the extremist activities as a way of forcing the government to address poverty in their country.

? Questions

1. **Describe** what is meant by 'religious extremism'.
2. **Explain** what the group Islamic State (IS) stands for and how it tries to achieve its aims.

Political motivations

Dictatorship and human rights violations

The type of political system used by a country can make terrorist behaviour and attacks more likely; in countries which are not democratic, people feel they do not have a say in how their country is run and terrorism is more likely to occur (see Figure 12.5 below). Oppressive governments often make decisions that are not favourable to their citizens and people may resort to terrorist activity to try to make their voices heard in order to bring about some sort of change.

Country	Government type
Afghanistan	Authoritarian regime
India	Flawed democracy
Iraq	Hybrid regime
Nigeria	Authoritarian regime
Pakistan	Hybrid regime
Philippines	Flawed democracy
Russia	Hybrid regime
Somalia	Unclassified
Thailand	Flawed democracy
Yemen	Authoritarian regime

Figure 12.5: *Top 10 countries affected by terrorism and their governments*

Political extremism

Political extremism is usually characterised by which side of the political spectrum it sits on. In politics, parties are sometimes referred to as being 'left wing' or 'right wing' (see page 66). Left wing politics has traditionally been linked to high levels of tax (especially for the rich), and a greater commitment to welfare programmes, such as the NHS for example. Right wing politics has traditionally been associated with low tax levels (especially for the rich), and individual responsibility for welfare.

Any political party or movement can become extreme in its beliefs if it moves too far on either side of the political spectrum. UKIP (United Kingdom Independence Party) is often cited as an example of an extremist right wing party in UK politics. While the party has no elected representatives in Scotland, it has nine MEPs representing English constituencies, three members in the House of Lords and one member in the Northern Ireland Assembly.

Nationalism

There are some countries and regions in the world where people wish to be independent and govern themselves but they don't always believe it can be achieved peacefully. Those who support a nationalist cause can therefore be drawn into a terrorist organisation. Nationalism, like left and right wing politics, can become extremist in nature if it begins

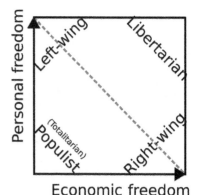

Figure 12.6: *The Nolan chart of political viewpoints*

> **GO!** Activity
>
> **Discuss**
> Discuss with your shoulder partner the reasons why not having a democratic government might make terrorism more likely.

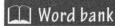

Word bank

• Nationalism

A devotion to the interests and culture of your home nation.

to use violence to achieve its stated goals. In the UK context the most obvious example of nationalist terrorism would be the IRA and the many affiliated organisations which support its goal of a united Ireland.

Palestinian terrorist groups have attacked Israel for many years. These organisations do not recognise Israel as a state and believe the land it occupies belongs to the state of Palestine.

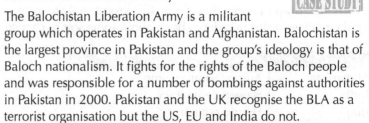

Balochistan Liberation Army

CASE STUDY

The Balochistan Liberation Army is a militant group which operates in Pakistan and Afghanistan. Balochistan is the largest province in Pakistan and the group's ideology is that of Baloch nationalism. It fights for the rights of the Baloch people and was responsible for a number of bombings against authorities in Pakistan in 2000. Pakistan and the UK recognise the BLA as a terrorist organisation but the US, EU and India do not.

Figure 12.7: *The flag of the Balochistan Liberation Army*

Attacks include the killing of 16 soldiers in Marwar and Chamalang in December 2015, where a further 13 soldiers were wounded, and the killing of 10 labourers in Gwadar in May 2017, in response to the China–Pakistan Economic Corridor, which will impact on the area that the BLA attempts to protect.

? Questions

1. Consider the case study about the BLA. Outline the reasons why the BLA carries out terrorist attacks.
2. Summarise the individual causes of terrorism in a mind map. You should use the previous subheadings to help you.

Tactics of terror

Terrorist organisations use a variety of different tactics to achieve their aims. One of their most important tactics is often the element of surprise; this means that terrorist tactics are often unpredictable. However, many terrorist organisations use similar tactics in order to achieve their goals.

Bombs

Terrorists often use bombs. Just one person with a bomb can make a whole city feel scared. Bombs can be hidden in busy places, on trains or even planes. A timer usually sets off the explosion when the bomber has left the area.

Suicide bombs

Suicide bombs are explosives attached to someone's body and hidden beneath clothing. The bomber positions themselves next to their target and then detonates the bomb. Palestinian terrorists often use this tactic. The attack at Manchester Arena in 2017 was carried out by a suicide bomber.

Chemical terrorism (Anthrax)

Anthrax is a naturally occurring disease that can be lethal. In 2001, terrorists in the USA sent anthrax bacteria in the form of white powder through the US mail system. This caused huge disruption in the country and many people were very scared. Five people died and 17 others were infected by the disease.

Gas attacks

Lethal poison gas is released into the air in a gas attack. It has been alleged that chemical warfare has been used many times in Syria, especially as part of state-sponsored terrorism. In August 2015, 35 Kurdish fighters were wounded in a chemical attack while fighting IS terrorists near Erbil, in Iraq. Laboratory tests later revealed that mustard gas had been used. In the same month, IS launched a chemical attack on the town of Marea, in northern Syria, against women and children.

Hijacking

Hijackers use force to take control of boats, planes and buses. They may take passengers hostage or use the vehicle as a weapon. Hijackers carried out the terrorist attacks in the USA in September 2001. More recently, in December 2016, a plane carrying 118 passengers from Libya to Tripoli was diverted to Malta International Airport with two men on board claiming to have guns and a hand grenade. The hijackers eventually surrendered to authorities with no deaths or injuries.

Cyber-terrorism

Cyber-terrorists use information technology to attack civilians and draw attention to their cause. This may mean that they use computer systems as a tool to make an attack. More often, cyber-terrorism refers to an attack on information technology itself in a way that would disrupt networked services. For example, cyber-terrorists could disable networked emergency systems or hack into networks storing financial information.

Car bombs

Car bombs are explosives packed in cars and vans and set off with a timer or by remote control. For example, in May 2017, a truck bomb exploded in Kabul, Afghanistan, near the German embassy during

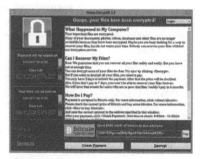

Figure 12.8: *The ransomware 'WannaCry' infected computers in over 150 countries and caused disruption to organisations like the NHS*

rush hour. More than 150 people were killed and over 400 were injured, mostly civilians. Several buildings in the embassy were damaged. The attack was the deadliest terror attack to take place in Kabul. No group has claimed responsibility for the attack.

Letter and mortar bombs

Letter bombs are explosives sent in an envelope or a parcel that explodes when opened. This form of attack has been used in the UK by the IRA and extreme animal rights groups.

A mortar is a bomb that is fired from a metal tube or pipe. It is detonated by a timer and flies a short distance. This type of bomb is cheap to make.

? Questions

1. Copy and complete the table below. You may wish to use this textbook and the internet to find relevant, up-to-date **examples** of the different terrorist tactics used across the world. Some of the examples and explanations have been filled in for you to get you started.

Tactic	Explanation	Example
Bombing	This is when terrorists use bombs to cause mass destruction and loss of life in order to highlight their cause.	
Hijacking	This is when terrorists take control of something, such as a plane, in order to draw attention to their cause.	
Suicide bombing		
Assault		
Kidnapping		For example, in 2010 Scottish aid worker Linda Norgrove was kidnapped and killed by the Taliban in Afghanistan.
Cyber-terrorism		

2. Terrorists use a variety of different tactics in order to achieve their goals. **Describe** these tactics. In your answer you must:

   • refer to at least two different tactics used by terrorists
   • provide relevant **examples** that explain your response

Activity

Research

Working individually, use the internet to research a recent example of a terrorist attack. Provide a written one-page report to your teacher. In your report you may wish to consider:

- when the attack happened
- where the attack happened
- a description of what happened
- who accepted responsibility for the attack
- how many people were injured/killed as a result of the attack
- the reason the attack happened (try to link your report to one of the individual factors identified)

Summary

In this chapter you have learned:

- how to identify the factors that make individuals become involved in terrorism
- how to identify the factors that make terrorist groups most likely to attack
- how to explain the different tactics used by terrorists

Learning Summary

Now that you have finished **The nature and causes of terrorism** chapter, complete a self-evaluation of your knowledge and skills to assess what you have understood. Use the checklist below and its traffic lights to draw up a revision plan to help you improve in the areas you identified as red or amber.

- I can explain what 'radicalisation' means.

- I can explain the social and economic causes of terrorism.

- I can explain the political causes of terrorism.

- I can explain what the terms 'left wing' and 'right wing' mean.

- I can explain the different tactics used by terrorists.

- I can describe what is meant by a 'political goal'.

- I can identify how terrorists try to achieve their aims.

Examples

In Modern Studies it is essential that you are able to back up any point you make with relevant evidence. When you are considering the statements above try to think of relevant examples for each response. You may wish to note these examples under each statement in your revision notes.

13 Theories of terrorism

What you will learn in this chapter

- Be able to identify and explain theories surrounding terrorist behaviour, specifically:
  - lone wolves
  - terrorist cells
  - home-grown terrorism
  - state-sponsored terrorism

Theories of terrorism

📖 **Word bank**

• Hypothesis

A proposed explanation for something that can be tested and therefore proved or disproved.

Theories in social science are usually based upon a hypothesis (a statement) which can be proved or disproved. A theory is a statement that tries to explain things. In Modern Studies, theories might be used to explain why things happen within a society.

In order to understand terrorist motivations and behaviours you need to think about the theories that exist. Terrorists have a variety of different reasons that they might use to justify their actions. Just as there is not one universal motivation for terrorist acts, there is no one theory that can explain why terrorism continues to exist.

'Lone wolves' or organised terrorists?

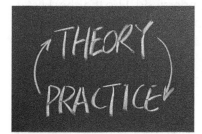

Figure 13.1: *Theories have to be put into practice to prove them*

Some terrorists are working from within a terrorist organisation. However, recently changes in the UK and America have suggested that an increasing number are becoming 'lone wolf' terrorists. These individuals may say that they support the beliefs of a terrorist group, such as al-Qaeda, but act completely independently. Such attacks tend not to involve much long-term planning and are difficult to predict.

In May 2013, British soldier Lee Rigby was attacked with knives and a meat cleaver in the street. The two men responsible claimed that they were acting to avenge the killing of Muslims by the British Army. Similarly, a month earlier in America, two individuals acted independently by planting pressure cooker bombs on the route of the Boston marathon. Three people were killed in the attacks and 264 were injured. One of the two brothers responsible for the Boston attacks claimed later that they were acting to avenge the wars in Afghanistan and Iraq. In 2017, three men armed with knives and a van killed seven people and wounded 48 on London Bridge.

Cells

'Terrorist cells' are organised groups of terrorists. It is thought that due to the global spread of support for its cause Islamic State has many terrorist cells operating in a number of different countries.

Figure 13.2: *Lee Rigby*

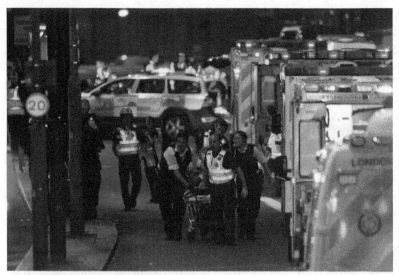

Figure 13.3: *Emergency services attend the London Bridge terror attack in 2017*

? Questions

1. **Explain** what a 'theory' is in social science.
2. Outline, with **examples**, what the expression 'lone wolf terrorist' means.
3. **Describe**, with **examples**, what terrorist 'cells' are.

Home-grown terrorism

Home-grown terrorism is carried out by individuals who live in the country that they have attacked or plan to attack. It is perhaps the greatest security risk to developed countries, such as Scotland, because it means that there are individuals living lawfully in the country who feel so frustrated that they see terrorist activity as the only way to have their opinions heard. This may include individuals who turn to Islamic terrorism but may also include groups such as the Animal Liberation Front (ALF).

Figure 13.4: *British nationality is no guarantee that a person will not commit an act of terrorism*

 Hint

You can find information on how to carry out your own social research for the Added Value Unit or Assignment on page 214.

 Hint

The Department of Homeland Security in the USA maintains a list of all organisations that it considers to be terrorist organisations.

Figure 13.5: *Boston Marathon bombing*

Make the Link

You may learn more about social theories in other subjects such as History.

Activity

Discuss

Discuss Sir David Omand's statement with your shoulder partner. **Do you agree** with Sir David Omand? **Explain your view** to your partner.

Word bank

• **Jihad**

An Islamic term often used to refer to a war or struggle against non-believers.

We know that terrorist sympathy exists in developed countries such as the United States and the United Kingdom. In 2016, Omar Mateen, a 29-year-old security guard who was born and raised in New York, killed 49 people and wounded 53 others in a terrorist attack inside Pulse, a gay nightclub in Orlando. Orlando Police Department officers shot and killed him after a three-hour stand-off. It was the deadliest terrorist attack in the US since the September 11 attacks in 2001. In a recording of a 911 call made shortly after the shooting began, Mateen can be heard swearing allegiance to the leader of the Islamic State of Iraq and the Levant (ISIL, or IS), Abu Bakr al-Baghdadi. Mateen said the killing of Abu Waheeb in Iraq by US forces the previous month 'triggered' the shooting. He later told a negotiator he was 'out here right now' because of the American-led interventions in Iraq and in Syria, and that the negotiator should tell the United States government to stop bombing.

Former UK security coordinator, Sir David Omand, commented: 'the most effective weapon of the contemporary terrorist is their ideology', but as Sir David notes, the ideology of committing jihad is far more difficult to tackle than one lone gunman.

? Questions

1. Outline what the expression 'home-grown terrorist' means.
2. **Describe** why home-grown terrorists exist in developed countries.

State-sponsored terrorism

State-sponsored terrorism is government support of organisations engaged in terrorism. Most governments do not take kindly to being accused of terrorism and such claims are often subject to political dispute amid different definitions of 'terrorism'. The US government maintains a list of 'State Sponsors of Terrorism', countries which it says have 'repeatedly provided support for acts of international terrorism'. The countries currently on the list are Iran, North Korea, Sudan and Syria.

Over the past 10 years, the Syrian government has played a considerable role in the growth of terrorist networks in the country. These networks of extremist groups terrorised the Syrian and Iraqi populations in 2016. President Assad has allowed al-Qaeda and other terrorist groups to use Syria to gain access to Iraq for the purpose of fighting the US-led coalition there and foreign terrorist fighters aligned with Iran continue to travel to Syria from around the world to fight for or with the regime.

Figure 13.6: *The city of Homs has been reduced to piles of rubble and dust after airstrikes, artillery and rocket attacks*

Chemical attacks in Syria

CASE STUDY

There have been several alleged chemical attacks by the Syrian government on the Syrian people, despite the fact that President Assad agreed to join the 1997 Chemical Weapons Convention in 2013.

On 7th April 2018, more than 40 people were killed in the town of Douma in the Eastern Ghouta region. The town was under the control of anti-government rebels at the time of the attack. Tests carried out by the organisation responsible for implementing the Chemical Weapons Convention detected 'various chlorinated organic chemicals'. More than 500 people were admitted to hospital showing symptoms of exposure to chemicals: cyanosis, foaming of the mouth and eye irritation. Most of the victims were women and children.

📖 Word bank

- **Cyanosis**
Discolouring of the skin due to a lack of oxygen.

America's use of drone strikes has been questioned. Drones are unmanned aircraft that attack a certain target. When President George W. Bush left office in January 2009 the US had been responsible for approximately 45 drone strikes. Under President Obama the US reportedly carried out more than 563 strikes. Due in part to this, American academic Noam Chomsky has called the United States 'a leading terrorist state'. There followed a period of 10 months with very few strikes until shortly after President Trump took office. In 2017-2018, the US carried out more than 12,000 manned and unmanned air strikes.

Figure 13.7: *Protest against US drone attacks in Pakistan*

? Questions

1. **Explain** what 'state-sponsored terrorism' means.
2. **Summarise** the case study of chemical attacks in Syria.
3. **Explain** why Noam Chomsky has called America 'a leading terrorist state'.
4. Consider Figure 13.8 below. **Identify:**
   - the percentage of US nationals who believe the US government should launch airstrikes in other countries against suspected terrorists
   - the percentage of US nationals who believe the US government should launch airstrikes in the US against suspected terrorists living there

   What **conclusions** can be drawn from the **evidence** you have identified?

Do you think the US government should or should not use drones to:	% Yes, should	% No, should not	% No opinion
Launch airstrikes in other countries against suspected terrorists*	65	28	8
Launch airstrikes in other countries against US citizens living abroad who are suspected terrorists*	41	52	7
Launch airstrikes in the US against suspected terrorists living here**	25	66	9
Launch airstrikes in the US against US citizens living here who are suspected terrorists**	13	79	7

* Based on Sample A of 502 national adults
** Based on Sample B of 518 national adults

Figure 13.8: *Survey of US citizens, 20–21 March 2013*

? Questions

1. **Explain** what is meant by 'counter-terrorism'.
2. **Describe** why some people are critical of counter-terrorism strategies such as drone strikes.

N5 GO! Activity

Discuss

Some civil liberties groups have criticised the UK government's policies on dealing with terrorism. Read the extract from the *Liberty* website below and discuss with your shoulder partner whether or not you believe that people should be made to give up certain rights in order to have greater security from the threat of terrorism. Feed back your answers to the whole class.

Human rights law requires the State to take steps to protect the right to life – which includes measures to prevent terrorism. However, any measures taken to counter terrorism must be proportionate and not undermine our democratic values. In particular, laws designed to protect people from the threat of terrorism and the enforcement of these laws must be compatible with people's rights and freedoms. Yet, all too often the risk of terrorism has been used as the basis for eroding our human rights and civil liberties:

- *After the tragic events of September 11th 2001, emergency laws were passed which allowed for the indefinite detention of foreign nationals who were suspected of being terrorists. Under this law individuals could be detained for an unlimited period at a maximum security prison despite never being charged, let alone convicted of any offence.*

- *Before it was repealed, section 44 of the Terrorism Act 2000 allowed people to be stopped and searched without suspicion. This overly broad power was used against peaceful protesters and disproportionately against ethnic minority groups.*

- *Broad new speech offences impact on free speech rights and non-violent groups have been outlawed.*

📖 Word bank

• The State
A nation or territory considered as an organised political community under one government.

• Proportionate
Corresponding in size to something else.

• Foreign national
A person who is not a citizen of the host country in which they are staying.

• Repeal
To officially cancel a law.

• Disproportionately
Out of proportion; not corresponding in size.

• Speech offences
Speaking to a group in order to incite violence or hate.

Summary

In this chapter you have learned:

- to identify and explain theories surrounding terrorist behaviour
- to identify and explain lone wolf terrorists
- to identify and explain terrorist cells
- to identify and explain home-grown terrorism
- to identify and explain state-sponsored terrorism

Learning Summary

Now that you have finished the **Theories of terrorism** chapter, complete a self-evaluation of your knowledge and skills to assess what you have understood. Use the checklist below and its traffic lights to draw up a revision plan to help you improve in the areas you identified as red or amber.

- I can understand what a 'theory' is in social science.

- I can explain what is meant by a 'lone wolf terrorist'.

- I can describe what terrorist 'cells' are.

- I can outline what is meant by 'home-grown' terrorism.

- I can explain why support for terrorism exists in developed countries.

- I can explain what 'state-sponsored terrorism' is.

Examples

In Modern Studies it is essential that you are able to back up any point you make with relevant evidence. When you are considering the statements above try to think of relevant examples for each response. You may wish to note these examples under each statement in your revision notes.

14 The War on Terror

What you will learn in this chapter

- How to identify why the war in Afghanistan happened.
- How to identify why the war in Iraq happened.
- To understand how the War on Terror has affected global security today.

The War on Terror

The term 'War on Terror' was first used by former American President George W. Bush in response to the terrorist attacks of September 11th 2001. The phrase characterises the international military campaign that began in response to those attacks. One of the biggest supporters of America's War on Terror was the then UK Prime Minister, Tony Blair.

On 20th September 2001 President Bush made a speech in which he directly linked the terrorist organisation al-Qaeda to the attacks. While this information is now largely historical, it is important to recognise the roots of the current global terrorism strategy.

Who are al-Qaeda?

Al-Qaeda is an extremist Sunni Muslim movement founded by Osama bin Laden. Al-Qaeda is a global terrorist organisation and has a network of supporters and active members across the world. The group are in favour of global jihad – which translates as 'to struggle' – and are often interpreted as justifying a 'holy war'. Al-Qaeda also supports sharia law, which is a very strict form of religious law laid down by Islam.

Figure 14.1: *Tony Blair and George W. Bush*

? Questions

1. **Explain** the role of George W. Bush and Tony Blair in the War on Terror.
2. **Explain** who the organisation al-Qaeda are and why they exist.

Invading Afghanistan

The first military target of the War on Terror was the country of Afghanistan. Afghanistan is a war-torn nation where 42% of the population live below the poverty line. Until 2001 the country was governed by the Taliban, an Islamic fundamentalist political movement which had spread into Afghanistan from Pakistan and had managed to form a government.

⚡ Make the Link

In RMPS you may learn that those who follow Islam are of the Muslim faith. It is important to understand that religious extremism exists in many other faiths – including Christianity. The word Islam, which means 'surrender', is related to the Arabic salam, or 'peace'.

📖 Word bank

- **Holy war**
A war declared in support of a religious cause.

Word bank

- **Ultimatum**

A final demand attached to a threat (e.g. of retaliation).

- **NATO**

North Atlantic Treaty Organization, an international organisation composed of an alliance of a number of countries.

Hint

You should remember the word coalition from Section 1, it means an alliance.

Word bank

- **Insurgency attacks**

Attacks against the government or authority by rebel forces.

- **Guerrilla war**

Small independent groups fighting against powerful forces, using tactics such as ambush and sabotage.

Figure 14.3: *Taliban fighters display their weapons*

American intelligence suggested that Afghanistan and the Taliban were harbouring key members of al-Qaeda, including Osama bin Laden. President Bush issued an ultimatum to the Taliban regime in Afghanistan to hand over bin Laden and the leaders of al-Qaeda.

Figure 14.2: *George W. Bush: 'By aiding and abetting murder, the Taliban regime is committing murder'*

While recommending to bin Laden that he leave the country, the Taliban would not hand him over without direct evidence to link him to the attacks. The United States refused to negotiate and for the first time in its history NATO invoked Article 5 of its constitution – that an attack on one member country is an attack on all (for more information on NATO's role in combating terrorism, see page 195). America decided to act with its own coalition – including the United Kingdom, France and Spain. In October 2001 allied forces invaded Afghanistan under the umbrella 'Operation Enduring Freedom'. Their aim was to remove the Taliban regime, find Osama bin Laden and destroy al-Qaeda's networks. Members of al-Qaeda and the Taliban quickly went into hiding in Afghanistan's mountains.

The Taliban were removed from formal political power relatively quickly. However, the Taliban have not disappeared and have been proactively engaged in a series of insurgency attacks since 2001. Their guerrilla war tactics and knowledge of the mountains of Afghanistan means they have been able to hide and build support easily.

In 2006, NATO's International Security Assistance Force (ISAF) took control of military operations in the country. In 2010, NATO announced it would withdraw all international troops from Afghanistan in 2014 and control would pass to the new Afghan army and police force. This handover went ahead in December 2014 and since January 2015, NATO has led the Resolute Support Mission – a non-combat mission serving simply to train and advise the security forces.

Osama bin Laden managed to escape capture for many years until he was discovered in Abbottabad in Pakistan in 2011. In May that year, intelligence led US Navy SEALs to a building where bin Laden was shot and killed. Al-Qaeda have promised to avenge bin Laden's death. A statement posted at the time on an al-Qaeda-supporting website read 'we will remain, God willing, a curse chasing the Americans and their agents, following them outside and inside their countries'.

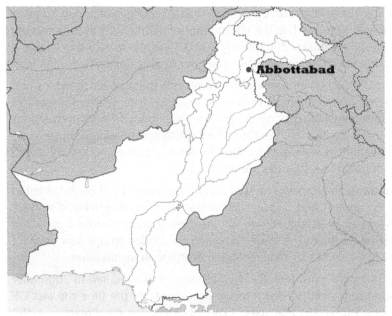

Figure 14.4: *Map of Pakistan showing location of Abbottabad where Osama bin Laden was killed*

> ## 📖 Word bank
>
> • **Navy SEALs**
> Members of a US naval special warfare unit.
>
> • **Avenge**
> Inflict harm in return for wrongdoing.

❓ Questions

1. **Describe** who the Taliban are.
2. **Explain** why Afghanistan was invaded in 2001.
3. **Explain** the current role of NATO in Afghanistan.
4. 'The Invasion of Afghanistan was extremely successful.'
   Identify and explain three pieces of **evidence** from the text above to **oppose** this statement.

The invasion of Iraq

In 2003 America led a 'coalition of the willing' in the invasion of Iraq. The purpose of this mission was to find weapons of mass destruction which it was alleged that the Iraqi leader, Saddam Hussein, had been developing. Newspaper reports at the time claimed that these weapons could be deployed to reach the UK within 45 minutes of launching.

> ## 📖 Word bank
>
> • **Coalition of the willing**
> A group of nations prepared to engage in military operations outside of the United Nations peacekeeping operations.
>
> • **Weapons of mass destruction**
> Nuclear, biological or chemical weapons able to cause widespread devastation and loss of life.

Figure 14.5: *Iraqis pass by a mosaic of their President, Saddam Hussein, in 1999*

George W. Bush's administration directly linked Iraq to the War on Terror. The President used the term the 'axis of evil' in early 2002 to describe 'rogue' nations, such as Iraq, he believed were harbouring terrorists and building up weapons of mass destruction. Later evidence would prove that Iraq had no weapons of mass destruction. Saddam's government additionally had no proven links to al-Qaeda.

International support

Unlike the invasion of Afghanistan in 2001, military action in Iraq was not well supported. In the UK millions of people took to the streets to protest; in February 2003 nearly 100,000 people marched in Glasgow against the UK government's support for American intervention in Iraq.

The UN had taken many different actions in Iraq over the years and had supported attempts in the past to allow their weapons inspectors to find out whether or not Iraq had the capability to develop weapons of mass destruction. As George W. Bush gave Saddam Hussein an ultimatum to leave power, the UN removed all weapons inspectors from Iraq. Days later the invasion began.

Following the invasion in April 2003 the capital city of Baghdad fell to allied control and Saddam Hussein's government quickly dissolved. However, as in Afghanistan, an insurgency quickly arose against the US-led coalition. The insurgency, which included groups supportive of al-Qaeda, led to far more coalition deaths than the invasion.

Iraq's former president, Saddam Hussein, was executed in 2006 after being sentenced to death in an Iraqi court. By the time the last US forces left in 2011 at least 116,903 Iraqi 'non-combatants', 4,487 Americans and 179 British troops had lost their lives.

Since the start of the Iraq invasion the number of global terrorist incidents has quadrupled.

? Questions

1. Outline the key events which led to the Iraq invasion in 2003.
2. Outline why **you think** the invasion was unpopular.

The end of the War on Terror?

Figure 14.6: *US President Barack Obama*

Perhaps the two strongest supporters of the War on Terror were the UK Prime Minister Tony Blair and American President George W. Bush. While neither of these individuals are in power today, the legacy of the War on Terror remains. The **Counter-Terrorism and Border Security Bill 2018** states that 'the nature of [terrorist] offences is ever changing ... [and these changes] allow us to continue to adapt to combatting the threat from international terrorism in a modern digital world'.

In May 2013, President Barack Obama declared that the 'global war on terror is over'. President Obama used this speech to focus on the 'networks' of terrorists and ways in which the international community can stop them gaining support.

The War on Terror has cost America substantially: in total it has cost more than a trillion dollars and more than 7,000 lives have been lost. President Donald Trump has resurrected the War on Terror, stating that stricter border controls and better internet vetting are the way to reduce incidents of terrorism.

Of the term 'War on Terror' some people would say that a war against terrorism was unwinnable. These people would argue that terrorism has always existed in some form and there will always be individuals who will use violence in order to make a political statement.

? Questions

1. Has the threat posed by international terrorism worsened since 2001? **Justify** your response with **evidence** from this chapter.
2. **Describe** America's new approach towards tackling international terrorism.
3. **Explain** why some people have been critical of the term 'War on Terror'.

Summary

In this chapter you have learned:

* why the war in Afghanistan happened
* why the war in Iraq happened
* the ways in which the War on Terror has affected global security today

Learning Summary

Now that you have finished **The War on Terror** chapter, complete a self-evaluation of your knowledge and skills to assess what you have understood. Use the checklist below and its traffic lights to draw up a revision plan to help you improve in the areas you identified as red or amber.

* I can explain where the term 'War on Terror' comes from.

* I can explain who al-Qaeda are.

* I can understand why al-Qaeda exist.

* I can explain who the Taliban are.

- I can describe the tactics used by the Taliban.

- I understand who Osama bin Laden was.

- I can outline why Afghanistan was invaded in 2001.

- I can outline the current role of NATO in Afghanistan.

- I can explain why some people think invading Afghanistan was unsuccessful.

- I can outline why Iraq was invaded in 2003.

- I can explain who Saddam Hussein was.

- I can explain why some people were opposed to the Iraq invasion.

- I can describe how the threat of global terrorism has changed since 2001.

- I can outline America's approach toward tackling global terrorism.

- I can explain why some people have been critical of the term 'War on Terror'.

Examples

In Modern Studies it is essential that you are able to back up any point you make with relevant evidence. When you are considering the statements above try to think of relevant examples for each response. You may wish to note these examples under each statement in your revision notes.

15 The consequences of terrorism

The impact on those immediately affected

The most serious consequence of terrorism is loss of life. According to the Global Terrorism Database, there were 10,900 terrorist attacks worldwide in 2017, resulting in more than 26,000 deaths.

Death and injury

Many terrorist attacks have the immediate impact of causing horrific injuries and deaths. As previously discussed, this could be to try to generate high levels of fear among the population or to try to force governments into action. On 13th November 2015, 15 gunmen and suicide bombers attacked a number of locations in Paris, including bars, a theatre and a stadium. They launched their attacks simultaneously and 130 people were killed and countless others injured. In the Bataclan theatre, three men wearing suicide belts stormed the building and fired automatic rifles into the crowd. A shoot-out with police followed and they activated their suicide vests and killed themselves. Eighty-nine civilians died in the theatre. Tourist numbers to Paris fell following the attack because people feared a repeat attack.

Fear

Terrorism causes fear and panic, which can make individuals' lives very stressful. Governments across the world have responded to the threat posed by international terrorism by stepping up security measures. Panic and social unrest can make individuals feel unsafe in their own homes and suspicious of people they may have previously trusted.

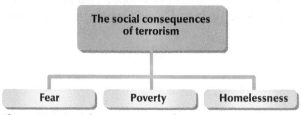

Figure 15.1: *Social consequences of terrorism*

Islamophobia

Islamophobia is prejudice against those of the Muslim faith. The Runnymede Trust (who promote a multi-ethnic Britain) have defined Islamophobia as the 'dread or hatred of Islam and therefore, [the] fear and dislike of all Muslims'.

Following the Manchester Arena attack in May 2017, hate crimes in the city increased by 500%. However, religious extremism also exists in many other religions, including Christianity. Some critics argue that the media have sensationalised Islam and portrayed it, unfairly, as a violent religion.

Breakdown in social cohesion

Social cohesion is the glue that binds a community together. People feel connected to a place if they feel their opinion matters – for example, if they are able to vote in regular elections. While terrorist attacks cause damage to property and loss of life it has been argued that this is not their primary aim. Indeed, a UN report stated in 2002 that 'the purpose [of terrorism] is not to take lives or destroy property. That is the mechanism, not the goal. The goal is to weaken the sense of cohesion that binds communities together, to reduce its social capital and to sow distrust, fear and insecurity.'

Poverty

Poverty is a consequence of terrorism. In Syria, which is ranked at number four in the Global Terrorism Index, 80% of the population are in poverty and 69% are considered to be in extreme poverty. Similarly in Somalia, ranked number seven in the Global Terrorism Index, poverty levels stand at over 70% and the unemployment rate is more than 40%. It is clear therefore that there is a link between poverty levels and the threat that terrorism poses.

Homelessness/refugees

Homelessness is an obvious consequence of terrorism. Not only are individuals removed from their home in the immediate aftermath of a terrorist attack, many also have to flee their country due to the ongoing consequences of terrorism. Around 5 million refugees have fled Syria to other countries due to the ongoing state-sponsored terrorism there. The numbers are similar for those fleeing Afghanistan, where around 6 million have fled to neighbouring countries. It is estimated that there are around 22.5 million refugees worldwide and this impacts on the countries where the refugees arrive as they have to provide resources for them. Refugees do not only flee to developed countries; many arrive in developing nations such as Uganda where resources are already scarce.

Make the Link

In History or RMPS you may have learned about the Second World War and the ideologies of Hitler, including that of anti-Semitism.

Word bank

- **Anti-Semitism**
When individuals have a distrust or irrational hatred of those from the Jewish faith.

Figure 15.2: *Anti-Muslim graffiti defaces a mosque in the USA*

Think point

You learned about state-sponsored terrorism in Chapter 11. Do you think the events in Syria should be described as state-sponsored terrorism?

THE CONSEQUENCES OF TERROR

❓ Question

Archbishop Desmond Tutu has stated 'you can never win a war against terror as long as there are conditions in the world that make people desperate – poverty, disease, ignorance'. Do you agree with the Archbishop's opinion? **Explain** your answer with relevant **evidence** from this chapter.

The impact on other countries and their governments

The cost of terrorism peaked in 2014 and has remained relatively high. The Global Terrorism Index puts the cost of terrorism in 2016 at $84 billion. The costs associated with terrorism include increased budgets for defence, personal security and the impact of terrorism on tourism within the countries it has affected.

Figure 15.3: *Archbishop Desmond Tutu, South African social rights activist*

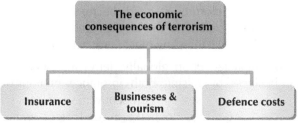

Figure 15.4: *Economic consequences of terrorism*

Direct economic impact of terrorist attacks

Terrorism is costly for governments across the world. Estimates have put the direct cost to America of the September 11th attacks at over $2 trillion. The direct cost of the 2017 Manchester Arena attack is thought to be more than £38 million.

Insurance against terrorism

Companies have recently begun offering insurance against terrorism. This protects owners against any losses they might have due to a terrorist attack. The odds of a terrorist attack happening remain unlikely – but if a terrorist attack did happen the insurance company might have to pay out a lot of money, making it very difficult to insure against terrorism. Most travel insurance now protects people against being stranded as the result of a terrorist attack (80% of all travel insurance now includes cover against situations arising due to terrorist attacks) and the cost of travel insurance has increased as a result.

▶ Activity

Research
Sometimes the media may report on terrorism in a way that deliberately causes fear in order to support their political point of view. Research different case studies of terrorist attacks and how they have been presented by the mainstream media. Focus on the use of **exaggeration and/or bias**. Present your findings to your class.

Figure 15.5: *Most travel insurance includes a terrorism clause*

Businesses and tourism

Terrorism is more likely to affect poorer developing countries where the effects of the loss of income to their businesses and tourism industry as a result of terrorism can be devastating.

Tourism is an example of an industry directly affected by terrorism; indeed, research in Spain has shown that a typical terrorist act scares away over 140,000 tourists. Since September the 11th 2001 it is now much more expensive to fly due to security fees which are added on to ticket costs by airports and airlines.

When terrorist attacks occur and tourists are put off from visiting it can have a negative impact on that country's income.

In 2015, IS attacks in two Tunisian cities – Sousse and Tunis – killed 60 people. The majority of the victims were European tourists. The attacks took a heavy toll on the country's tourism sector, which accounts for around one-sixth of GDP and provides employment for more than 200,000 people. Visitor numbers fell by 25% to 5.4 million in 2015, and revenue from tourists dropped by 35% to $1.1 billion. Mass unemployment and business closures ravaged the resorts. Tunisia's government urged tourists to return to the country and stated that Tunisia was no more under threat than any other European country.

Business can also be impacted upon globally. Terrorism increases the cost of doing business by raising both insurance premiums and security costs, which decreases the competitiveness of goods. This means businesses will struggle to make a good profit while also remaining competitive. Terrorism slows the flow of goods and resources through ports due to greater inspections and safeguards, again meaning companies will struggle to make a good profit.

Figure 15.6: *Memorials left on the beach in Tunis after the 2015 attacks*

📖 Word bank

- **Profit**

The money left over after a business has paid all its bills, staff and other costs.

Defence costs

In 2017–18 the total cost of anti-terrorist initiatives in the UK stood at £2 billion, more than double what it was at the start of the decade in the UK. The US alone now spends about $100 billion annually on departments directly engaged in preventing terrorism. Terrorism costs governments across the world as they are required to have effective counter-terrorism strategies to try to protect their populations from the effects of a terrorist attack. More information can be found on counter-terrorism in chapter 16.

GO! Activity

Research
Carry out a mini-investigation with your peers, family and/or teachers about holiday destinations.

- For this task you will need to design a questionnaire. Information on how to conduct a questionnaire can be found on page 219.
- Design no more than 10 questions to help you find out about how the issue of international terrorism affects tourism.
- Present your information in the form of a blog entry. You should have at least two different sources that show your results, such as a bar graph or a bullet point list.
- The blog page should also contain at least two conclusions from your research.

Regional and wider international consequences

Global instability

The world has become increasingly unstable in recent years; some political analysts would argue that this is directly due to the threat of international terrorism.

Figure 15.7: *Political consequences of terrorism*

Arab Spring

In late 2010, 26-year-old Tunisian street vendor Mohamed Bouazizi set himself on fire. Local police had prevented him from selling fruit which was his main source of income. Protests against the corrupt authorities in Tunisia began and over the next 12 months the revolution spread, affecting Tunisia, Egypt, Libya, Bahrain, Yemen and Syria, as people stood up to their countries' long-established regimes. The 'Arab Spring', as it became known, created substantial global instability. While it was not caused by terrorism, the consequences of changes in political leadership have led to opportunities for extremists, who have used the instability it has created to gain political power and support for their cause. In Syria, state-sponsored terrorism is creating global uncertainty and most countries no longer have a trading relationship with the country.

Figure 15.8: *Protests in Egypt during the Arab Spring*

Figure 15.9: *Word cloud for the Arab Spring uprising in the Middle East*

Increased security

Security has increased as a result of international terrorism. Today when travelling on a plane, for example, travellers can expect the following restrictions:

- specific ID required; ID name must match name on ticket
- shoes must be removed at checkpoints
- all baggage, both carry-on and checked, must be screened
- no liquids (above 100 ml) allowed through checkpoints
- special items must be pulled from luggage (laptops)
- jackets/outerwear must be removed
- body scan machine screening
- enhanced pat-downs
- no more non-ticketed visitors allowed at airline gates

Figure 15.10: *Airport security scanners*

Terrorism has also affected security in public buildings and areas; for example, in 2010 the Scottish Parliament had security bollards built outside the perimeter of the building to prevent an attack similar to the Glasgow airport bombing of 2007. In 2017, the key locations in Edinburgh had anti-terrorism barriers installed during the Edinburgh Festival to prevent vehicle attacks on pedestrians.

? Questions

1. Use the information in this chapter to summarise the consequences of terrorism using the headings below:
   - those immediately affected
   - other countries and their governments
   - wider international consequences

Hint

In the National 5 exam, remember to state that your international issue is terrorism.

2. **Explain**, **in detail**, three consequences of an international issue or problem you have studied. You must use the Point, Explain, Example structure (see page 236) and include at least **three examples**.

Counter-terrorism – compromising rights?

The threat posed by international terrorism in recent years has meant that countries across the world have had to develop ways of dealing with terrorism before it has a chance to happen. These strategies – often known as 'counter-terrorism' – can be controversial if they mean that individuals have to give up some of their human rights for the sake of 'security'.

 Hint

Counter-terrorism strategies are discussed in more detail in chapter 16 of this Section.

Summary

In this chapter you have learned:

- the impact of terrorism on those immediately affected
- the impact of terrorism on other countries and their governments (including the UK)
- the regional and wider international consequences of terrorism

Learning Summary

Now that you have finished **The consequences of terrorism** chapter, complete a self-evaluation of your knowledge and skills to assess what you have understood. Use the checklist below and its traffic lights to draw up a revision plan to help you improve in the areas you identified as red or amber.

- I can describe the impact of terrorism on those immediately affected.

- I can describe the impact of terrorism on other countries and their governments.

- I can describe the regional and wider international consequences of terrorism.

- I can explain what is meant by 'counter-terrorism'.

- I can describe why some people are critical of counter-terrorism strategies.

Examples

In Modern Studies it is essential that you are able to back up any point you make with relevant evidence. When you are considering the statements above try to think of relevant examples for each response. You may wish to note these examples under each statement in your revision notes.

16 Governments: responding to and resolving terrorism

What you will learn in this chapter

- To understand how the UK and Scottish governments have responded to terrorism.
- To explain the problems that they have faced in responding to terrorism.

Government response to terrorism

Terrorism is, in the main, a reserved power as it is related to defence. This means that it is the UK government's responsibility to ensure that Scotland is protected against the threat posed by international terrorism.

The ways in which governments and organisations respond to terrorism directly affects the threat that terrorism will pose in the future. Governments often like to be seen to be 'cracking down', with tough measures on terrorism. They may do this by introducing a 'threat level' or by introducing new laws regarding terrorist suspects.

Figure 16.1: *People may feel vulnerable when governments talk about threats*

However, this can often have a negative effect on a population: increasing the 'threat level' can frighten people, and as a result they feel less protected. Also some critics argue that introducing 'threat levels' and asking people to be vigilant doesn't actually target terrorists and would-be supporters.

The main way in which any government can respond to terrorist activity is through passing relevant laws:

Make the Link

You will have learned about reserved and devolved powers in Section 1.

Think point

Think about the ways in which you keep safe in school. Consider the following:
- does your school have a security policy?
- are there secure doors?
- do staff wear identity badges?

Make the Link

In Section 1 you learned about how laws are made.

An overview of UK government counter-terrorism legislation	
Terrorism Act 2000	Expands the definition of terrorism; it now includes action, used or threatened, for the purpose of advancing any "political, religious, ideological or racial" cause. Terrorist action is defined: violence against a person, damage to property, serious risk to the health or safety of the public or a section of the public and behaviour designed seriously to interfere with or seriously to disrupt an electronic system. All subsequent terrorism legislation and powers for the police and courts flow from this definition.
The Terrorism Act 2006	• Drafted in the aftermath of the 7th July 2005 London bombings. • Created new offences related to terrorism, and amended existing ones. • Increased the number of days a suspect can be held without charge from 14 to 28 days.

The Counter-Terrorism Act 2008	• Allows the UK government to force the financial sector to take action on suspected money laundering or terrorist financing.
	• Allows police to enter – by force if necessary – and search the premises of individuals subject to control orders.
	  • Allows police to take fingerprints and DNA samples from individuals subject to control orders.
	  • The number of days someone detained for suspicion of terrorism can be held without charge was increased to 42.

Terrorism Prevention and Investigation Measures Act 2011	• Introduced Terrorism Prevention and Investigation Measures (TPIMs) (see page 188). • Some critics have argued that TPIMs are simply a watered down version of control orders.
Protection of Freedoms Act 2012	• Allows the power to search people and vehicles.

The UK government's counter-terrorism strategy is called 'CONTEST'. It is split into four parts that are known within the counter-terrorism community as the 'four Ps': Pursue, Prevent, Protect and Prepare.

This translates to:

1. The government will work to **pursue** terrorists and disrupt their work by detecting, prosecuting and otherwise disrupting those who plot to carry out attacks against the UK or its interests overseas.

2. The government will **prevent** terrorism by stopping people from becoming terrorists or supporting terrorism. This includes countering terrorist ideology and challenging those who promote it, supporting individuals who are especially vulnerable to becoming radicalised, and working with sectors and institutions where the risk of radicalisation is considered to be high. This has involved training staff in the NHS and in schools.

3. The government will **protect** by strengthening protection against a terrorist attack in the UK or against its interests overseas. The work focuses on border security, the transport system, national infrastructure and public places.

📖 Word bank

• **Money laundering**
A way of hiding the fact that money has been gained in an illegal way.

4. The government will **prepare** by lessening the impact of a terrorist attack where that attack cannot be stopped. This includes bringing a terrorist attack to an end and increasing the resilience of the country so that it can recover from the aftermath.

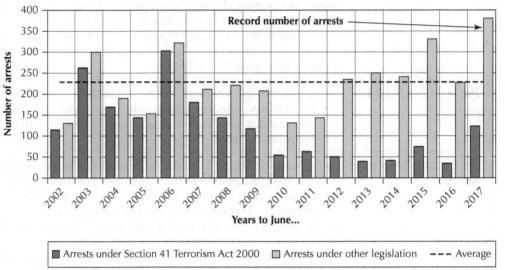

Figure 16.2: *Arrests related to terrorism 2003 to 2017*

? Questions

1. **Explain** why terrorism is mainly dealt with by the UK government.
2. Using the information in the table above, make a time-line showing the name of each of the acts and the year in which they were passed.
3. Summarise the four parts of the 'CONTEST' strategy.
4. Look at the dates the laws were introduced. Outline what might have led to their introduction.
5. Look at Figure 16.2. What conclusion can you draw about the number of terrorism arrests?

Terrorism prevention and investigation measures CASE STUDY

Control orders were put in place to be used by the Home Secretary with the aim of restricting the freedom of individuals suspected of involvement in terrorist activities. They were introduced by the **Prevention of Terrorism Act 2005**. In 2011 control orders were replaced in the **Terrorism Prevention and Investigation Measures Act 2011**; the Coalition government argued they are fairer than the old control orders.

Terrorism prevention and investigation measures (TPIMs) are very similar to control orders in that they restrict an individual's freedom and are imposed directly by the Home Secretary. Those subject to a TPIM are not able to:

• leave their house overnight
• go beyond the geographical boundaries decided by the Home Office

- remove their electronic monitoring tag
- talk to or meet with whoever they want
- stop the police or staff from the monitoring company entering and searching their home without a warrant
- have friends or family to their home unless approved by the Home Office, approval of which can be removed at any time
- travel overseas

The UK government also monitors the 'threat level'. The threat level shows the likelihood of a terrorist attack happening in the UK and is calculated in response to any known 'terrorist activity'.

There are five levels of threat:

- low – an attack is unlikely
- moderate – an attack is possible but not likely
- substantial – an attack is a strong possibility
- severe – an attack is highly likely
- critical – an attack is expected imminently

The threat level is currently set separately for Northern Ireland and Great Britain.

The Scottish government

While counter-terrorism policy is reserved to the Westminster government, many aspects of preventing and dealing with a potential terrorist act in Scotland are managed by the Scottish government. The Specialist Crime Division has responsibility for counter-terrorism in Scotland.

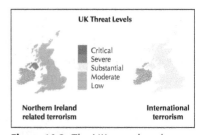

Figure 16.3: *The UK was placed on 'critical' alert after the Glasgow airport bombing (see page 155)*

Think point

While Defence is currently a reserved issue, the Scottish government has a role in dealing with the problems and issues associated with terrorist behaviour. Can you think why this might be the case?

❓ Questions

1. Visit the UK's security service website: https://www.mi5.gov.uk (QR code below) and find out what the current threat levels are for:
   - international terrorism
   - Northern Ireland-related terrorism

   Explain why you think the two terror threat levels might be different.

Hint

You can find more information about internet research on page 222.

2. Using a suitable search engine, try to find two recent **examples** of counter-terrorism in action in:
   - the UK
   - Scotland

   Describe whether or not you think the examples you selected have been successful in decreasing the threat posed by terrorism. You may wish to present your findings using a PowerPoint presentation to illustrate your answer.

Summary

In this chapter you have learned:

- to understand how the UK and Scottish governments have responded to terrorism
- to explain the problems that they have faced in responding to terrorism

Learning Summary

Now that you have finished the **Governments: responding to and resolving terrorism** chapter, complete a self-evaluation of your knowledge and skills to assess what you have understood. Use the checklist below and its traffic lights to draw up a revision plan to help you improve in the areas you identified as red or amber.

- I can explain why the UK government is responsible for dealing with terrorism.

- I can describe relevant laws which have been passed by the UK government to try to stop terrorism.

- I can describe the UK government's counter-terrorism strategy.

- I can explain which organisation is responsible for counter-terrorism strategies in Scotland.

- I can explain what a terrorism prevention measure is.

Examples

In Modern Studies it is essential that you are able to back up any point you make with relevant evidence. When you are considering the statements above try to think of relevant examples for each response. You may wish to note these examples under each statement in your revision notes.

17 Multilateral organisations: responding to and resolving terrorism

What you will learn in this chapter

- To understand how multilateral organisations have responded to terrorism.
- To explain the problems these organisations have faced in responding to terrorism.

Multilateral organisations

Multilateral organisations are groups of countries, working together for a stated goal.

The opposite of multilateralism would therefore be unilateralism, where countries work completely independently of each other in their own self-interest.

International organisations such as the European Union (EU), the United Nations (UN) and NATO (the North Atlantic Treaty Organization) are multilateral organisations of which the UK has membership. Each organisation has a role to play in international relations and therefore a role to play in responding to the threat of international terrorism.

The United Nations

The UN is an international alliance formed in 1945 following the end of the Second World War. It is organised through six main bodies: the General Assembly, the Security Council, the Economic and Social Council, the Trusteeship Council, the International Court of Justice and the Secretariat.

Today the UN has a total of 193 member countries. The most recognisable figure in the UN is the Secretary General who acts as the leader and spokesperson for the organisation.

In 2006 all member countries of the UN adopted its Global Counter-Terrorism Strategy with the stated aim to co-ordinate counter-terrorism strategies across the world. Specifically the strategy aims to:

- tackle the conditions that support the spread of terrorism
- prevent and combat terrorism
- build countries' capacity to prevent and combat terrorism and to strengthen the role of the UN system
- ensure respect for human rights for all and the rule of law while countering terrorism

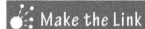

Make the Link

In History you may learn about the League of Nations, the multilateral organisation that preceded the United Nations.

Figure 17.1: *Flag of the United Nations*

Figure 17.2: *António Guterres, Secretary General since 2017*

The UN's Counter-Terrorism Implementation Task Force helps member states with implementing the strategy. The Task Force is organised into a number of 'working groups'. These groups look at different aspects of counter-terrorism such as addressing radicalisation, protecting human rights and tackling the financing of terrorism.

Figure 17.3: *Denying financial support, or money freezing*

❓ Questions

1. **Explain** why the UN was first formed.
2. Outline the UN Global Counter-Terrorism Strategy.

The UN against terrorism

The UN is a diplomatic organisation; this means that it provides a place for countries to discuss and debate international issues of global importance. However, the UN can take action and has done so in recent years in response to the threat of international terrorism.

Non-military resolutions

A resolution is a commitment to take action. This might be to raise awareness or to send a warning to a country or an organisation. For example, Resolution 2396 (2017), passed in December 2017, encourages countries to investigate and prevent international terrorists from travelling and spreading hateful ideology.

Peacekeeping

Figure 17.4: *A UN peacekeeper at work*

UN peacekeepers monitor the peace process in countries all over the world. UN peacekeepers (often known as Blue Berets because they wear blue helmets) can include soldiers, police officers and civilian personnel.

UN peacekeepers are currently positioned worldwide. As of September 2018 the United Nations had in place:

- 90,454 uniformed peacekeepers
- 12,932 international civilian personnel
- 1,294 volunteers

Uniformed peacekeepers come from a variety of different countries including America, China and Nepal. UN peacekeepers are therefore directly involved in the peace process worldwide.

Military action

Perhaps the strongest action that the UN can take is military intervention. In 2011 the UN passed a resolution that authorised air strikes against tank columns and naval ships in Libya. The UN wanted to support the 'rebels' who had staged an uprising against the Libyan government, led by Colonel Muammar Gaddafi. Gaddafi ruled the country of Libya for 42 years in total. It has been claimed that his time in power was characterised by torture and human rights abuses and that he was a supporter of international terrorism.

Figure 17.5: *Colonel Gaddafi*

No-fly zones

No-fly zones are areas over which aircraft are not allowed to fly. This stops the military from gaining information by flying overhead, or from dropping bombs for example. The UN has used such zones in Libya, Bosnia and Herzegovina, and in Syria.

? Question

Using the headings below, summarise the main ways in which the UN has taken action in the global fight against international terrorism in recent years:

- resolutions
- peacekeeping
- military action
- no-fly zones

Criticisms of the UN's counter-terrorism strategy

Critics of the UN say that the organisation has failed as an international peacekeeper. Wars continue today and global threats such as terrorism remain. Other criticisms include the fact that the UN is seen as an elitist institution governed by the most powerful countries in the world and only works in their self-interests.

GO! Activity

Research
- Visit the UN website and look at the list of its 193 members:
  http://www.un.org/en/member-states
- Then visit the Freedom House members list, which lists those countries deemed to be 'free' (based on the political and civil rights of its citizens):
  https://freedomhouse.org/report/freedom-world/freedom-world-2018
- Note down the countries which are not classed as free and yet are part of the UN.

Discuss
If countries are not classed as free how **do you think** that might affect dealing with the issue of international terrorism?

Elitism

The Security Council is the key place in which decisions surrounding international security are made. According to the 'post Second World War' political make-up, there are five permanent members of the UN Security Council: China, France, Russia, the UK and the USA.

 Hint

Think about the ways in which support for terrorism develops.

📖 Word bank

- **Sanction**

A threatened penalty for disobeying a law.

- **Invoke**

To activate something, or state that it is now in effect.

The Security Council deals with maintaining peace, issuing sanctions, and authorising military action. Critics contend that the permanent members, who all have nuclear capabilities, are able to act in any way they wish without question because of their permanent status. Others argue that permanent membership is an outdated idea, with currently powerful countries such as Germany excluded from the top table. The Security Council has also been criticised in the past for responding slowly to international disputes.

The veto

A final criticism of the power of the Security Council is the power of veto held by the five permanent members. The veto means that even if just one of the five vote against a resolution, such as military action or imposing sanctions for example, the vote will be unsuccessful. Since 1982 the USA has vetoed 43 Security Council resolutions against Israel, which is more than the total number of vetoes cast by all the other Security Council members put together. Critics argue that the American government's 'pro-Israeli' view has led to human rights violations that the international community, through the Security Council, could have stopped from happening.

⚙️ Think point

Think about the ways in which the USA conducts herself as a global power. Has this impacted upon the ways in which international organisations have been able to respond to terrorism?

❓ Question

Using the headings below, summarise the main criticisms of the UN's counter-terrorism strategy:

- undemocratic membership
- elitism
- the veto

NATO

The North Atlantic Treaty Organization (NATO) is a military alliance created in 1949 following the end of the Second World War. NATO is based on the idea of collective defence – Article 5 of the NATO treaty states that an attack on one member country is an attack on all. Following the events of September 11 2001, NATO invoked Article 5 for the first and only time.

Figure 17.6: *The NATO flag*

🔗 Make the Link

You may have learned about the principles of communism in History.

NATO and terrorism

When NATO was formed in 1949 the main threat to global security was communism.

Communism no longer presents as much of a threat today, but international terrorism has increased in recent history; in response to this NATO has had to adapt and develop new ways to protect international security. Russia is still not a member of NATO but the NATO-Russia Council (established in 2002) handles security issues and joint projects. Today NATO has 29 member countries in total.

NATO's counter-terrorism strategy

NATO's counter-terrorism strategy is based on:

- awareness of the threat of terrorism
- the shared capabilities of member countries
- engagement with partner countries

NATO now conducts a number of operations that support the fight against terrorism; three examples are shown in the figure below.

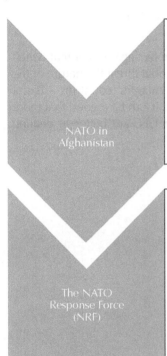

NATO in Afghanistan

- NATO's main role in Afghanistan is to support the Afghan government. This is done through the Resolute Support Mission (RSM) by training and assisting the Afghan forces to best protect themselves from terrorism and the threat of support for terrorism from developing ever again.
- Since January 2015, NATO has had over 16,000 troops from 39 countries in Afghanistan working to strengthen democracy and prevent terrorism.
- NATO troops provide training in civil emergency planning and disaster preparedness to help Afghan troops deal with a terrorist attack, should one happen.

The NATO Response Force (NRF)

- The NATO Response Force (NRF) is a rapid-reaction multinational force which was created following the events of September 11th 2001.
- The NRF has access to 40,000 troops which NATO can deploy with speed as and when required and is comprised of land, air and sea troops all provided by NATO members.
- The NRF rotates its troops – this means that countries commit their land, air, naval or Special Operations Forces to the NRF and they rotate on a 12-month cycle.
- The NRF not only works against terrorist activity but has been utilised for disaster relief, protecting infrastructure and security operations.
- Within the NRF is the Very High Readiness Joint Task Force (VJTF), created in 2014 and ready to deploy within two days.

Operation Sea Guardian

- In November 2016, NATO launched a maritime security operation – called Operation Sea Guardian – which can perform a broad range of tasks.
- It aims to protect ships moving goods from terrorist attacks, protect the communication cables which lie under the sea from terrorist attacks and prevent the transport of weapons of mass destruction.
- Operation Sea Guardian is currently operating in the Mediterranean. It conducts tours that last for three continuous weeks every two months, which represents a total of six operations per year. There are usually three ships and a submarine involved.

Figure 17.7: *NATO's counter-terrorism strategy*

? Questions

1. **Explain** why NATO was first formed.
2. Outline NATO's counter-terrorism strategy.
3. Summarise the three missions in which NATO is currently involved in countering the threat of international terrorism.

Criticisms of NATO's actions on terrorism

Communism

Critics argue that NATO was formed to protect against a threat which doesn't exist anymore. As terrorism is a global threat the nature of the alliance – which only represents 'North Atlantic' countries – is not helpful in tackling this problem. Therefore it can be argued that more representative organisations, such as the UN, are better at dealing with the threat of terrorism.

Figure 17.8: *This map shows the NATO member countries: far from a global spread*

Cost

Member countries pay money to NATO for the provision of military training and for their protection as part of the alliance. Countries pay an amount of money based on their Gross National Income – in 2017 Albania paid the least and America the most. Critics say that countries who pay more into NATO may expect to get more out of it and therefore smaller countries who pay less, such as Albania, will feel that they have a smaller say in the way in which the organisation is run. President Trump has been very critical of the unequal system of payments and his comments may also make these countries feel less powerful. This may mean that when it comes to dealing with international threats such as terrorism countries will not be treated equally.

Illegal wars

NATO is often drawn into conflicts which it did not start. In recent history this has been the case with the wars in Iraq and Afghanistan.

In 2017, NATO undertook a bombing campaign against Syria in an anti-terror campaign. This was criticised by some as a 'humanitarian disaster'. The bombing campaign included targeting electricity and water supplies. The fact that civil war continues in Syria suggests that the campaign was unsuccessful.

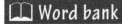

Word bank

- **Gross National Income**
The sum of a nation's Gross Domestic Product (money made within the country) plus Net Income received from overseas.

Figure 17.9: *The flag of the European Union*

? Question

Using the headings below, summarise the main criticisms of NATO's counter-terrorism strategy:

- communism
- cost
- illegal wars

The European Union

The European Union (EU) is an economic and political alliance and is made up of 28 member countries in total. The origins of the EU can be traced back to the 1950s when it was then known as the European Coal and Steel Company. The organisation was formed on the basis of trade and a common market in which European nations could trade with limited sanctions and export tariffs.

The EU internal market (sometimes known as 'the single market') tries to guarantee the free movement of goods, capital, services and people (the EU's 'four freedoms') within the EU's 28 member states.

Think point

Why do you think we entered into a political and economic union with our EU neighbours?

Word bank

- **Export tariffs**

Taxes on goods going out of the country.

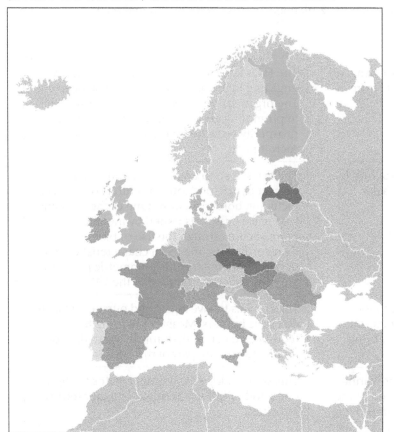

Figure 17.11: *Map of Europe showing the EU member states*

Figure 17.10: *Belgian EU Counter-Terrorism Coordinator Gilles de Kerchove*

Citizens across Europe elect MEPs (Members of the European Parliament) every five years to sit in the European Parliament and make decisions on their behalves. The UK has 72 MEPs in total; Scotland is currently designated as a 'region' of this total and is allocated six MEPs.

Make the Link

In Section 1 we looked at different parliaments.

As discussed on page 30, Britain is due to leave the EU in March 2019. This will affect the terrorism strategy of the EU because it is unlikely that the UK will be allowed access to the sharing of information which currently goes on. The rest of this section discusses the EU counter-terrorism strategy as it currently stands in 2018. Your teacher may ask you to research the changes to this after the UK has left the EU.

? Question

Explain why the European Union as we know it today was first founded.

The EU and terrorism

After the terrorist attacks in London in 2005 it was decided that the EU needed to take a more planned approach to managing terrorism (see the table below). The EU also appointed a Counter-Terrorism Coordinator to help member states in the fight against terrorism.

The EU has had some notable success in tackling terrorist activity. Europol's Terrorism Situation and Trend Report 2017 states that the EU made 1,002 arrests for terrorist offences and 77 arrests for travelling to conflict zones for terrorist purposes. It is also reported that it prevented 142 planned attacks, including 70 in the UK.

EU counter-terrorism strategy

Prevent people from turning to terrorism and stop future generations of terrorists from emerging.	The EU is keen to 'prevent' individuals from engaging in terrorism in the first instance. The organisation is keen to 'lead by example' in promoting good governance, promoting prosperity elsewhere and by challenging recruitment.
Protect citizens and critical infrastructure by reducing vulnerabilities against attacks.	The EU is keen to upgrade measures that protect people and infrastructure from attack, including border security. One of the key aims is to make passports issued by member states more secure through the use of biometrics (i.e. by recording unique facial characteristics, iris patterns and fingerprints). Biometric passports are now issued as standard in the UK.
Pursue and investigate terrorists, impede planning, travel and communications, cut off access to funding and materials and bring terrorists to justice.	The EU aims to investigate and pursue terrorists across its borders. Measures to bring terrorists to justice, to cut off their funds and to disrupt their networks are part of this agenda.
Respond in a co-ordinated way by preparing for the management and minimisation of the consequences of a terrorist attack, improving capacities to deal with the aftermath and taking into account the needs of victims.	This strand allows EU member states to support one another in the aftermath of major terrorist atrocities.

The European Council reviews progress on the above strategy every six months.

? Question

Using the headings below, summarise the main ways in which the EU has taken action in the global fight against international terrorism in recent years:

- prevent
- protect
- review
- respond

Figure 17.12: *A biometric chip in a British passport*

Criticisms of the EU

The EU is made up of 28 member states and therefore passing laws or attempting to jointly 'solve' any issue can be difficult as there are 28 countries with 28 different governments of their own. The interests of the individual countries often take priority over working as part of a union. Criticisms of the EU's policy on terrorism often relate to civil liberties.

Proposals on data retention

Proposals on data retention have been criticised both in the European Parliament and in member states and countries often have a poor record of sharing intelligence.

The EU has requested on numerous occasions to use information stored by companies to track terrorists from country to country. For example, the Passenger Name Record (PNR) is a database that includes a passenger's name, address, phone number and credit card details. It is used in the airline and transport industry. In April 2013 a EU proposal to allow the use of PNR data for investigating serious crime and terrorist offences was rejected.

Figure 17.13: *Millions of files would be made available via the PNR database*

Biometric security standards for ID cards and passports

Critics argue that while the EU can suggest all countries use a form of biometric security for their passports and ID cards, they can't actually 'enforce' a European Policy. Article 18 of the EC Treaty allows for freedom of movement meaning European citizens can live and work in any European country they want to.

Freedom of movement has been criticised for allowing terrorists to attack in many states. Those who carried out the attacks in Paris in 2016 had moved from Belgium to France and had been to Syria prior to the attack.

Human rights

Others believe that the EU is interfering in countries' domestic affairs by creating laws in country-specific cases of terrorism. The newspaper article below considers this argument in more detail.

📖 Word bank

- **EC Treaty**

A document that lays out how the union of member states operates; EC being European Community, a former name.

DAILY NEWS

world - business - finance - lifestyle - travel - sport

Al-Qaeda terrorists launch human rights bid

Two al-Qaeda terrorists, one of whom plotted to kill thousands of people in a bomb attack on a British shopping centre, have launched an attempt to have their convictions quashed on human rights grounds.

The pair have applied to the European Court of Human Rights after claiming MI5 was complicit in their torture by Pakistani security services, a claim that has already been rejected by British courts.

Officials at the European Court have allowed their application to go ahead rather than declaring it inadmissible, as they do with thousands of cases a year.

The government must now respond to the claims, and if its explanation does not satisfy the court it will order a full hearing which, if successful, would almost certainly lead to the British courts being forced to quash the convictions.

The new development raises further questions about the influence of Strasbourg over British sovereignty, and the way human rights legislation is being exploited by defence lawyers.

[Source: http://www.telegraph.co.uk/news/uknews/terrorism-in-the-uk/9499541/Al-Qaeda-terrorists-launch-human-rights-bid.html]

GO! **Activity**

Show your knowledge
To support your learning and to help you revise, make a mind map which shows the major problems each organisation has faced. You should detail:
- key dates in which the organisation has faced opposition
- the counter-terrorism strategy of each organisation
- a summary under each explaining whether or not you believe the organisation has been successful in countering the threat posed by terrorism

Conclusion

Since the September 11th attacks in the US in 2001, terrorist activity has increased exponentially around the world. The Global Terrorism Index 2017 shows Islamic State (IS) to be the deadliest terrorist group in the world. There were over 6,141 deaths caused by IS in more than 250 cities in 2016. This suggests that no organisation or country has been successful in tackling international terrorism. While some individual programmes have had some success, the issue continues to grow worldwide.

? Question

1. Using the headings below, summarise the main criticisms of the EU's counter-terrorism strategy:
   - data retention
   - biometric security standards, ID cards and passports
   - human rights
2. Explain why some may say international organisations have been unsuccessful in tackling terrorism.

Summary

In this chapter you have learned:

- how multilateral organisations have responded to terrorism
- the problems these organisations have faced in responding to terrorism

Learning Summary

Now that you have finished the **Multilateral organisations: responding to and resolving terrorism** chapter, complete a self-evaluation of your knowledge and skills to assess what you have understood. Use the checklist below and its traffic lights to draw up a revision plan to help you improve in the areas you identified as red or amber.

- I can explain why the UN was first formed.

- I can outline the UN counter-terrorism strategy.

- I can describe the ways in which the UN has acted to prevent terrorism.

- I can explain the main criticisms of the UN's counter-terrorism strategy.

- I can explain how NATO was first formed.

- I can outline NATO's counter-terrorism strategy.

- I can describe the ways in which NATO has acted to prevent terrorism.

- I can explain the main criticisms of NATO's counter-terrorism strategy.

- I can explain why the EU was first founded.

- I can outline the EU's counter-terrorism strategy.

- I can describe the ways in which the EU has acted to prevent terrorism.

- I can explain the main criticisms of the EU's counter-terrorism strategy.

Examples

In Modern Studies it is essential that you are able to back up any point you make with relevant evidence. When you are considering the statements above try to think of relevant examples for each response. You may wish to note these examples under each statement in your revision notes.

18 Interested organisations

What you will learn in this chapter

- To identify how interested organisations have responded to terrorism.
- To understand how you can contribute to this international issue as a global citizen.

Interested organisations

Alliances such as the EU or organisations such as the UN are formal organisations that use the governments of their members to try to change things. Other interested organisations and individuals, however, can also help by responding to the issues surrounding terrorism.

Civil liberties groups

Civil liberties are rights and freedoms that individuals are entitled to. Examples of civil liberties include freedom from torture and freedom of expression. Civil liberties groups therefore exist to protect these freedoms.

Figure 18.1: *Freedom of expression is guarded by civil liberties groups*

Liberty

Liberty is a pressure group that campaigns to protect civil liberties and promotes human rights.

'Human rights law requires the State to take steps to protect the right to life – which includes measures to prevent terrorism. However, any measures taken to counter terrorism must be proportionate and not undermine our democratic values. In particular, laws designed to protect people from the threat of terrorism and the enforcement of these laws must be compatible with people's rights and freedoms. Yet, all too often the risk of terrorism has been used as the basis for eroding our human rights and civil liberties. We believe that terrorism can and must be fought within the rule of law and the human rights framework. Repression and injustice, and the criminalisation of non-violent speech and protest, make us less safe, not more.

Figure 18.2: *Liberty logo*

These measures act as a recruiting sergeant to the extremist fringe and marginalise those whose support is vital to effectively fight the terrorist threat.

They also undermine the values that separate us from the terrorist, the very values we should be fighting to protect.'

[Source: http://www.liberty-human-rights.org.uk/human-rights/countering-terrorism]

? Questions

1. Summarise what civil liberties groups do.
2. Consider the above case study. **Explain** the work of Liberty in countering terrorism.

Charities

Charities are organisations that exist in support of a cause. Charities can serve a vital role, therefore, in combating issues surrounding international terrorism. The charity Amnesty International is looked at in the below case study.

Amnesty International

[CASE STUDY]

'The so-called 'war on terror' has led to an erosion of fundamental human rights, highlighted by the increasing use and acceptance of torture and other cruel, inhuman and degrading treatment.

Figure 18.3: *Amnesty International logo*

We have seen and heard testimonies of 'terrorist suspects', held or formerly held in places of detention such as Guantánamo Bay and Bagram. We know that such places of detention exist in several locations globally. We know that this new trend for torture must stop.

We are campaigning to hold governments accountable for their actions and to uphold international law and the absolute prohibition of torture under any circumstances.'

[Source: http://archive.is/tCgl]

? Questions

Consider the above case study. **Describe** the work of Amnesty International in countering terrorism.

⁖ Make the Link

You can find more information about pressure groups in Section 1 on page 75.

Pressure groups

Pressure groups are organisations that try to influence government by encouraging them to pass laws or to change laws they do not agree with. They are sometimes referred to as 'lobby groups' or interest groups.

Scotland Against Criminalising Communities (SACC)

CASE STUDY

SACC campaigns against Britain's terrorism laws, against torture and detention without trial, against laws that criminalise political and community activity, against the so-called 'War on Terror'. SACC stands up for human rights and civil liberties. SACC's aims are:

Figure 18.4: *SACC logo*

- To campaign against the use of excessive state powers to criminalise political activity which are contained within the Terrorism Act 2000, the Anti-Terrorism, Crime and Security Act 2001, the Prevention of Terrorism Act 2005, the Terrorism Act 2006 and the Counter-Terrorism Act 2008; to campaign for the repeal of these acts; to campaign against any other legislation that has a similar effect; to monitor the use of such legislation and to work in close association with the communities most affected by these acts in order to highlight their discriminatory nature.

- To demand that everyone must be treated as innocent until proven guilty; that habeas corpus (the right of a person to be brought before a judge to determine if their detention is lawful) be fully respected and to demand those imprisoned without trial are released or granted a fair trial.

[Source: http://www.sacc.org.uk/about-sacc]

? Questions

1. Summarise what pressure groups do to counter terrorism.
2. Consider the case study above. **Explain** the work of the SACC in countering terrorism.

📖 Word bank

- **Hustings**
A meeting at which candidates in an election address their voters.

GO! Activity

Research

Under the provisions of the Curriculum for Excellence you need to become aware of how what you learn in class can have an impact on the wider world.

Select one of the three organisations from the case studies provided (or you may wish to choose your own civil liberties group or charity). Contact the charity/organisation via email and ask how you might be able to help effect change in countering international terrorism through their work.

To extend your learning, you may like to invite a speaker from your charity to discuss the issues in this Section in depth. With your teacher's support you could even broaden this out into a hustings with your local MP, for example, to provide a response to the government's actions (or a critique depending on their party) in dealing with international terrorism.

This research could also be very helpful for your Added Value Unit.

Summary

In this chapter you have learned:

- how interested organisations have responded to terrorism

- how you can contribute to this international issue as a global citizen

Learning Summary

Now that you have finished the **Interested organisations** chapter, complete a self-evaluation of your knowledge and skills to assess what you have understood. Use the checklist below and its traffic lights to draw up a revision plan to help you improve in the areas you identified as red or amber.

- I can explain the role of charities in combating terrorism.

- I can explain the role of pressure groups in combating terrorism.

- I can explain the role of civil liberties groups in combating terrorism.

Examples

In Modern Studies it is essential that you are able to back up any point you make with relevant evidence. When you are considering the statements above try to think of relevant examples for each response. You may wish to note these examples under each statement in your revision notes.

19 The future of terrorism

What you will learn in this chapter

- To understand how the future of terrorism might develop.
- To explain how terrorists might be able to use technology to support their ambitions.

The future of terrorism

When governments, NGOs and interested organisations think about the best ways to respond to terrorism, they cannot do so in isolation. This means that they need to think one step ahead of terrorists, or would-be supporters. Terrorism today is international and support for different terrorist organisations can probably be found in every country in the world at some level. Terrorism in the future, however, may look very different. Countries and governments across the world need to think about how they will plan for the development of terrorism and the changing tactics terrorists will use to create fear and panic.

Figure 19.1: *Using tactics to stay one step ahead*

Cyber-terrorism

Cyber-terrorism is the use of the internet to disrupt computer systems, for example by creating an online virus, or through hacking into a network. Some experts believe that the more reliant we become on computers, the more likely we are to see some sort of cyber-terrorism as the key to the end of the world. Through hacking, terrorist supporters and organisations can access government materials online which might help them to destabilise a regime. In 2002, Scottish man Gary McKinnon was accused of the 'biggest military computer hack of all time'. The US government claimed that Mr McKinnon hacked into US Army, Navy, Air Force and Department of Defence computers, as well as 16 NASA computers. They have claimed his hacking caused over $700,000 worth of damage to government systems. Mr McKinnon, who has been diagnosed as suffering from Asperger's Syndrome, has maintained his innocence and claimed he was simply looking for information on UFOs. In October 2012, after a series of court battles in the UK, the British government withdrew an extradition order to the United States. This means that he will not have to stand trial for the alleged offences in America where he could have faced up to 70 years in prison.

> **📖 Word bank**
>
> - **NGO**
>
> A non-governmental organisation; any non-profit, voluntary citizens' group that is organised on a local, national or international level.
>
> - **Network**
>
> A group of two or more computers linked together.
>
> - **Destabilise**
>
> To upset or cause unrest.
>
> - **Extradition**
>
> Handing over someone to the foreign state in which they are suspected of having committed a crime.

Figure 19.2: *An online virus could cause untold damage*

Gary McKinnon said 'I was convinced, and there was good evidence to show, that certain secretive parts of the American government intelligence agencies did have access to crashed extra-terrestrial technology which could, in these days, save us in the form of a free, clean, pollution-free energy'.

? Questions

1. **Explain, in detail,** what the term 'cyber-terrorism' means.
2. Summarise the case of Gary McKinnon. Come to a **conclusion** as to whether or not you believe the British government was correct to refuse to extradite Mr McKinnon. **Justify** your response with **evidence** from this chapter.

Why cyber-terrorism?

The internet is a valuable tool for terrorists because it allows them to share materials and brainwash would-be supporters. Members of terrorist organisations often use internet chat rooms to make contact with those that are weak and vulnerable, especially young people. Terrorists often think that the internet is a 'safe place' because they can remain anonymous; however, in 2008 the youngest person in Britain ever arrested and convicted under the Terrorism Act was sentenced to two years in a young offenders' institution based on his internet activity. Hammaad Munshi was 16 when he was arrested in 2006 when police found a guide to making napalm (used for making bombs) on his computer. Sentencing him, the judge said he had been influenced by 'fanatical extremists'.

Social media

Millions of people across the world use social media to interact with friends, show support for certain causes and to share information.

Think point

Think about your own internet usage – have you ever regretted something that you might have said while online?

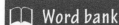

Word bank

• **Brainwash**

To cause someone to alter his or her beliefs, by forcible methods.

Websites like Facebook, Twitter and YouTube have all been used by terrorists and terrorist supporters to encourage support for their causes. The internet allows terrorists to spread propaganda worldwide. Islamic State (IS) uses sites such as Twitter and Facebook to recruit new members by posting videos of fighters filmed and professionally edited to look like Hollywood movies.

Social media is an extremely useful tool for terrorists to gain support: it is free of charge and it allows them access to a huge pool of individuals they might never have been able to connect with using other techniques, such as holding meetings. The UK government's security services monitor all social media and gather information on who is following who on sites like Twitter. It is much more difficult to monitor terrorist communication on Snapchat due to the short-term nature of posts.

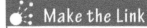

Figure 19.3: *Social media is an effective means of mass communication*

Nuclear terrorism

If terrorists were ever able to find a way to produce a nuclear device political analysts say it could lead to substantial loss of life and devastation.

Make the Link

You may have learned about the science behind nuclear weaponry in Physics.

Figure 19.4: *A nuclear missile*

While no nuclear attacks have taken place, threats have been made and intelligence suggests that terrorist groups are interested in nuclear warfare. For example, in October 2015 it was reported that Moldovan authorities working with the FBI stopped four attempts by gangs to sell radioactive material to IS and other Middle Eastern extremists, between 2010 and 2015. The last reported case came in February 2015 when a smuggler with a large amount of radioactive caesium specifically sought a buyer from IS.

In March 2016, it was reported that IS suspects were monitoring a senior Belgian nuclear official. These suspects had been linked to the November 2015 attacks in Paris, leading Belgian authorities to suspect that IS had been planning to abduct the official to obtain nuclear materials for a dirty bomb.

📖 Word bank

• **Radiological weapons**
Any weapon that is designed to spread radioactive material with the intent to kill and cause disruption.

Terrorist interest

Intelligence evidence has suggested that al-Qaeda have the capability to produce radiological weapons, but that they would need to find nuclear material and recruit rogue scientists to build 'dirty bombs'. A 'dirty bomb' is made of radioactive material and could kill potentially thousands of individuals and contaminate the area of its detonation for many years after.

❓ Questions

1. **Explain** why terrorist organisations have been drawn to the use of social media in recent years.
2. **Outline** the evidence that suggests terrorists have attempted to use nuclear tactics.
3. **Explain** what a 'dirty bomb' is.

Summary

In this chapter you have learned:

• how the future of terrorism might develop

• how terrorists might be able to use technology to support their ambitions

Learning Summary

Now that you have finished **The future of terrorism** chapter, complete a self-evaluation of your knowledge and skills to assess what you have understood. Use the checklist below and its traffic lights to draw up a revision plan to help you improve in the areas you identified as red or amber.

• I can describe what is meant by 'cyber-terrorism'.

• I can explain the role of social media in terrorism.

• I can explain what is meant by 'nuclear terrorism'.

Examples

In Modern Studies it is essential that you are able to back up any point you make with relevant evidence. When you are considering the statements above try to think of relevant examples for each response. You may wish to note these examples under each statement in your revision notes.

Assessment

20 Added Value Unit/Assignment

What you will learn in this chapter

- What is required for your National 4 AVU or National 5 Assignment.
- How to formulate a research question.
- The different kinds of research methods you can use.
- The different kinds of information you can collect.
- How to create and conduct an interview.
- The advantages and disadvantages of using an interview as a method of research.
- How to construct a questionnaire.
- The advantages and disadvantages of using a questionnaire as a method of research.
- How to use the internet for research.
- The advantages and disadvantages of using internet research.
- How to conclude your research and present your findings.

Figure 20.1: *Research is essential in proving a theory*

Social research

For the Added Value Unit (AVU) of your National 4 course or your National 5 Assignment, you will be asked to carry out some social research in order to prove or disprove a theory. A theory is an idea you might have that can be proved or disproved through carrying out research; in Modern Studies we sometimes call a theory a hypothesis.

Your research

Stage one: identify your topic

First, you should select the section you wish to focus your research on. You need to think about the issues that interest you the most; you can do this by brainstorming your prior knowledge on the section, and you can also find a list of suggested ideas for your research topic at the end of this chapter on page 231.

Stage two: formulate your research question/hypothesis

You now need to formulate a research question. When you are deciding on your research question you should focus on two different elements that will help you to form aims for your social research. For example:

- 'Should Scotland become an independent country?'
- 'Community Payback Orders are a very effective punishment.'
- 'Terrorist attacks have increasingly affected the UK in recent years.'

From your research question you should be able to make a list of aims that will help you in finding out the information you require. For example:

1. To find out what a Community Payback Order is – what crimes it is used as a punishment for, and what does it entail.

2. To find out how many people who are given CPOs go on to reoffend.

3. To find out what other punishments might be used instead.

4. To find out how effective the alternative punishments are.

Stage three: selecting your research methods

You now need to select at least two different research methods to help you find out the information you have listed in your aims. There are many different types of research methods used in social research but they are all based on gathering, evaluating and interpreting information. You need to select the methods most suited to your AVU/Assignment topic.

Differences between sources of information

There are different kinds of information you could collect. Quantitative and/or qualitative methods, and primary and/or secondary data – you should gather a few different types of information so that you have lots of things to talk about.

Quantitative methods

- Those that focus on numbers and frequencies.
- Quantitative methods include questionnaires, surveys etc.
- Provide information that is easy to analyse statistically and fairly reliable.
- These methods can be cost- and time-effective as there is a lack of involvement from the researcher – i.e. they do not need to make face-to-face contact with participants.
- However, in order for the results to be reliable they usually involve a high number of people being questioned.

Qualitative methods

- Those that focus on descriptive data, which is usually written.
- Qualitative methods include case studies and interviews.
- May be less reliable than quantitative methods, but the information collected is usually more in-depth and descriptive.
- Qualitative methods usually involve a lot of input from the researcher, e.g. they will need to have more face-to-face contact with participants.
- However, this research usually involves a lower number of people being questioned.

Make the Link

Social research is carried out by social scientists. You might have come across social science in Modern Studies, Geography, History and Business Management. Social scientists use social research to help them investigate different questions they may have about society. Scientists carry out experiments to prove or disprove theories; social scientists carry out social research to do exactly the same thing.

Make the Link

Create a list of the different research methods you may already know of; think of the ways you have researched information in Modern Studies and other subjects.

Figure 20.2: *Take time to research using materials available to you*

Primary data

- The researcher goes out and collects new data.
- Examples include interviews, letters and questions/surveys.

Secondary data

- The researcher uses existing sources of information.
- Examples include webpages, books, newspapers and TV/radio programmes.

Your research topic might be better suited to one type of data over another so you need to think carefully about the best ways to find the most useful and reliable information for your topic. For example, if your topic is about terrorism you might not be able to find anyone who knows a lot about this topic to provide you with an interview and secondary data, such as internet research, might therefore be more appropriate.

Over the next few pages you will find step-by-step guides to using three different research methods: interviews (a primary source), questionnaires (a primary source) and internet research (a secondary source).

Interviews

An interview is a conversation between two or more people where questions are asked by the interviewer to gain information from the interviewee (the person being asked). Carrying out an interview is a great way for you to develop your knowledge and skills in a topic or issue from within any section in Modern Studies.

How to plan and conduct an interview

Step one: research

The best way to construct effective questions is to know as much as you can about your subject. Research your chosen topic/issue using secondary sources of information such as webpages, books, newspapers and TV/radio programmes.

Step two: who to interview?

Make a list of people who might be able to help with your research question, for example your MSP, MP or local councillor perhaps.

Contact the person(s) you wish to interview – ensure you do this in plenty of time. Arrange a time and place that would be appropriate to conduct the interview. If it isn't possible to meet the person face-to-face you may wish to conduct the interview via webcam or phone. If the person(s) agree you may be able to record the conversation so that you can transcribe (make a full written copy of) what was said. You may wish to use the transcription as a source of information for your National 4 AVU or during your National 5 Assignment write-up.

Step three: the questions

Read over your research and create a set of questions. Simple questions can be 'closed'; this means they will be answered with a simple 'yes or

Hint

When completing your National 5 write-up it is very important to refer to the findings of your research. Do not just write about generic research methods.

Figure 20.3: *Planning is very important when preparing for an interview*

Hint

You may wish to contact one of your representatives to arrange an interview with them.

no' response. However, most questions will be 'open' meaning they will produce different responses depending on the interviewee. Many open questions begin with 'how', 'what', 'when', 'where', 'why' etc., or ask for an opinion. Ensure you have your questions written down so you don't forget what you want to ask. Become very familiar with your questions before you go into the interview – you could try out the interview with a classmate beforehand. This is known as a 'pilot' interview and will allow you to 'road test' your questions to see how effective they are at gathering the information you require.

Step four: conducting the interview
Make sure you take the following with you:

- your questions
- a pen/pencil
- a notebook to record your notes
- possibly a recording device (remember that you must always ask permission before recording an interview)

Step five: after the interview
After the interview review your notes alongside your existing research. If you recorded the interview you may wish to type it up.

- What do your findings show?
- Are there any patterns in the views expressed?
- Is there evidence of bias?
- Does your own research support the views of the interviewee?
- Does your own research contradict the views of the interviewee?

Key features of interviews

- Can create qualitative and quantitative data.
- A primary source of data.
- Carried out face-to-face by the researcher.
- Researcher can ask a set of pre-prepared questions about a specific topic. However, there is also the option to ask further questions depending on the interviewee's responses.
- Researcher can use both 'open' and 'closed' questions to gain information.
- Interviewee can elaborate on any of the areas covered.

Advantages and disadvantages of interviews

Advantages

- Allows the researcher to explore issues in an in-depth way.
- Researcher can create pre-prepared questions but can also ask supplementary questions.
- It is easy to quantify the results of 'closed' questions (by creating a pie chart of responses, for example).

- Researcher can clarify if there is any confusion about the questions posed.
- Interviewee can explore certain points in more detail.
- Good way of finding out what people think and feel about particular topics.

Disadvantages

- Can be time-consuming for researcher and interviewee as it involves face-to-face contact.
- Interviewee may digress into irrelevant areas.
- Can be difficult to quantify the results as much of the data may be descriptive.
- May be difficult to compare answers given by different individuals.
- People may not answer honestly. This may be because they are too embarrassed to say what they really think, or they may give an answer that they think the researcher wants to hear.

GO! Activity

Use your skills

1. Create a list of the topics and issues from the Democracy in Scotland and the United Kingdom section that you are interested in. You can include the examples on page 231 or use them to help you think of others.
2. Decide on one topic or issue that you are interested in researching and create a research question. Make a list of aims which will help you find out the information you require.
3. Conduct research into your chosen topic or issue using a variety of different sources and methods.
4. Select a relevant representative or representatives and arrange an interview with them; your teacher will be able to help you find out how to get in touch with the person(s) if you are unsure.
5. Prepare questions to be asked at the interview. Ask your teacher, a family member or a friend to read over your questions and provide you with some feedback.
6. Conduct the interview. Remember to be prepared!
7. Write up your research and show how it has helped you to gain a better understanding of your chosen topic or issue.

Checklist

- Pick someone who you would like to interview – how can they help you achieve the aims you have for your AVU/Assignment?
- Arrange an interview with that person either face-to-face, or over the phone or internet – make sure you don't leave it until the last minute to ask them.
- Carry out research on the topic for your interview and, if possible, background research on the person you are interviewing.

- Think carefully about your questions and practise them before the real interview.

- During the interview take lots of notes, or record it if the person you are interviewing is happy for you to do so.

- After the interview look at your notes and draw conclusions based on your research – remember to focus on your aims.

Questionnaires

Questionnaires are a valuable way of collecting a wide range of information from a number of people. This section will help you with conducting a questionnaire for a topic from the Social Issues in the United Kingdom section. However, you can apply the techniques to all of the sections within the Modern Studies course.

How to construct a questionnaire

Step one: planning your questionnaire

When constructing a questionnaire it is important to have an idea of what information you want to get from the results. Do you want to find out the public's opinion on a topic? Do you want to find out specific information? You can ask many different questions that may have different aims in order to get a wide range of opinions; by designing your questions carefully you can gain some very useful information for your AVU or Assignment.

Figure 20.4: *A questionnaire can be written out by hand or compiled online*

Step two: writing your questionnaire

When planning your questionnaire you need to carefully consider how you word the questions as this will affect the replies that you get. People may not understand a question properly, or the wording of a question may encourage them to give one answer rather than another (this is known as a 'leading question'). An example of a leading question is 'do you agree that prisons are really unsuitable for people that have drug addictions?' By using the word 'agree' this question encourages the respondent to think that prison is not suitable for people with drug issues. The questions should be clear, precise and not be full of 'jargon' that people might not understand.

Types of question

An effective questionnaire will have lots of different types of questions.

'Closed' questions are specific and have a set choice of answers. They are therefore more likely to communicate similar meanings to all respondents. Closed questions take less time for the interviewer, the participants and the researcher and so are a less expensive survey method for large-scale surveys. Generally, more people return surveys that use closed questions than those that use open questions as it is quicker and easier to answer multiple-choice questions.

'Open' questions do not give respondents answers to choose from, but are worded so that the respondents are encouraged to explain their answers and reactions to the question with a sentence, a paragraph, or

🔵 Make the Link

You may be asked to construct a questionnaire in other subjects while carrying out your Added Value Unit or Assignment.

Hint

A questionnaire is a form of primary research – the collection of data that does not already exist.

Hint

Your teacher will help you develop a research question before you carry out your questionnaire so that you have a focused topic that you are trying to investigate.

even a page or more, depending on the survey. Open questions allow the respondents to express a wider range of opinions than closed questions; however, they can be more difficult to draw results from as their answers cannot be compared as easily.

When constructing your questionnaire try to include a variety of open and closed questions and at least one of each of the following types of questions:

1. Knowledge questions: used to find out how much people know about a particular subject, for example, 'what do you know about the court system in Scotland?'

2. Factual questions: straightforward questions with 'yes', 'no' or 'don't know' answers. Other factual questions may be answered with a number, for example, 'what age are you?'

3. Opinion questions: used to find out how people feel about a topic, for example, 'do you think there are enough police on the streets?'

4. Motivation questions: ask for people's reasons for doing something. They can also usefully follow an opinion question, for example, 'if you answered 'yes' to the last question, tick the boxes that indicate your reasons why.'

Step three: choosing who to send the questionnaire to
You need to be able to draw conclusions from your results so it is important you survey a range of different people, sometimes called a 'sample'. This means asking people from a range of backgrounds, for example men and women, varying age groups and people of different ethnicities, religions and social classes. Using a questionnaire is the quickest and cheapest way to ask a large sample of the population as it will only cost the price of a stamp for each person, or may even be free if you put it online.

Step four: send out the questionnaire
You could do this by post, or if you have put your questionnaire online you could send the link to your sample via email.

Step five: record the findings of your questionnaire
You could make a pie chart or graph to demonstrate your conclusions.

Key features of questionnaires

- Produces mainly quantitative data, but qualitative data can also be produced.
- A primary source of data.
- Can be carried out face-to-face by a researcher, or sent to the respondent in the post or via email.
- All the respondents answer the same list of questions.
- Closed questions are normally used in questionnaires – respondents choose from a range of possible answers given on the questionnaire; for example, 'yes', 'no' or 'sometimes'.
- Respondents may also be asked to express an opinion or attitude; for example, 'what is your attitude to sentencing criminals to time in prison? – strongly in favour, in favour, neutral, against, strongly against?'

Advantages and disadvantages of questionnaires

Advantages

- Once you have written your questionnaire it can be sent to lots of people, which will give you a good idea of what the widespread opinion on a certain issue is. This is an inexpensive way of gathering a lot of data.

- It will mainly produce quantitative data (numerical evidence), which can be used to draw conclusions. Quantitative data is easier for researchers to draw conclusions from than qualitative data (more descriptive and varied information) as you can simply add up the results, display it in graphs and pie charts, and draw conclusions accordingly.

- As all respondents are asked the same list of questions it is easier to compare people's answers.

- Can be less expensive and time-consuming than other primary research methods, such as interviews.

Disadvantages

- Not everyone who you send a questionnaire to will respond.
- Some respondents may not answer all of the questions.
- If the questionnaire is not conducted face-to-face then there is no opportunity for the researcher to clarify if the respondent doesn't understand one of the questions.
- There is often no chance for the respondent to elaborate if they would like to answer a question in more detail.

GO! Activity

Use your skills

Work with a partner and re-word the following questions to make them effective questions using the techniques above. Some of the questions might need to be removed altogether.

- 'Do you agree with the prison system?'
- 'Should all knife crime offenders get a jail sentence?'
- 'Why are people in prison responsible for their own situation?'
- 'Why are young males more likely to go to prison than other people?'
- 'How many people do you know that are in prison?'

Explain why each of the questions is not suitable in their current form.

Checklist

- Express questions clearly, making sure that they can be understood.
- Questions should be brief but specific; avoid using 'ifs' and 'buts'.
- If you ask people to tick categories make sure that they do not overlap.

- Have a mixture of open and closed questions.
- Consider your sample.
- Keep a note of the number of people you ask.
- Make conclusions based on your research; remember to focus on your aims.

Internet research

The internet gives you a variety of opportunities in social research. With one click of a button you have access to millions of different websites that might be able to offer relevant information for your research question. The trick to carrying out internet research, however, is to be highly selective in what information you are looking for. You also need to be cautious about the type of information you find.

Figure 20.5: *The internet puts libraries' worth of information at your fingertips*

How to use the internet for research

Step one: choosing a search engine

There are many different search engines that can help you in finding the information you require. Common examples include Google, Yahoo and Ask Jeeves. You can also use search engines that combine search results, known as 'metasearch engines'. Common examples include SurfWax, Search.com and Ixquick.

Figure 20.6: *Choose the best search engine for your purposes*

Step two: searching appropriately

Search engines are easy to use – you *could* simply type your research question into the search box and it would no doubt generate thousands of different 'hits'. However, you can narrow your search area and access more high-quality results if you focus on the relevant key words you're interested in. You can do this by simply typing in the words of interest, for example 'terrorism fatalities 2018'. Some search engines, such as Google, have 'keyword search' tools that you may also wish to make use of.

You can also try using a 'search operator' through the advanced search page on your chosen search engine.

What you would like to search for	What to type	For example
Search for an exact word or phrase.	Use double quotes: *"[the word or phrase you are looking for]"*	This can be useful if you are looking for a particular phrase or perhaps information about a certain act of parliament: *"Terrorism Act 2008"* You should only use this if you are looking for the exact phrase as this kind of search can exclude otherwise helpful results.

Exclude a word.	Put a '-' before a word to exclude results that include that word: -[the word you would like to exclude]	You might do a search and get lots of information you don't need. For example, if you are researching terrorism but are not interested in attacks that took place on public transport you could search: terrorism -"public transport" As with the above, you should be careful when using this as you may exclude useful information.
Search within a site or domain.	Include the address of the site you would like to search within using 'site:': [search] site:[the site you would like to search within]	You could use this for example, if you wanted information from the Scottish Parliament website about the referendum: referendum site:scottish.parliament.uk You can also use this if you just want to search for information from sites that end in a certain 'domain' (the .com, .co.uk, .gov etc.); if you wanted to search only within .gov sites you could search referendum site:.gov
Search for pages that link to a certain other page.	Put 'link:' in your search to find pages that include a certain link: link:[the link you want to be included on the page]	If you are investigating drugs laws you might look for sites that link to the Talk to Frank site: link:talktofrank.com You can also look for links to specific pages: link:talktofrank.com/legalhighs
Search for pages that are similar to another.	Use 'related:' to find sites similar to ones you have found useful: related:[site you would like to find similar sites to]	You might have found a useful site and want to see if you can find other similar sites. For example, if you have used the Liberty site for looking at human rights issues you could find other sites like it by entering: related:liberty-human-rights.org.uk
If there are gaps in your search term.	Use an asterisk '*' to replace unknown words: [part 1 of search term]*[part 2 of search term]	This can be useful if you are not sure of a word in your search term. For example, if you couldn't remember what the 'P' in CPO stands for you could search: "Community * Orders"
Search for either word.	Use 'OR' to find pages that only include one of the words you list: [search term 1] OR [search term 2]	Use this if you only want to look at a page that has certain information. For example if you wanted pages that only included information on trade unions **or** pressure groups you could search: "trade union" OR "pressure group"
Search for a number range.	Use '..' to find pages that include numbers within that range: [number]..[number]	You can use this for all kinds of numbers including dates, prices and measurements. For example, if you wanted to find information on terrorism between 2010 and 2018 you could search: terrorism 2010..2018 You can also just use the one number with the two full stops to search for an upper or lower limit; so to find information on terrorism after 2002 you could search: terrorism 2002..

An advanced search can be completed by combining words and search terms, choosing to search by date, by country or even by limiting your search to the number of results displayed.

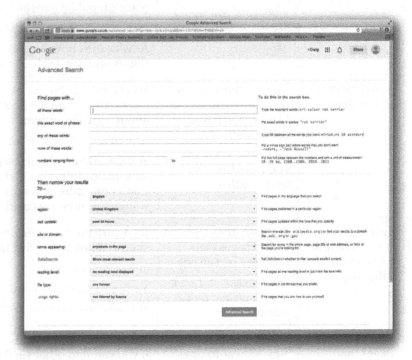

Figure 20.7: *An advanced search*

Using an advanced search is handy if you are considering searching within a website – such as the BBC, for example. Newspapers, such as the *Scotsman*, often have their own search engines that can again help to narrow your results. For example, you might wish to consider the *New York Times* website and use its search engine to find relevant news articles about terrorist attacks in America.

Figure 20.8: *The* New York Times *is one of the most respected news sources in the USA*

You might also want to consider academic results – these could provide you with search results for social research that has already been carried out in your field by social scientists. Academic search engines you could try include Google Scholar, RefSeek and Gooru Learning.

Hint

Your school/college may have an account with academic journals such as JStor that you may wish to access.

Step three: selecting the information

The information that you use from the internet needs to be treated critically. This means that you should be careful and select information that has come from a reliable source. Websites such as Wikipedia, for example, can contain inaccurate information because anyone who has access to the internet can update or change the content and you therefore have no sure way of knowing if the information is reliable and factual. You might like to consider:

- who is the author of the page?
- is there any reason the page might contain bias?
- is there contact information available to ask further questions of the information presented?

Hint

Remember to bookmark the most useful websites you find.

Step four: recording your evidence

When you are carrying out internet research it's important that you keep a record of the different sites you have visited and the dates on which you did so. This will be helpful for your teacher but it will also be helpful for you in deciding which sites you might want to revisit, and which were not as helpful. You may wish to record your research in a log or a table, like this one:

Date visited	URL	Usefulness	Notes
12/05/14	http://www.visionofhumanity.org/sites/default/files/Global_Terrorism_Index_Fact_Sheet.pdf	✓	• From 2002 to 2011 over one-third of all victims killed in terrorist attacks were Iraqi. • Western Europe experiences many more terrorist incidents than the US, having also suffered 19 times more fatalities than the US.

Step five: using your research

You now need to take the internet research you have gathered and use it to inform your research. For the National 4 Added Value Unit is entirely up to you to decide how your findings can be best presented; you may wish to do so visually in the form of a wall chart with associated explanations. You may wish to write up your findings in a word document. You may even wish to record your findings in a podcast. For the National 5 assignment you will only be able to use 2 sides of A4 paper in the write-up.

Hint

To shorten URLs you may wish to use the website: https://bitly.com

Your research needs to link directly to the task in hand, so you need to use what you have found to answer the questions you posed at the beginning of your research. For example, if you were researching terrorist attacks in America, you might have found statistics on the number of attacks and fatalities in recent years and could write 'the evidence shows that terrorist attacks in America have reduced substantially since the 1970s, with the exception of September 11th 2001. In 2011 there were no recorded fatal terrorist incidents compared to over 470 attacks in 1970. Therefore, in recent years the number of terrorist attacks has decreased, as has the number of fatalities resulting from terrorist incidents in the US'.

When drawing written conclusions from the evidence you have gathered you should be sure to quote the relevant piece of evidence you would like to cite and to mention the conclusion you wish to draw. For example:

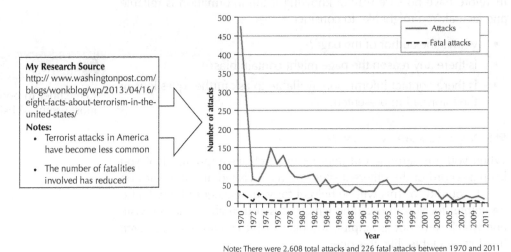

Note: There were 2,608 total attacks and 226 fatal attacks between 1970 and 2011

Figure 20.9: *An example of how you could draw a conclusion from your research*

Key features of internet research

- Secondary data.
- You can find both quantitative and qualitative information.
- Can be carried out alone.
- Search engines will be used to find a wide variety of data.

Advantages and disadvantages of internet research

Advantages

- Lots of different kinds of information are available, including official government data, reports from news organisations from around the world, and the results of primary research carried out by other social scientists.
- You can cross-reference information with other websites to check its accuracy.
- You can find out the opinions of people who you probably wouldn't be able to contact for primary research like questionnaires or interviews.

Hint

When completing your National 5 write-up you should refer to specific websites and not the internet as a whole.

Disadvantages

- There may be too much information for you to pick out the most relevant pieces.
- It can be difficult to tell which information is reliable.
- Some results may contain high-level language that is difficult to understand.

 Activity

Show your skills

With your shoulder partner, come up with a question you would like to find the answer to; for example 'how has the UK responded to the threat posed by international terrorism?'

Use the internet to try and find out the answer.

- Try several different search engines.
- Try typing the full question in, then use just keywords, or an advanced search. Which gives you the most useful response?
- Make a list of the websites you visit; which do you think has the most reliable information and why?

Checklist

- Consider carefully what information you would like to find.
- When carrying out your search think about which search engines and searches might provide the most useful information; should you use key words or an advanced search?
- Think about which websites will offer reliable sources of information.
- Make a note of all the websites you visit, what information you got from them, and how useful and reliable you found them.
- Make conclusions based on your research; remember to focus on your aims.

Concluding your research

Depending upon the level you are sitting the expectations of how you conclude your research will be different.

National 5 learners will be expected to complete a final write-up, demonstrating evidence of your research and reflecting on this process.

National 4 learners will be required to complete similar social research, however you will not have to produce a write-up to reflect this process. This means that you have a range of options in terms of how you present your final research: from PowerPoint to a poster display to a podcast, for example.

National 5 learners are not prevented from doing likewise; however you should be aware that the final write-up is a requirement at

Figure 20.10: *You have reached the end point of your research*

National 5 because the Assignment is marked externally by the SQA and is worth 20% of your final mark.

The Outcome and Assessment Standards should be used as your success criteria. The information below considers each standard and how you might reflect upon the requirements.

National 4 – Added Value Unit

1.1: Choosing, with support, an appropriate Modern Studies topic or issue for study

You need to be able to explain why you chose the topic or issue you selected for your AVU. Remember, for National 4 this doesn't need to be in written format; it could be in the form of a talk, an interview with your teacher, or in poster format for example.

1.2: Collecting relevant evidence from at least two sources of different types

You should have evidence from two different sources. It's up to you how you show this to your teacher: you might have a graph from a recent opinion poll, or a screen-shot of a website you used; either way you need to be able to show your teacher the evidence you have gathered and make sure this comes from two different sources, for example a questionnaire you carried out, a newspaper cutting, notes taken from a television documentary etc.

1.3: Organising and using the information collected to address the topic or issue

You should organise your research in a logical way. So, if you carried out a questionnaire there might be certain questions where you will focus your attention. In a questionnaire there might be 10 questions – three of these could have been on age, gender and race and it might not be appropriate to look at these in detail. Rather, a question later in your questionnaire might be more suitable, because it looks at the topic or issue your AVU is focused on. If your AVU was focused on the issue of youth crime, for example, you may have asked a question about youth crime in that person's area. The answers to that question could be highlighted in a pie chart.

1.4: Drawing on a factual knowledge and understanding to describe and briefly explain some key features of the topic or issue

You will have background knowledge from your work in class about the issue or topic you selected and you will have found key information in the research stage. So, you need to evidence the key areas of your AVU – show your teacher where your starting point was. Explain how carrying out research improved your knowledge by describing this in more depth. Make sure you reference your sources when you use evidence.

1.5: Apply the skills of either detecting bias and exaggeration, or making decisions, or drawing conclusions

In National 4 you have a choice of which skill-set you would like to address. Remember, these skills are all assessed in every section in

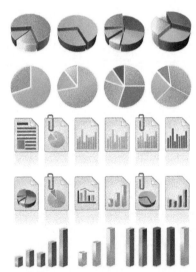

Figure 20.11: *Different ways to present data*

Modern Studies. So, think about the two different sources you've used. You might wish to consider:

- was there bias or exaggeration present in a website?
- are you able to make a decision?
- can you draw a conclusion from carrying out a questionnaire?

1.6: Presenting findings about the topic or issue
National 4 provides you with the freedom to present your findings in a very flexible way.

Some examples include:

- a PowerPoint presentation
- a poster display
- a talk
- a podcast
- a role play

You can, of course, provide a written write-up of your research for the AVU. However, unlike National 5 this does not need to be completed under timed exam conditions and it will be marked internally by your teacher.

National 5 – The Assignment

Supporting evidence
The requirements for National 5 differ slightly from those of National 4 where Added Value is assessed as a separate section. One hour is allocated to carry out the write-up of the N5 assignment. Candidates will produce a research sheet (two A4 sides). It is not permitted to copy any information from these sheets onto the assignment. If information is copied, no marks will be awarded. This evidence will be sent to the SQA along with your final write-up for your assignment, which will be carried out in your school under exam conditions.

Your evidence should not be in the form of a plan. It should show the marker your two different research methods clearly.

Your research may be either primary or secondary. It may include statistics from a recent government survey, for example, or a newspaper article, results from research you have carried out, such as an online survey, notes taken from a recent TV documentary, or any other form of valid information which you have gathered from a reliable source.

A: Choosing, with minimum support, an appropriate Modern Studies topic or issue
You simply need to describe your issue/give your hypothesis or research question and explain why you chose the issue you selected. For example, you may choose 'Police Scotland is not effective at preventing crime'.

B: Evaluating the effectiveness of two research methods used, commenting on their strengths and weaknesses where appropriate
In this section you need to mention the two research methods that you used – you should directly mention the evidence you brought into the

Figure 20.12: *Use the MADE acronym to help structure your answer*

write-up at this stage. It might be useful to provide two separate paragraphs on each method and to consider the advantages and disadvantages of each and then come to a conclusion. An acronym to help you structure this answer is shown below:

M Explain the **m**ethod you selected. For example:

'One research method I chose for my Assignment was to carry out a questionnaire.'

A Outline the **a**dvantages of this method. For example:

'An advantage of my questionnaire was that it provided me with a large number of responses from which I was able to draw conclusions about Police Scotland. I was able to tailor the questions so that I could ask specifically about Police Scotland and didn't have to waste time looking at other sources that might not have been relevant or important.'

D Outline the **d**isadvantages of this method. For example:

'A disadvantage of my questionnaire is that I only asked people I know as I posted it on my social media. This means they were all about my age and from my area so the results are not representative of the whole of Scotland. They might have answered how they thought I wanted them to.'

D Say something you would do **d**ifferently next time. For example:

'Next time I carry out any research I will hand out my questionnaire in a local supermarket as this way I might get responses from different age groups and could see what the elderly think of Police Scotland.'

E **E**valuate this research method. For example:

'Therefore, while my questionnaire provided me with lots of data specific to my research question, I cannot use the data to apply conclusions to the whole of Scotland so it is unreliable.'

C: Drawing on knowledge and understanding to explain and analyse key features of the topic or issue

This part again allows you to directly explain your research and link it to the knowledge you have gained from researching this topic. You may have included aims in your research plan and this is where you should answer them. For example, if your Assignment has focused on the police, describe and explain the key features of policing in Scotland. Link this knowledge to your research. You may wish to use the 'PEE' method (Point, Explain, Example, see page 236) to structure this response. In the 'example' section, make sure to reference your own knowledge AND your research evidence for full credit.

If your aim is 'to find out how community policing works', your paragraph might develop as follows:

P 'Police Scotland places community police officers in all schools in Scotland.'

E 'The community police officer is there to build trust with the community and deal with young people.'

E 'For example, in my interview with PC Campbell I …' (You should include at least one more example like this.)

D: Reaching a well-supported conclusion, supported by evidence, about the topic or issue

You now need to come to a conclusion based on your evidence.

Make it What's the conclusion you're drawing? For example:

'One conclusion I can draw from my research is that most people do not think there are enough police officers on the streets.'

Back it Use your evidence and research to prove your point. For example:

'From my research, 88 respondents out of 100 said that they had not seen a police officer in their community/street in the last year. Furthermore, from Scottish government research in 2017, 56% of those polled did not think the police patrolled regularly enough.'

Link it Link your evidence to form a valid conclusion. For example:

'Therefore, the conclusion is that the police in my community are not visible enough – this is supported by national research which shows that the government needs to invest more money in community policing.'

Note: You need to make a minimum of two conclusions at National 5 level.

Ideas for your research question

Democracy in Scotland and the United Kingdom

- 'Scotland should become an independent country.'
- 'The voting age should be lowered to 16 in all elections.'
- 'MSPs should work more within their constituency.'
- 'Pressure groups are effective/ineffective in influencing decision-making in the Scottish Parliament.'
- 'Trade unions are effective/ineffective in influencing decision-making in the Scottish Parliament.'
- 'Political parties are all the same.'
- 'Women and/or ethnic minorities are under-represented in the Scottish Parliament.'
- 'The work of the Scottish Parliament has helped it achieve its founding principles.'

Crime and the Law

- 'Prisons are not suitable for offenders under 25.'
- 'Poverty is the biggest single factor in influencing criminal behaviour.'

- 'Drug use is a big problem in Scottish society.'
- 'More money should be spent on prisons.'
- 'Community Payback Orders are a very effective punishment.'
- 'Minimum pricing for alcohol will have a positive impact on society.'
- 'CCTV is an effective way to prevent crime.'
- 'The Children's Hearing system effectively deals with young people.'

Terrorism

- 'Religion causes terrorism.'
- 'Terrorism is the greatest threat to global security.'
- 'The UK has dealt effectively with the threat posed by terrorism.'
- 'Counter-terrorism strategies do not infringe on an individual's civil liberties.'
- 'The international community has dealt effectively with the threat posed by terrorism.'
- 'Individuals' rights and responsibilities are weakened because of terrorist activities.'
- 'Terrorism decreases life expectancy in countries where support is widespread.'
- 'Most terrorists are members of terrorist organisations.'
- 'Terrorism attacks are most likely to occur on public transport.'
- 'Religious extremism is the greatest cause of terrorism.'

Learning Summary

Now that you have finished the **Added Value Unit/Assignment** chapter, complete a self-evaluation of your knowledge and skills to assess what you have understood. Use the checklist below and its traffic lights to draw up a revision plan to help you improve in the areas you identified as red or amber.

- I know what I will need to do for my National 4 AVU or National 5 Assignment.

- I can identify a topic I would like to research as part of my National 4 AVU or National 5 Assignment and make a list of aims to help me identify the information I require.

- I can explain the difference between quantitative and qualitative data.

- I can explain the difference between primary and secondary sources of information.

- I can explain what an interview is.

- I can describe how to construct an interview.

- I can describe how to conduct and record an interview.

- I can state advantages and disadvantages of using an interview as a method of research.

- I can draw conclusions from my interview to help me with my AVU or National 5 Assignment.

- I can explain what a questionnaire is.

- I can describe how to construct a questionnaire and the different types of questions that might be included and how they might be used:

  - Closed questions

  - Open questions

  - Knowledge questions

  - Factual questions

  - Opinion questions

  - Motivation questions

- I can explain what a sample is.

- I can draw conclusions from my questionnaire to help me with my AVU or National 5 Assignment.

- I can state advantages and disadvantages of using a questionnaire as a method of research.

- I can choose a search engine and search appropriately to find a website.

- I can distinguish which information is useful and reliable on a website.

- I can record evidence from a website.

- I can draw conclusions from a website to help me with my AVU or National 5 Assignment.

- I can state advantages and disadvantages of using the internet as a method of research.

- I understand how to complete my AVU/Assignment.

21 Unit assessments and exam skills

What you will learn in this chapter

- How to answer knowledge questions.
- At National 4 to detect and briefly explain bias or exaggeration using evidence from up to two sources of information.
- At National 5 to support and oppose a view using evidence from between two and four sources of information.
- At National 4 to make and justify a decision using evidence from up to three sources of information.
- At National 5 to make and justify, in detail, a decision based on evidence from between two and four sources of information, showing an awareness of alternative views.
- At National 4 to draw and support a conclusion using evidence from up to two sources of information.
- At National 5 to draw and support, in detail, a conclusion using evidence from between two and four sources of information.

In National 4 and 5 Modern Studies you will be assessed according to the knowledge you have gained and the skills you have acquired. It is important that you understand how to apply your knowledge in a written context; however, at National 4 level it will not always be necessary to write your answers – your teacher may, for example, allow you to work in a group.

Knowledge questions

Knowledge questions assess your understanding of what you have learned. These questions will ask you to 'explain' or 'describe'. For 'describe' questions you should give descriptions of things you have learned about during the course. For 'explain' questions you should clearly show the connections between the different points you make.

Using the correct structure is important when answering knowledge questions. Firstly, make a point in relation to the question. You should try to make your first sentence link back to the question – this will make the point of your paragraph clear. Secondly, you need to go on to explain the point you've made by including relevant information. Remember you need to demonstrate your knowledge but don't waste time by writing too much. Finally, you should include an up-to-date example such as a person's name, a statistic or a place.

Make the Link

In all National 4 and 5 social subjects you will be assessed by a mixture of knowledge and skills questions.

Figure 21.1: *The knowledge you have gained will help you answer questions*

Some people find the '**PEE**' method useful when structuring knowledge questions: for every three marks on offer you should make a **P**oint, **E**xplain that point, and give an **E**xample of that point. A really good PEE paragraph might get four marks, but to be safe you should include a PEE paragraph for every three marks. The wording of the question will usually tell you how many paragraphs you need to write. For example, the question below asks for three reasons so you should write three paragraphs. The answer which follows is an example of one paragraph and would be awarded three marks.

> 'The use of the prison system has been criticised in recent years.'

Explain, in detail, three reasons why the use of the prison system has been criticised in recent years. (8)

Point: The prison system has been criticised in many years because some people believe that a stay in prison will make someone more likely to reoffend.

Explain: Many employers do not want to hire people who have been in prison so ex-prisoners may feel forced to commit more crimes in order to survive.

Example: It has been calculated that three of every four prisoners go on to reoffend.

 Activity

Try writing another two PEE points to get the full eight marks available for this question.

Democracy in Scotland knowledge questions

Here is an example of a knowledge question that could be asked about the Democracy in Scotland and the United Kingdom section:

Groups that try to influence the Scottish government		
Pressure groups	Trade unions	The media

1. Choose **one** of the groups above.

   Describe, **in detail**, **two** ways in which the group you have chosen tries to influence the Scottish government. (4)

The first paragraph of your answer could be:

'One way in which pressure groups try to influence the Scottish government is by holding a demonstration. Pressure groups march through the streets holding signs and banners, handing out leaflets etc. Large demonstrations usually attract lots of media attention and this can influence the government. For example, in September 2013

 Activity

Show your knowledge
This question is worth four marks, so try to produce another paragraph that answers the question. You could use the PEE method to help you.

thousands of pro-independence campaigners marched through the streets of Edinburgh in support of their cause.'

Now attempt the following questions. Pay attention to the number of marks available and make sure you make the correct number of points. When you have finished, swap your answers with another pupil and mark each other's.

> 'The Additional Member System (AMS) has several disadvantages.'

2. Explain, **in detail**, the disadvantages of the Additional Member System (AMS).

   You should give a **maximum** of **three** disadvantages in your answer. (8)

> 'Members of the Scottish Parliament (MSPs) represent their constituents in many ways.'

3. Describe, **in detail**, **two** ways in which MSPs can represent their constituents in the constituency. (4)

> 'People in Scotland can participate in many ways.'

4. Describe, **in detail**, **two** ways in which people in Scotland can participate in politics. (6)

Crime and the law knowledge questions

Here is an example of a knowledge question that could be asked about the Social Issues in the United Kingdom section:

> 'The police in Scotland try to reduce crime.'

1. Describe, **in detail**, **two** ways in which the police try to reduce crime levels. (6)

The first paragraph of your answer could be:

'The police try to reduce crime levels by working in the community. They visit schools to talk to pupils and some schools have 'campus' officers who try to get to know pupils and stop them from getting involved in trouble. The Scottish government reported that crimes in schools have gone down because campus officers are good role models.'

Now attempt the following questions. Pay attention to the number of marks available and make sure you make the correct number of points. When you have finished, swap your answers with another pupil and mark each other's.

 Activity

Show your knowledge
This question is worth six marks, so try to produce two more paragraphs that answer the question. You could use the PEE method to help you.

'People commit crime for lots of different reasons.'

2. Explain, **in detail**, **two** reasons why some people might commit crime. (6)

'Crime can impact on victims in many ways.'

3. Describe, **in detail, two** ways crime can impact on victims. (6)

'Courts in Scotland have the power to punish offenders.'

4. Describe, **in detail**, **three** ways courts can punish offenders. (8)

Terrorism knowledge questions

In this section the questions will ask about an international issue. In your answers you should make it clear that your international issue is terrorism. Here is an example of a knowledge question that could be asked about the International Issues section:

'International conflicts and issues have many causes.'

1. Describe, **in detail**, **two** causes of an international issue or conflict you have studied.

   In your answer you must state the world issue or conflict you have studied. (6)

The first paragraph of your answer could be:

'One cause of **terrorism** is religious extremism. Religious terrorists may use terrorism to punish what they see as 'ungodly' behaviour in society, or to avenge what they see as attacks on their beliefs. For example, divisions between Shia and Sunni Muslims have led to terrorist attacks.'

Now attempt the following questions. Pay attention to the number of marks available and make sure you make the correct number of points. When you have finished, swap your answers with another pupil and mark each other's.

 Activity

Show your knowledge
This question is worth 6 marks, so try to produce another paragraph that answers the question. You could use the PEE method to help you.

'International conflicts and issues can have far-reaching consequences.'

2. Describe, **in detail**, **two** consequences your international conflict or issue has had on the wider world.

   In your answer you must state the world issue or conflict you have studied. (4)

> 'International organisations are sometimes successful in tackling international conflicts and issues.'

3. Explain, **in detail**, **two** reasons why an international organisation has been successful in tackling an international conflict or issue you have studied.

   In your answer you must state the world issue or conflict you have studied. (4)

> 'International organisations try to solve international conflicts and issues.'

4. Describe, **in detail**, **two** ways in which an international organisation has attempted to solve an international conflict or issue you have studied.

United Nations Organization	NATO	World Bank
European Union	African Union	Charities and other NGOs

   In your answer you must state the world issue or conflict you have studied. (6)

Skills questions

For these types of questions you will be given two, three or four sources and asked to do one of the following.

At National 4:

- detect and explain bias and exaggeration
- make and justify a decision
- draw and justify a conclusion

At National 5:

- support and oppose a view
- make and justify a decision
- draw and support a conclusion

Figure 21.2: *Skills questions give you a chance to show the skills you have built up over the course*

Support and oppose a view

You will usually be given a number of sources on an issue, followed by a statement(s) that has been made by an individual. You will then be asked to give information from the sources to support and oppose the view of the individual. You must include both sides of the explanation.

Example question

Study sources 1, 2 and 3 then answer the question which follows.

Source 1

Key points on the European Union membership referendum

The United Kingdom European Union membership referendum, also known as the EU referendum, took place in the United Kingdom on 23 June 2016. Membership of the European Union has been a topic of debate in the United Kingdom since the country joined … in 1973.

The final result of the referendum for the United Kingdom and Gibraltar was declared at Manchester Town Hall at 0720 BST on Friday 24 June 2016 after all the 382 voting areas and the 12 UK regions had declared their results …

With a national turnout of 72% the target to secure the majority win for the winning side was 16,788,672 votes. The decision by the electorate was to 'Leave the European Union' [51.9%] which won by a majority of 1,269,501 votes … over those who had voted in favour of 'Remain a member of the European Union' [48.1%] with England and Wales voting to 'Leave' while Scotland and Northern Ireland voted to 'Remain'.

Voters aged 24–49 narrowly opted for 'Remain' (54%) over 'Leave' (46%), while 60% of voters aged 50–64 opted to 'Leave'.

Source 2

Result of referendum on membership of the EU

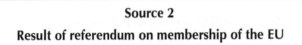

Leave
51.9%
17,410,742 VOTES

Remain
48.1%
16,141,241 VOTES

0 results left to declare

How the parts of the UK voted

England

Leave **53.4%**
15,188,406 VOTES

Remain **46.6%**
13,266,996 VOTES

Northern Ireland

Leave **44.2%**
349,442 VOTES

Remain **55.8%**
440,707 VOTES

Scotland

Leave **38.0%**
1,018,322 VOTES

Remain **62.0%**
1,661,191 VOTES

Wales

Leave **52.5%**
854,572 VOTES

Remain **47.5%**
772,347 VOTES

Source 3

Opinions on Brexit

UK Today

THE OVERALL PICTURE IS A NEGATIVE ONE

Slightly more of the British public think that voting to leave the EU was the wrong decision than think it was the right decision, and on most measures more people think it will have a negative impact than think it will have a positive impact.

DAILY BLOG

GOVERNMENT DOING A BAD JOB

A large majority think that the government is doing a bad job of negotiating the UK's withdrawal from the European Union. People aren't clear about what either of the main parties really think about Brexit and don't much support either Theresa May's or Jeremy Corbyn's stances towards Europe.

The Star

It will happen!

Most people still think the government should go ahead with Brexit. Seventy per cent of 54–60-year-olds think it should still go ahead.

The Mail Today

A raw deal?

Half (50%) of people think that the European Union has the upper hand in negotiations and that the UK has generally accepted its demands. Just 3% of under-25-year-olds think that Britain is getting the better deal.

Using Sources 1, 2 and 3, **give reasons to support and oppose** the view of Stephen Thomson.

'The British public supports the plan to leave the EU.'
View of Stephen Thomson

In your answer you must:

- give evidence from the sources that supports Stephen Thomson's view
- give evidence from the sources that opposes Stephen Thomson's view

Your answer must be based on all three sources. (10)

How to answer the question

- In order to achieve full marks you must show evidence from the sources that supports Stephen Thomson's view, and evidence from the sources that does not support Stephen Thomson's view.
- Make sure you show evidence that both supports and opposes the view; an answer that deals with only one side of the explanation will only be awarded a maximum of six marks.
- Make sure you have used all of the sources at least once.
- Your answer should show an understanding of the information and statistics used in the sources – use words and phrases that show you understand, for example 'only half' and 'massive'.

GO! Activity

Use your skills
Attempt to answer the rest of this question. Give one other reason to support and one other reason to oppose the view of Stephen Thomson.

Hint

Remember that in skills questions you will only get marks for using information that is in the sources.

Model Answer

'One reason to support Stephen Thomson's view that 'The British public supports the plan to leave the EU' is that in Source 1 it says 'The decision by the electorate was to 'Leave the European Union' [51.9%]'. The results in Source 2 confirm this as they also show that 51.9% of Britain voted to leave. This supports the view of Stephen Thomson as it shows that a majority of the people who turned out to vote support the decision to leave the EU.

One reason to oppose Stephen Thomson's view that 'The British public supports the plan to leave the EU' is that in Source 1 it says 'Voters aged 24–49 narrowly opted for 'Remain' (54%)'. This is confirmed in Source 3 where is says that 'Just 3% of under-25-year-olds think that Britain is getting the better deal.' This opposes the view of Stephen Thomson as it shows that a majority of younger people do not support the plan to leave the EU.'

Making and justifying decisions

You will usually be given two options and will have to pick one and explain why it is the best option, using the sources available. You need to provide evidence from all the sources to support the decision that you reach. You need to explain why the evidence supports your decision; this means you must give at least three reasons why you chose your option.

In the National 5 exam, you should also identify evidence that supports the alternative decision and state why you chose to reject this option.

Example question

Option 1
Spend more money on prisons

Option 2
Spend more money on alternatives to prison

Source 1

Facts and viewpoints

The Scottish government spends around £325 million a year on the Scottish Prison Service. In February 2011 the Scottish government decided to get rid of almost all sentences below three months and has given out many alternative sentences.

- Scotland's prisons are overcrowded. The Scottish Prison Service says the average daily population of Scotland's prisons was 7,665 in 2018; Scotland's prisons are only designed to hold 7,330 prisoners.

- Having a convicted person at home keeps families together and stops innocent family members from being punished by having a loved one taken away.

- Taking away someone's freedom is a good form of punishment; it lets the victims see that something has been done.

- Prisons are very expensive and alternatives to prison are a cheaper option. The cost of keeping someone in prison for 16 weeks is around £10,000, compared to the cost of electronic tagging which is approximately £1,700.

- Spending more money on prisons would improve the facilities and increase the number of spaces available.

- Most criminals in Scotland's prisons have previous convictions. Around 70% of the prison population are repeat offenders.

- A recent study by Glasgow University suggests that when criminals work in the community where they have committed a crime they start to realise the impact of their actions and are less likely to reoffend.

- A recent government document suggests reoffending rates have reduced in the last two years; some people think this is because electronic tags are being used more regularly.

- Alternatives to prison do not always work; many people commit crimes while on Community Payback Orders and of those that complete the Community Payback Order many go on to reoffend later.

- Over half of criminals reoffend after being released from prison.

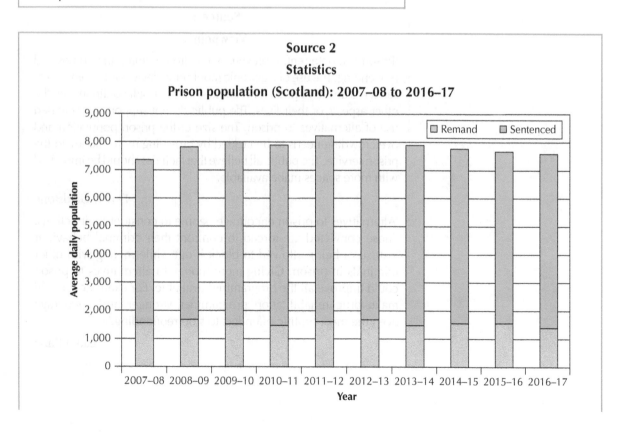

Source 2

Statistics

Prison population (Scotland): 2007–08 to 2016–17

Results of a poll asking Britons' opinions on the prison system

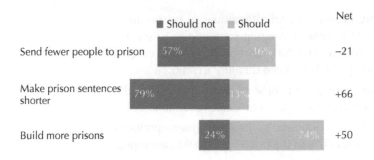

	■ Should not ■ Should	Net
Send fewer people to prison	57% 36%	−21
Make prison sentences shorter	79% 13%	+66
Build more prisons	24% 74%	+50

Results of a poll asking Britons if community service should be used more as an alternative to prison

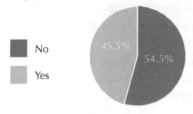

■ No

■ Yes

45.5% 54.5%

Source 3

Viewpoints

'Prison is a deterrent; it prevents some from committing crimes and reoffending. The use of electronic monitoring devices and community service is an easy option for criminals; they can still continue with the other aspects of their lives. The public do not support an increased use of alternatives to prison. The size of the prison population and overcrowding needs to be tackled by providing more money to the prison service. The public all believe that facilities should be improved with more spaces made available.'

David Gladstone

'Alternatives to prison encourage people to consider their actions. Those convicted are forced to confront their criminal behaviour instead of being allowed to block it out while mixing with other criminals in prison. Giving more money to alternatives to prison could improve all the programmes available. For example it could make drug rehabilitation programmes stronger and encourage even the most prolific offenders to stop reoffending.'

Laura Kane

You must decide which option to recommend to the Scottish government; either they should spend more money on prisons **(Option 1)** or they should spend more money on alternatives to prison **(Option 2)**.

- Using Sources 1, 2 and 3, **which option would you choose?**
- Give reasons to **support** your choice.
- **Explain** why you did not choose the other option. **(National 5 only.)**

How to answer the question

- Pick your option.
- Underline or highlight all the evidence that supports your option. Make sure you have used all of the sources at least once. You can draw lines on your question paper between your highlighted bits and the correct information to help you do this.
- Write at least three paragraphs explaining why you chose your option, including quotes from the evidence that supports your option.

N5
- In the National 5 exam, you also need to write at least one paragraph explaining why you rejected the other option. Include a piece of evidence from the sources which supports your decision to reject this option.
- In the National 5 exam this question will be worth 10 marks; in order to achieve full marks you should give three reasons to support your decision and two reasons to reject the other option. You would also need to use all the sources to get full marks.

Model Answer

Below is an example of a paragraph you might write explaining why you picked Option 1:

'Source 1 states that prisons are overcrowded and that money needs to be spent to increase the numbers available. Source 2 backs this up by showing an increase of the number of people in prison to over 8,000 in 2011–12. Therefore prisons are too full and more money should be spent on prisons.'

N5 For National 5, below is an example of a paragraph you might write explaining why you rejected Option 2:

'Some people might say we should choose Option 2 because Source 3 says 'Giving more money to alternatives to prison could improve all the programmes available.' These people are wrong because Source 1 says 'Alternatives to prison do not always work'.'

 Activity

Use your skills
Attempt to answer the rest of this question by writing at least one more paragraph in support of Option 1. Try writing another answer supporting Option 2. This will help you practise the skill of justifying a decision.

Drawing and supporting conclusions

You will usually be presented with 2–4 sources from which to draw your conclusions; these will be supplemented by bullet points in the question itself that you can use as a guide to frame your answer.

Example question

Source 1

Terrorism in the UK, 2017

The UK's intelligence services are facing an 'intense' challenge from terrorism, the head of MI5 has warned.

Andrew Parker said there was currently 'more terrorist activity coming at us, more quickly' and that it can also be 'harder to detect'.

The UK has suffered five terror attacks this year [2017 – an increase on 2016], and he said MI5 staff had been 'deeply affected' by them.

He added that more than 130 Britons who travelled to Iraq and Syria to fight with so-called Islamic State had died.

MI5 was running 500 live operations involving 3,000 individuals involved in extremist activity in some way, he said.

Speaking in London, Mr Parker said the tempo of counter-terrorism operations was the highest he had seen in his 34-year career at MI5.

Twenty attacks had been foiled in the last four years, including seven in the last seven months, he said – all related to what he called Islamist extremism …

The Home Office said: 'In summary, we expect the threat from Islamist terrorism to remain at its current, heightened level for at least the next two years, and that it may increase further.'

The impact of terrorism on the UK may be lower than other countries worldwide but the threat is very real and serious.

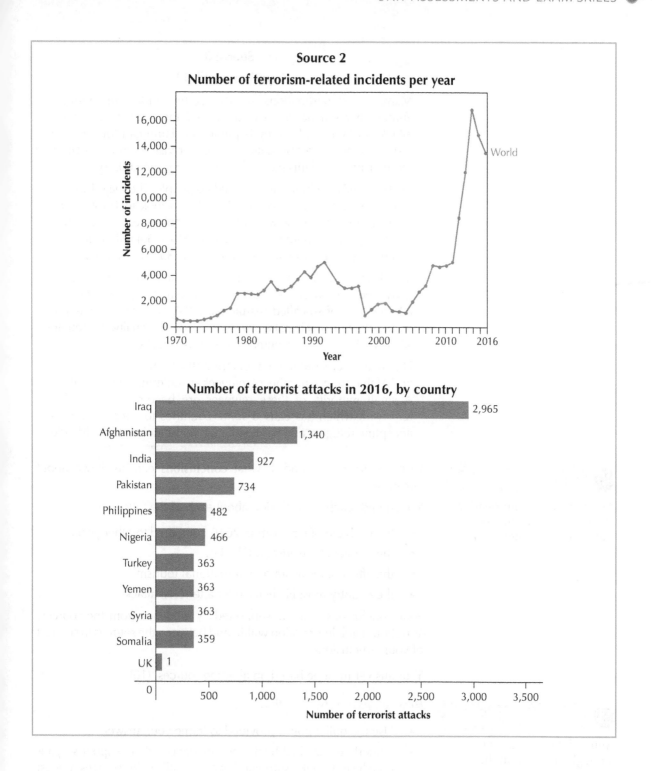

Source 2

Number of terrorism-related incidents per year

Number of terrorist attacks in 2016, by country

Source 3

Terrorism worldwide

Many tourist destinations are feeling the impact of terrorism. Turkey shares a border with Syria and the number of terrorist attacks in Syria and Turkey is putting off European tourists from visiting. Hotels are also cutting prices for visitors to try to attract more visitors, and this means less money for the country.

In 2015, ISIS attacks in Tunisia killed 60 people. The majority of the victims were European tourists. The attacks took their toll on the country's tourism sector, which provides employment for more than 200,000 people. Visitor numbers fell by 25% to 5.4 million in 2015, and money raised from tourists dropped by 35% to $1.1 billion.

In 2017, Iraq says it hanged, in a mass execution, 38 jihadist militants convicted of terrorism offences. The justice ministry said they were all members of so-called Islamic State (IS). Despite attempting to reduce the threat of IS in Iraq by using the death penalty, the country still experiences a large number of terrorist attacks.

Due to an increased number of terror attacks in countries like Iraq and Afghanistan, a number of refugees are entering other countries. A small minority of these refugees are becoming involved in terrorism, which has caused some countries to become wary of accepting refugees and has resulted in racist incidents worldwide.

Hint

You should use information from across the sources to support your conclusions.

Using Sources 1, 2 and 3, what **conclusions** can be drawn about terrorism?

You should reach a conclusion about each of the following:

- the problem of terrorism in 2016 compared to other years
- the impact of terrorism on the UK
- the effect of terrorism on international tourism
- the country most likely to suffer a terrorist attack

Your conclusions must be supported by evidence from the sources. You should link information within and between the sources in support of your conclusions.

Your answer must be based on all three sources. (10)

How to answer the question

Hint

You will be able to find enough evidence in the sources to support your conclusion. Make sure you link the evidence to your conclusion.

- Use the bullet points provided to frame your answer.
- Underline or highlight the evidence that supports your conclusion. Make sure you have used all of the sources at least once. You can draw lines on your question paper between your highlighted bits and the correct information to help you do this.
- Work across the sources to identify relevant evidence that will support the conclusion you are making.
- Start your paragraph by spelling out what the conclusion that you have reached is.
- Complete your paragraph by making an evaluative comment. This may be to comment on how the figures you have used indicate a majority/minority, significant increase/decrease, etc.

Model Answer

Each of the points provided will be worth three marks in the final National 5 exam. Below is an example of a paragraph you might write drawing conclusions on the question above:

'One conclusion that can be drawn about the problem of terrorism in 2016 compared to other years is that it was lower. Source 2 shows that the number of terrorist attacks in 2016 worldwide was roughly 13,000, compared to over 16,000 in 2015. Source 1 also states that 'The UK has suffered five terror attacks this year [2017 – an increase on 2016]'. Therefore the number of terrorist attacks in 2016 is 3,000 lower, which is a significantly large decrease.'

> **GO! Activity**
>
> **Use your skills**
> Attempt to answer the rest of this question by writing at least three more paragraphs using the bullet points to frame your answer.

Learning Summary

Now that you have finished the **Unit Assessment and exam skills** chapter, complete a self-evaluation of your knowledge and skills to assess what you have understood. Use the checklist below and its traffic lights to draw up a revision plan to help you improve in the areas you identified as red or amber.

- I know how to structure and answer knowledge questions.

- When asked to detect and explain bias, exaggeration and/ or support and oppose a view I can show an understanding of the statistics from the sources.

- When asked to make and justify a decision I can give at least two pieces of evidence taken from the sources to support my decision.

- At National 5 level when asked to make and justify a decision I can explain why I rejected the alternative option.

- When asked to make and justify a decision I can link the evidence from the sources to the option I have chosen.

- When asked to draw a conclusion I can select appropriate evidence to support my view.

- When asked to draw a conclusion I can use appropriate evidence and link it to supporting evidence from another source.

- When asked to draw a conclusion I am able to use the evidence selected to support a valid conclusion.